Andreea Hilda Kosorus

Learning-oriented Question Recommendation

Andreea Hilda Kosorus

Learning-oriented Question Recommendation

Short- and Long-term Question Recommendations based on Semantic Similarity, VLMCs and Bloom's Taxonomy

Südwestdeutscher Verlag für Hochschulschriften

Imprint
Any brand names and product names mentioned in this book are subject to trademark, brand or patent protection and are trademarks or registered trademarks of their respective holders. The use of brand names, product names, common names, trade names, product descriptions etc. even without a particular marking in this work is in no way to be construed to mean that such names may be regarded as unrestricted in respect of trademark and brand protection legislation and could thus be used by anyone.

Cover image: www.ingimage.com

Publisher:
Südwestdeutscher Verlag für Hochschulschriften
is a trademark of
Dodo Books Indian Ocean Ltd. and OmniScriptum S.R.L publishing group

120 High Road, East Finchley, London, N2 9ED, United Kingdom
Str. Armeneasca 28/1, office 1, Chisinau MD-2012, Republic of Moldova, Europe
Printed at: see last page
ISBN: 978-3-8381-3415-4

Zugl. / Approved by: Linz, JKU, Diss., 2013

Copyright © Andreea Hilda Kosorus
Copyright © 2014 Dodo Books Indian Ocean Ltd. and OmniScriptum S.R.L publishing group

Abstract

The information overload in the past two decades has enabled question-answering (QA) systems to accumulate large amounts of textual fragments that reflect human knowledge. Therefore, such systems have become not just a source for information retrieval, but also a means towards a unique learning experience. Meanwhile, the success of recommender systems has motivated research on deploying recommendation techniques also in educational environments to facilitate access to a wide spectrum of information. However, the adopted methods were rather traditional, generally applicable to any recommendation need.

QA systems distinguish themselves from search engines by the type of manipulated data – well-formed grammatical units endowed with semantic content – and its purpose: not just for retrieving facts, but also for more complex learning activities. Current conceptions about learning assume learners as active agents and not passive recipients or simple recorders of information. Therefore, the sequence in which knowledge is assimilated is of high importance. Recently developed recommendation techniques for search engine queries try to leverage the order in which users navigate through them. Although a similar approach might improve the learning experience with QA systems, questions are still considered as any other recommendation item.

In this thesis, two categories of recommendation techniques are defined. The first type, the short-term recommender, considers only the most recently asked question to produce semantically related suggestions using a new semantic similarity measure. The second one, the long-term or learning-oriented question recommender is a novel approach that exploits not only the user's history log, but also two important question attributes: its topic and learning objective. For this purpose, a domain-specific topic-taxonomy and Bloom's learning framework is employed, whereas for modeling the order in which questions are selected, variable length Markov chains are used.

Both recommendation techniques, as well as the semantic similarity measure, were evaluated and their results are discussed in detail. Results show that the short-term recommender is well-suited for particular user needs, but, on the long-run, the learning-oriented recommender can provide more useful, meaningful recommendations for a better learning experience. The learning-oriented recommender was also compared to other predictive models that don't rely on any domain knowledge. The outcome confirms the initial hypothesis that the learning-oriented recommender can model better the users' learning process and that it can be successfully deployed to guide the user on his/her learning journey.

Contents

Abstract i

1. Introduction 5
   1.1. Background 5
   1.2. Relevance 6
   1.3. Contribution 7
   1.4. Approach 8
   1.5. Benefits 11

2. State of the Art 15
   2.1. Overview 15
   2.2. Recommender systems 15
       2.2.1. General overview 16
       2.2.2. Query recommendation 24
       2.2.3. Graph-based query recommendation 25
       2.2.4. Query recommendation using probabilistic models 31
       2.2.5. Summary 34
   2.3. Semantic text similarity 35
       2.3.1. Concept similarity 36
       2.3.2. Concept-set similarity 39
       2.3.3. Document similarity 40
       2.3.4. Short-text similarity 43
       2.3.5. Syntactic similarity measures 48
       2.3.6. Summary 49
   2.4. Predictive models for sequential data 50
       2.4.1. Sequential event prediction 50
       2.4.2. Temporal probabilistic models 52
       2.4.3. Summary 60
   2.5. The learning taxonomy 61
       2.5.1. Overview 61
       2.5.2. The knowledge dimension 63
       2.5.3. The cognitive process dimension 64
       2.5.4. Summary 65

3. Semantic Short-Text Similarity 67
   3.1. Overview 67
   3.2. Definition 67

3.3. Knowledge-base description 68
        3.3.1. General overview 68
        3.3.2. The topic taxonomy 69
        3.3.3. Topic mappings 71
   3.4. The four-layered semantic short-text similarity 71
        3.4.1. Topic similarity 72
        3.4.2. Keyword similarity 72
        3.4.3. Keyword-set similarity 73
        3.4.4. Short-text similarity 74
   3.5. Example 74
   3.6. Summary 76

4. **Short-term Recommendation**   **77**
   4.1. Overview 77
   4.2. Definition 77
   4.3. Semantic utility 78
   4.4. Recommendation generation 78
   4.5. The conversation recommender 79
   4.6. Summary 81

5. **Learning-oriented Recommendation**   **83**
   5.1. Overview 83
   5.2. Knowledge-base description 84
   5.3. Learning-oriented recommendation 87
        5.3.1. Preliminaries 87
        5.3.2. Models 89
   5.4. Summary 102

6. **Results and Evaluation**   **105**
   6.1. Overview 105
   6.2. Semantic short-text similarity measures 105
   6.3. Short-term recommendation 109
   6.4. Learning-oriented recommendation 113
        6.4.1. Data 113
        6.4.2. Experimental setup 115
        6.4.3. Evaluation metrics 117
        6.4.4. Evaluation parameters 120
        6.4.5. Results 120
        6.4.6. Comparison with the short-term recommendation 127
        6.4.7. Summary and conclusions 128

7. **Conclusion and Future Work**   **135**
   7.1. Summary 135
   7.2. Conclusions 136
   7.3. Impact and future work 138

Contents

A. Appendix	**141**
B. Appendix	**143**
C. Appendix	**147**
Bibliography	**161**
List of Notations	**175**
Index	**179**

List of Figures

1.1. Learning model 11

2.1. Situation of this research work 15
2.2. Different relations among queries 26
2.3. Search engine interaction cycle 27
2.4. Graphical structure of the vlHMM 34
2.5. The online grocery store problem 51
2.6. First-order Markov chain 55
2.7. Examples of l-th order Markov chains 56
2.8. Graphical structure of a hidden Markov model 60
2.9. Bloom's taxonomy 62

3.1. Knowledge-base structure of a QA system 69
3.2. A topic-tree with keywords 70
3.3. Example of question similarity 75

5.1. Question-topic mapping 84
5.2. Simple question recommender 90
5.3. Topic-based question recommender 91
5.4. Knowledge- and cognitive process-based recommender 92
5.5. Mixed question recommender 93
5.6. Mixed learning-oriented question recommender 95
5.7. Simple hierarchical question recommender 96
5.8. Hierarchical knowledge-based question recommender 97
5.9. Hierarchical cognitive process-based recommender 98
5.10. Hierarchical knowledge- and cognitive process-based recommender . . 99
5.11. Hierarchical learning-oriented question recommender 100
5.12. Hybrid question recommender 101

6.1. Average log-loss 121
6.2. Accuracy 122
6.3. Coverage 122
6.4. Diversity 123
6.5. Model performance over the earth sciences dataset 124
6.6. Learning curves over the earth sciences dataset 125
6.7. Model performance over the nutrition dataset 126
6.8. Learning curves over the nutrition dataset 127
6.9. Model performance over the homeschooling dataset 128

6.10. Learning curves over the homeschooling dataset 129
6.11. Model performance with different mappings 130
6.12. Accuracy and learning utility over the earth sciences dataset 132
6.13. Accuracy and learning utility over the nutrition dataset 133
6.14. Accuracy and learning utility over the homeschooling dataset 133
6.15. Comparison of learning utility over the three datasets 134
6.16. Short-term versus learning-oriented recommendation 134

B.1. The cognitive process dimension of the revised version of Bloom's taxonomy [108]. 143

C.1. A taxonomy of the earth sciences domain 152
C.2. A taxonomy of the nutrition domain 153
C.3. A taxonomy of the homeschooling domain 154
C.4. Correlation of user answers over the earth sciences domain 155
C.5. Correlation of user answers over the nutrition domain 156
C.6. Correlation of user answers over the homeschooling domain 157
C.7. Learning curves for the earth sciences domain 158
C.8. Learning curves for the nutrition domain 159
C.9. Learning curves for the homeschooling domain 160

List of Tables

2.1.	Dimensionality of a full Markov chain	57
6.1.	User answer variance	106
6.2.	Correlation of survey answers with the semantic similarity	106
6.3.	Average rating of survey participants	107
6.4.	Sample question pairs	107
6.5.	Empirical survey results of the conversation recommender	111
6.6.	Overview of the question datasets	114
6.7.	Statistics on the knowledge mapping	114
6.8.	Statistics on the cognitive process mapping	114
6.9.	Statistics on the learning objective mapping	115
6.10.	Question coverage of survey sequences	116
6.11.	Survey answer statistics	117
6.12.	Overview of the topic mappings	126
6.13.	Summary of learning utility results	131
6.14.	Short-term recommendation accuracy	131
A.1.	Number of independent parameters for different Markov chains	141
A.2.	Recommendation techniques	142
B.1.	The knowledge dimension	144
B.2.	The cognitive dimension I	145
B.3.	The cognitive dimension II	146
C.1.	Examples of survey question ordering	147
C.2.	Question mappings for the earth sciences domain	148
C.3.	Question mappings for the nutrition domain	149
C.4.	Question mappings for the homeschooling domain	150
C.5.	Statistics of user answers	151

1. Introduction

1.1. Background

The research field of recommender systems is a very rich and rapidly growing knowledge domain. The variety of existing recommendation techniques is a consequence of an exceptionally fast development towards a computerized and automated environment. Recommender systems have proven to be successful in many domains where information overload is present [135]. Nowadays, personalized devices are integrated in almost every aspect of our life. Recommender systems, therefore, play an important role and determine, on some level, our efficiency and success during daily activities.

One of the four needs fundamental to human fulfillment is the need to *learn* – our mental demand to develop and to grow [48]. Aside of being a basic human need, learning and mental development is a socially recognized necessity for survival. We learn in order to integrate ourselves into the current society, to be able to communicate, earn a living and be fulfilled. From our birth we enter a learning process that continues until the end of our days.

In the past two decades, the learning aspect has become more and more subject to personalization and automation. New techniques and technologies have been developed to guide and help not just the learner but also the teacher, especially in the academic environment. From simple hand calculators to advanced systems, like intelligent tutoring systems [64], the educational technology or e-learning field has witnessed a dramatic growth in a short period of time. Additionally, the success of recommender systems has motivated research on deploying such techniques also in educational environments to facilitate access to a wide spectrum of information [135, 148].

While new technologies were being developed towards meeting different learning tasks, the information overload problem within the academic environment received less attention. This aspect has been identified not just within existing well-established domains, for which the fundamental building blocks have been naturalized for centuries (e.g., earth sciences, human biology, etc.), but also in emerging new fields of study (e.g., media studies, women's studies, etc.).

One of the consequences of information overload is the rise of question answering (Q&A or QA) systems, which are computer systems that aim at (automatically) answering questions posed by humans. Hence, these systems can also be considered as part of the educational technology field. Over time, the databases of QA systems have gathered large amounts of information – small reflections of human knowledge – from a variety of domains and it, therefore, represents a *potential source for learning and establishment of new fields of study.*

The main motivation behind the work presented in this thesis is to leverage the functionality of QA systems towards new learning techniques and use the "wisdom of the crowds" in order to convey useful information and guide the learner on a meaningful learning journey.

1.2. Relevance

Current QA systems integrate traditional content-based or collaborative recommendation engines with the goal to filter out for the user the items that might be of interest. Content-based recommendations are questions identified as relevant with respect to the user's past choices, while collaborative recommendations are questions that users with similar tastes visited in the past.

In both cases, the recommender engine works as a gray-box: there is some knowledge about the internal functionality, but no intuitive or logical interpretation of how or why certain recommendation decisions are made. Moreover, the recommender does not take into account explicitly the user's learning goals or the order in which questions are selected. Both aspects make the QA system very susceptible to fake information, typically inserted on purpose to influence recommendations. Nevertheless, the overload of information – therefore, the overload of questions in the QA system's database – would make it very difficult for the recommender to propose useful items, especially when there is no well-established goal-oriented approach behind it.

Recent research in the field of query recommendation for search engines are based on query search graphs that aim at extracting interesting relations from users' query logs [13, 15]. Some of these graphs are constructed based on relations between queries which are explored and categorized according to different sources of information (e.g., words in a query, clicked URLs, links between their answers). Other techniques rely on the co-occurrence frequency of query pairs which are part of the same "search mission" [16, 29, 30, 32]. However, these approaches do not take into account neither the semantic interdependence between temporally neighbored queries, nor the user's search intent. A recent attempt to tackle the latter issue is presented in [43].

Despite the extensive research in this area and the successful application of such methods, they are not suitable for QA systems for at least two reasons. First, the recommendation items are represented by questions as well-formed grammatical units endowed with semantic content, whereas search queries are usually a collection of keywords. Secondly, most QA systems are used with the purpose of learning (e.g., find an explanation for a particular phenomenon, understand a specific concept, etc.), while search engines are queried to simply retrieve information. The work presented in this thesis aims at improving question recommendation for QA systems by addressing these two aspects. However, a stronger emphasis is put on the learning capability.

As a motivational example, consider a user in search for answers for a particular question. Once an answer is found, the user might encounter unknown concepts related to his initial search goal that might raise new questions in his mind. In general, the transition from one question to the other is not influenced by their semantic relatedness alone, but it is also driven by a learning process – an interpretable sequence of learning goals.

If such learning patterns could be identified and integrated into a recommender system, the gain would be at least three-fold. First, the learner can efficiently reach his/her learning objectives by visiting only relevant information and in the order that enables better understanding and conceptualization of the topic of interest. Secondly, assuming that such patterns are formed under a controlled environment, they would increase the robustness of the recommender in the presence of fake information. Finally, these learning patterns could be used for the establishment of new fields of study and for (semi-)automated construction of curricula.

1.3. Contribution

Motivated by the aforementioned two features of QA systems, the work documented in this thesis aims at introducing two new recommendation techniques:

- **Short-term** – relies only on the user's current search goal and tries to produce recommendations which are *semantically* relevant to this particular search goal. This type of recommender addresses the first important aspect of QA systems, namely, that recommendation items are represented by questions as well-formed grammatical units endowed with semantic content. Its central component is a *semantic short-text similarity measure* based on a domain-specific taxonomy.

$$q_t \xrightarrow{?} q_{t+1}$$

- **Long-term** or **learning-oriented** – its objective is to model the users' *learning process* using the history log of the QA system – question sequences representing the order in which questions were asked/visited by users– and then use this model to generate meaningful, *learning-oriented* recommendations. This type of recommender is based on a domain-specific topic taxonomy and on Bloom's learning framework[28, 10]. In order to model question sequences, the learning-oriented recommender also uses variable length Markov chains [19, 38, 94].

$$\ldots, q_{t-2}, q_{t-1}, q_t \xrightarrow{?} q_{t+1}, q_{t+2}, \ldots$$

The contribution of this research work is three-fold. First, it introduces a new technique for measuring semantic similarity between short texts. Secondly, it uses the previously mentioned semantic similarity measure in combination with the hierarchical structure of a domain-specific taxonomy to develop a short-term recommendation technique called *conversation recommender*. Finally, it presents a novel collaborative recommender model – the *learning-oriented recommender* – with the objective to guide the user through a useful and meaningful learning process.

In order to show the relevance of these new techniques, an empirical evaluation is performed for each of the three approaches and their results are documented in detail. Additionally, for the evaluation of the learning-oriented recommender beyond the general metrics (e.g. accuracy, coverage, diversity, robustness, etc.), a new measure called *learning utility* was introduced. The aim of the learning utility is to measure how well the learning-oriented recommender reflects the users' learning process. In other words, it measures the *learning gain* of a user from a recommendation.

1.4. Approach

As previously mentioned, there are three key techniques discussed in this thesis. Let us briefly sketch the approach behind them.

Semantic short-text similarity

Research towards the discovery of semantic relatedness between words or concepts has witnessed great achievements in the past three decades. Many new techniques and improvements of existing methods have contributed to the maturation of this challenging research field [25, 39, 46, 52, 66, 77, 85, 89, 91].

Modeling text similarity between documents has also been a heavily researched subject in the IR field and it still represents a great theoretical and practical challenge for the cognitive science [86]. A variety of different methods were developed for measuring document similarity: word-based, keyword-based and n-gram measures [134].

Interestingly, there is little or almost no advancements recorded towards measuring semantic similarity between short fragments of texts (e.g., sentences, questions). In [76] it is argued that existing document similarity measures are not suitable for this purpose.

Motivated by this gap and its relevance for QA systems, i.e. for an efficient and effective question retrieval (i.e. searching for an existing similar question) and storage (i.e. avoiding redundancy), a new *four-layered semantic similarity* was defined. The idea behind this short-text similarity measure is to discover, within short fragments of text, interrelationships between concepts or keywords based on a domain-specific taxonomy and use them to compute the semantic relatedness.

Consider a domain-specific topic taxonomy as a hierarchical structure of key concepts within a particular field of study (e.g., nutrition, earth sciences, biology, etc.). The taxonomy is organized as a tree, where nodes represent topics, i.e. primal

1.4 Approach

concepts, while links between nodes represent IS-A or specification/generalization relationships (e.g., geology is a subtopic of earth sciences). To each of these topics, an extensive set of keywords is assigned, with weights that stand for the "relevance" of a keyword to the corresponding topic.

The four layered semantic similarity is defined, in this order, on the following submeasures:

- the *keyword-set similarity*, which uses
- the *keyword similarity* based on
- the *topic similarity*.

The topic similarity can be defined using one of the existing information content-based similarity measures between concepts [25, 52, 77, 89, 91, 157]. The keyword similarity is defined using the topic taxonomy, by selecting the two most relevant topics for the target keyword pairs. Then, the keyword-set similarity is determined based on a particular combination of keyword pairs and their corresponding similarity. Finally the semantic short-text similarity is expressed as the similarity between the keyword-sets, which are extracted from the corresponding text fragments.

Short-term recommender

The content-based short-term recommender is defined using a semantic utility function that determines how recommendations are generated and it is expressed with the help of the aforementioned semantic similarity measure.

This type of recommender does not leverage the entire history of questions visited in the past by the user, but instead provides suggestions based on the user's recent request.

Recommendations are generated in the following way: the semantic similarity between the user's last question and the rest of the existing questions is computed, and then based on this, the N most relevant questions are filtered out and returned to the user as suggestions.

Based on this technique, a more advanced short-term recommender is defined, which is called *conversation recommender*. The goal of this recommender is to generate recommendations in such a way, that the user feels like being in a conversation with another person.

The main idea behind the conversation recommender is to use the hierarchical structure of the topic taxonomy in order to allow the user to explore other topics of interest. Instead of simply recommending the most similar questions, it offers a variety of suggestions by following a simple pattern. It identifies the last question's topic and its position in the hierarchy of the taxonomy and then visits the neighboring nodes, selecting from each a given number of most similar questions. The nodes are visited after the following rule:

- first, the current topic,

- then, the parent topics,
- followed by the child topics and
- finally, the rest of the topics.

Additionally, the conversation recommender also looks for similar questions within the most popular topics and suggests some of the recently added ones in order to avoid the new item problem.

Learning-oriented recommender

The learning-oriented recommender was introduced for an improved user experience. It was generally observed, that questions are not visited at random and that, even though the user can return to review past topics, there is still an interpretable pattern behind the question sequence logs.

The first step towards modeling such learning patterns was to identify the *key question attributes* that contribute or determine the user's next choice. Two important features were associated with a question:

- the *topic* – refers to the main subject of the question, and
- the *learning objective* – describes the type of knowledge and the cognitive process level needed to answer the question.

According to Bloom's revised learning taxonomy, there are a total number of 24 distinct learning objectives derived from four knowledge (factual, conceptual, procedural, metacognitive) and six cognitive process types (remember, understand, apply, analyze, evaluate, create) [10] (see Appendix B).

The establishment of the learning taxonomy was driven by the need of a common framework to improve the communication between educators on the design of curricula and examinations. However, it was noticed that the same learning objectives can be identified also within questions and it is determined, more or less, by the expected answer.

For example, consider the following question within the earth sciences domain: *"How does the extraction of fossil fuels harm the environment?"*. On the knowledge dimension, this question requires *conceptual* understanding, because it involves the interrelationships between two basic elements – fossil fuels and environment. On the cognitive process dimension, it refers not only to a simple presentation of effects, but also demands either an *explanation* or an *analysis* on the influence of fossil fuels on the environment.

After identifying the main question attributes, the next step was to determine how the two aspects contribute to the sequential user choices. Several probabilistic graphical models, based on variable length Markov chains, were constructed and evaluated in order to find out which of them best capture the user learning behavior.

The results show that question sequences are first influenced by the underlying topic and the order in which these topics are tackled, then, within each topic, a particular order of learning objectives is observed. In other words, users tend to ask questions grouped by topic, but in a particular order which is given by the learning objective of the question (see Figure 1.1).

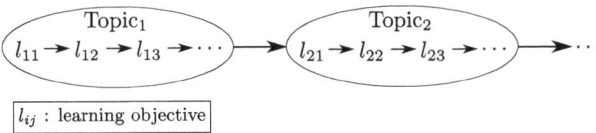

Figure 1.1.: Learning model.

1.5. Benefits

Semantic short-text similarity

The benefits of the semantic short-text similarity measure are multiple and diverse, not only within the information retrieval and natural language processing fields, but also for many other applications.

In particular within a QA system, it contributes to the efficient and effective question retrieval and storage. We mention here only a few:

- searching for existing answers for a particular new question,
- searching for questions similar to a set of keywords provided by the user,
- avoiding redundant questions or answers in the database,
- recommending questions to users [105].

Short-term recommender

To understand the advantages of the short-term recommender within the context of a QA system, consider the following two scenarios:

1. A user is in search for answers for a particular question and types in the search field of the system either the full question or the keywords relevant to this question. In return, the system queries the existing database of questions for semantically similar questions and recommends the users the first N most related ones.

2. In a different scenario, the user has recently learned about the answer for a question within a particular topic, but there are still open questions related to the same topic. In this case, the user might be interested to understand more about it.

In both cases, recommending the semantically most related questions to the user's last request can be of great help and relevance. However, it does not provide the user with the possibility to move from one topic to another and, therefore, the user might find himself/herself caught within the same subject.

Nevertheless, in an attempt to tackle this issue, an extended short-term recommender – the conversation recommender – was introduced, which can generate meaningful recommendations without having to know anything about the user's history nor his/her preferences. Additionally, it can generate suitable recommendations for new users as well, were no browsing history is available, and also "push" recently added questions to the front page.

Despite these benefits, it cannot provide personalized recommendations. We argue that users which faithfully use the services provided by a domain-specific QA system have, in general, a well-defined goal in mind. The conversation recommender cannot detect these needs and help the user follow his/her learning goal.

This is the point where the contributions of the learning-oriented recommender are acknowledged.

Learning-oriented recommender

Consider again a QA system designed to *guide* the user through a particular field of study, assimilating with each question new knowledge. The typical user is driven by a specific learning goal, which can differ or be similar to other users' learning objective. In order to accompany the user on a meaningful and helpful learning journey, the system should be able to detect the user's objective and provide suitable suggestions based on previous experiences.

The learning-oriented recommender is capable of meeting this user need. It can learn from the users' past question sequences and model their learning process based on them, assuming that these sequences actually follow a meaningful learning path. This means that the learner can *efficiently reach* his/her *learning objectives* by visiting only relevant information and in the order that enables better understanding and conceptualization of the topic of interest.

Besides the learning gain, this recommendation technique offers other relevant benefits:

- In general, both content-based and collaborative recommender systems can lack stability and be very sensitive to external attacks that attempt to influence recommendations. Assuming that the learning patterns are formed in a controlled environment, i.e. the question sequences truthfully reflect the users' learning process, they would increase the robustness of the recommender in the presence of fake information.

- Additionally, using the learning-oriented recommender model we could extract learning patterns and then use them for the establishment of new fields of study and for (semi-)automated curricula generation. In other words, these patterns

1.5 Benefits

could serve as a guide to determine the order in which different subjects are ought to be learned.

Road-map

The contributions of this work are grouped as follows:

- chapter 2 gives an overview of the current state-of-the-art within the key research fields subject to this thesis;
- chapter 3 introduces a new semantic short-text similarity measure used for matching and recommendation purposes;
- chapter 4 presents a semantic content-based recommendation approach called short-term or conversation recommendation;
- in chapter 5 a new collaborative, learning-oriented question recommendation is introduced;
- chapter 6 gives an elaborate analysis and evaluation of the three key approaches: semantic short-text similarity, short-term and learning-oriented recommendation;
- finally, in chapter 7 a summary accompanied by concluding statements and some key future perspectives of this work are presented.

2. State of the Art

2.1. Overview

The work documented in this thesis is situated in the overlapping area of four major research fields: recommender systems, semantic text similarity, predictive models and educational psychology. In this regard, the following sections capture some of the most relevant findings registered within these prominent areas. The goal of this chapter is not to give an exhaustive overview, but rather to present a selected collection of concepts, definitions, methods and results which will serve as a foundation for further understanding.

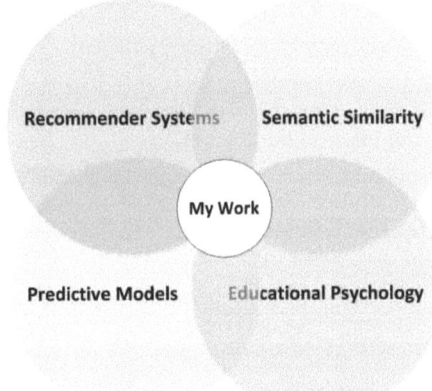

Figure 2.1.: Situation of this work in the overlapping area of four major research fields.

2.2. Recommender systems

This section contains an overview of the field of recommender systems and lists some of the current generation of recommendation methods, usually classified into three main categories: *content-based*, *collaborative* and *hybrid* recommendation approaches.

In the first part, we will shortly present the rationale behind these three approaches, overview some current state-of-the-art techniques and highlight the strengths and weaknesses of these methods. More emphasis will be put on the hybrid-based approaches, since our own method falls into the same category.

Secondly, we will review the latest query recommendation methods and finally, go into more details with graph-based query recommendation approaches.

2.2.1. General overview

Recommender systems (RS) were originally defined as systems in which *"people provide recommendations as inputs, which the system then aggregates and directs to appropriate recipients"* [126]. Since then, the meaning and purpose of RS has evolved and has now a broader connotation.

According to [129], recommender systems are *"software tools and techniques providing suggestions for items to be of use to a user (...) A RS normally focuses on a specific type of item (e.g., CDs, or news) and accordingly its design, its graphical user interface, and the core recommendation technique used to generate the recommendations are all customized to provide useful and effective suggestions for that specific type of item."*

Burke [41] defines RS as systems that produce individualized recommendations as output or has the effect of guiding the user in a personalized way to interesting and useful objects in a large space of possible options.

RSs are, therefore, primarily directed towards individuals who either lack experience, competence or time to evaluate the overwhelming number of items on a specific Web site. One of the most popular example is Amazon.com, which employs a RS to personalize the online store for each customer.

Personalized recommendations are often offered as a ranked list of items, which are predicted based on user preferences and constraints. Basically all RSs are developed based on the simple idea that *"individuals often rely on recommendations provided by others in making routine, daily decisions"*. Therefore, the first RSs tried to leverage recommendations produced by a community to deliver recommendations to the current user. This type or RS is often referred to as collaborative-filtering. But we will get into more details later in this subsection.

Recommender systems (RS) have become an important research area since the mid-1990s when researchers started focusing on recommendation problems that explicitly rely on the ratings structure [3]. The idea behind this approach is to estimate ratings for items that have not been seen by a user.

Let us formally define the recommendation problem. Consider $\mathcal{C}$ the set of all users and let $\mathcal{S}$ be the set of all possible items that can be recommended (e.g. books, movies, sites, etc.). The set $\mathcal{S}$ of items, as well as the set $\mathcal{C}$ of users can be extremely large, even millions in some applications. Let u be a utility function [3] that measures the usefulness of item $s \in \mathcal{S}$ to user $c \in \mathcal{C}$: $u : \mathcal{C} \times \mathcal{S} \to \mathcal{R}$, $\mathcal{R}$ being a

2.2 Recommender systems

totally ordered set (e.g. non-negative integers). Then, for each user $c \in \mathcal{C}$, we want to choose an item $s' \in \mathcal{S}$ that maximizes the user's utility:

$$\forall c \in \mathcal{C}, s'_c = \arg\max_{s \in \mathcal{S}} u(c, s).$$

The utility can be an arbitrary function, depending on the application, can either be explicitly defined by the user or can even be a profit-based function.

The main problem often encountered with recommender systems is that the utility function u is not defined on the entire $\mathcal{C} \times \mathcal{S}$ space, but only on a subset. This is the real challenge of RSs: in order to be able to estimate the utility for every user $c \in \mathcal{C}$ and every item $s \in \mathcal{S}$, it needs to extrapolate the function u to the entire $\mathcal{C} \times \mathcal{S}$ space.

Based on how the utility function is computed, recommender systems are classified into the following categories:

- *content-based* – recommend items based on what the user preferred in the past;
- *collaborative* – recommend items that people with similar tastes liked in the past;
- *hybrid* – combination of content-based and collaborative methods.

Additional to these types of recommendation techniques, Burke [41] identified another three:

- *demographic* – identifies users that are demographically similar to a given one and tries to extrapolate from their ratings the rating of a specific item;
- *utility-based* – uses a utility function over the entire item-set to describe the users' preferences and uses this function to determine a given item's ranking;
- *knowledge-based* – has knowledge about how a particular item meets a particular user need and then tries to suggest objects based on inferences about a user's needs and preferences.

Table A.2 summarizes the rationale behind these techniques and also provides information about the needed background and input in order to generate recommendations.

In the following, we will present in more detail the related work in the field of content-based, collaborative and hybrid recommender systems.

2.2.1.1. Content-based

Content-based recommender systems try to recommend items similar to the ones a certain user liked in the past [92].

In content-based recommendation methods, the utility $u(c, s)$ of item s for user c is calculated based on the utilities $u(c, s_i)$ assigned by user c to items $s_i \in S$

which are similar to s. The values $u(c, s_i)$ are either explicitly assigned by the user with a rating or can be implicitly assigned based on certain criteria (e.g. user c purchased/viewed/watched item s_i).

As an example, consider an online book store which is based on a content-based recommender system. When recommending books to a user c, the system would first try to identify similar books to the ones highly rated or purchased by the user in the past and then recommend only those books which have a high degree of similarity.

Many current content-based systems focus on recommending items containing textual information: documents, Web sites, news, etc.

Disadvantages

1. *Limited content analysis*

   Content-based techniques are limited by the features that explicitly describe an item. In order to get quality recommendations, one needs to have a sufficient set of features that describe the item and, therefore, the content itself must be either in a form that can be automatically parsed by a computer or the features need to be assigned to items manually.

2. *Overspecialization*

   When the system can only recommend items that score highly against a user's profile, the user is limited to being recommended items that are similar to those already rated. *Diversity* proved to be a desirable feature in RSs, hence new approaches have been developed to improve this aspect. Zhang et al. introduced in [161] five redundancy measures to evaluate whether a document that is suggested by the system as relevant contains some novel information as well. According to [3], the user should be ideally presented with a *range of options and not with a homogeneous set of alternatives*.

3. New User

   Being based on previous ratings, the user needs to rate a sufficient number of items before the system can offer reliable recommendations. A new user, therefore, with few or no ratings provided, would not be able to receive qualitative recommendations.

2.2.1.2. Collaborative

Collaborative RSs try to predict the utility of an item for a certain user based on the items previously rated by other users with similar tastes in the past.

Formally, the utility $u(c, s)$ of item s for user c is determined based on the utilities $u(c_j, s)$ assigned to item s by user c_j that are "similar" to user c.

Consider the same online book store example which is based on a collaborative recommender system. When recommending books to a user c, the system would

2.2 Recommender systems

first try to find other users that have similar tastes in books like user c and then, only the books that are most liked by these users would be recommended.

According to [37], collaborative recommendation algorithms can be divided into two groups: *memory-based* or *heuristic-based* and *model-based*.

The rationale behind **memory-based algorithms** is to use heuristics to make rating predictions based on the previously rated items.

To compute the similarity between two users c and c', many approaches have been developed, mostly based on the ratings of the items that both users rated. The two most popular approaches are *correlation*, *cosine-based* or the *mean squared difference*.

Such recommender systems tried to develop various approaches towards improving the performance of user similarity calculations and rating estimations, for instance, by calculating these values in advance and recalculating them only once in a while. Other improvements proposed extensions of these standard correlation-based and cosine-based techniques: default voting, inverse user frequency, case amplification [37] and weighted majority prediction [49, 107].

Model-based algorithms use the available user-specified ratings to learn a model which will then be used to make predictions [24, 37, 61, 71, 98].

In [37], the proposed probabilistic model calculates unknown user ratings based on the user's rating for the previously rated items:

$$r_{c,s} = \sum_{i=0}^{n} i \times Pr(r_{c,s} = i | r_{c,s'}, s' \in \mathcal{S}_c). \qquad (2.1)$$

where $r_{c,s}$ represents the rating of user c for item s. Here, it is assumed that rating values are integers between 0 and n. The probability expression in Equation 2.1 represents the probability that user c will give a particular rating to item s given that users ratings of the previously rated items $\mathcal{S}_c = \{s \in \mathcal{S} | r_{c,s} \neq \emptyset\}$.

In order to estimate these probabilities, two probabilistic models were proposed: Bayesian networks and cluster models. The experiments show that, in some applications, this model-based technique outperforms memory-based approaches in terms of accuracy of recommendations [24, 37].

Other proposed models-based collaborative recommendations are based on: statistical models, probabilistic relational models, linear regression, maximum entropy model, Markov decision processes [139], probabilistic latent semantic analysis [71], Latent Dirichlet Allocation [98], etc.

In [117] a combination of both memory-based and model-based approaches was introduced, which was experimentally demonstrated to provide better recommendations than memory-based or model-based collaborative approaches on their own.

A different approach towards improving existing collaborative filtering algorithms was proposed in [159]. The input of the set of user-specified ratings was carefully selected using some methods that exclude noise, redundancy and exploit the sparsity of the ratings data.

Disadvantages

1. *Memory-based approaches - few ratings*

   One of the limitations of memory-based approaches is that whenever there are relatively few user-specified ratings these methods would not work well when computing the similarity between two users since the similarity measures is based on the sets of items rated by both users.

2. *New user problem*

   As with content-based recommender systems, in order to make accurate recommendations, the system must learn first the user's preferences from introduced ratings. In case of a new user with few or no rating history, collaborative approaches will also perform weak. To address this problem, hybrid recommendation approaches were adopted (see subsubsection 2.2.1.3).

3. *New item problem*

   A similar problem arises when new items are added to the system: until a substantial number of users get to rate these items, the system would not be able to recommend it. Similarly, this problem was also solved using hybrid approaches.

4. *Sparsity*

   The problem of sparsity arises when the number of existing ratings is small in comparison to the number of ratings to be predicted. Therefore, users with unique preferences will receive poor recommendations, since no other user with similar tastes exists. There are a few techniques that try to solve this problem. One way would be to also use user profiles [116] when computing the similarity between users. Exploring the transitive associations among users using their past ratings and feedback also solves the sparsity problem [73]. Another approach is using a dimensionality reduction technique, Singular Value Decomposition (SVD) [24].

2.2.1.3. Hybrid

The development of hybrid recommendation approaches were primarily driven by the need of avoiding the limitations of content-based and collaborative systems. In [3], a classification of such hybrid methods is given:

1. implementing collaborative and content-based approaches separately and then combining their predictions,

2. incorporating some content-based characteristics into a collaborative approach,

2.2 Recommender systems

3. incorporating some collaborative characteristics into a content-based approach, and

4. constructing a general unifying model that incorporates both content-based and collaborative characteristics.

Combining separate recommender systems This technique is based on combining the ratings obtained from the individual methods into a final recommendation using either a linear combination or a voting scheme [116]. Another approach would be to use only one of the individual recommenders, at a given moment, by choosing the "better" one based on a specific "quality" metric (e.g. choosing the recommendation which is more consistent with the past ratings of the user).

Incorporating content-based characteristics into collaborative models The approach described in [116] is a traditional collaborative recommender method but it also incorporates content-based user profiles which are then used to calculate the similarity between two users. This method allows to overcome the sparsity-related problems.

A similar approach is used in [102], where the existing vector of user ratings is enriched with additional ratings which are calculated using a pure content-based recommender.

Incorporating collaborative characteristics into content-based models One of the most well-known approaches within this category is the dimensionality reduction technique used on a group of content-based profiles [142].

Unifying recommendation model In [118] and [137] a unified probabilistic approach is introduced for combining collaborative and content-based recommendations based on probabilistic latent semantic analysis. Another technique is proposed in [45], which uses Bayesian mixed-effects regression models that employ Markov chain Monte Carlo methods for parameter estimation and prediction.

In order to improve recommendation accuracy to address some of the limitations of traditional recommender systems, hybrid methods can also been augmented with knowledge-based techniques [40].

All in all, several papers, focused on comparing empirically the performance of hybrid approaches with pure collaborative and content-based approaches, showed that hybrid methods can deliver much more accurate results than pure approaches [102, 116, 142].

However, in [3] it is argued that in order to provide better recommendations for more complex applications, most of the previously mentioned methods would need significant extensions: improving the understanding of users and items, incorporating the contextual information into the recommendation process.

2.2.1.4. Extending the capabilities of recommender systems

As previously pointed out, most recommender systems produce ratings that are based on a limited understanding of the information in the user's transactional histories and other available data [3].

Additionally to using profile features or user demographics, more **advanced profiling techniques** based on data mining [54], sequences [96] and signatures [47] that describe a user's preferences can be used to build more complex user profiles.

After building the user and item profiles the rating estimation function can be defined as a function of the user profile, item profile and the previously registered ratings. Such a recommendation would clearly subsume the collaborative, content-based and hybrid methods.

As mentioned in the previous subsection, model-based approaches are based on various statistical and machine learning methods. Another possible extension for model-based recommender systems could be the use of other areas of mathematics, such as **mathematical approximation theory** (e.g. radial basis functions), for defining the rating estimation function.

According to [3], current recommender systems rely on a two-dimensional *User × Item* space and do not take into consideration any additional information, like context (e.g. time, place, circumstances, etc.), which might be crucial in some applications (e.g. vacation recommendation). In order to take contextual information into consideration, [2] proposes a new definition of the utility function over a **multidimensional space** as

$$u : D_1 \times D_2 \times, \ldots, \times D_n \to \mathcal{R}.$$

Although not many of the existing two-dimensional recommendation algorithms can be extended to a multidimensional one, there is another possible approach which allows this extension, namely using a hierarchical Bayesian network [12].

In [4] it is argued that relevant contextual information is of great importance when providing recommendations. Here, the authors discuss the general notion of context and how it can be modeled in recommender systems. They also introduce three different algorithmic paradigms – contextual pre-filtering, post-filtering, and modeling – for incorporating contextual information into the recommendation process.

Such contextualization has been extensively researched as a paradigm for building intelligent systems that can better predict and anticipate the needs of users, and act more efficiently in response to their behavior. In [148], a context framework that identifies relevant context dimensions for Technology Enhanced Learning (TEL) applications is presented. Promising prototypes illustrate the potential and opportunities that these systems create. Still, important challenges related to the capturing and use of contextual data remain open and need to be tackled in order to increase uptake and validate research efforts in realistic trial experiments.

2.2 Recommender systems

Other possible extensions for recommender systems can be considered any of the following [3]:

- **Multi-criteria ratings** – In some applications it is crucial to incorporate into the recommendation method not just single criterion ratings, but also multi-criteria ratings (e.g. restaurant recommendation based on food quality, decor and service).

- **Non-intrusiveness** – Recommender systems are considered intrusive when they require explicit feedback from the user and often with a significant user involvement. One possible way of exploring the intrusiveness problem is to determine an optimal number of ratings the system should ask from a new user.

- **Flexibility** – Most recommender systems are considered inflexible, in the sense that they support only a predefined and fixed set of recommendations. Another view of this limitation is the fact that most recommender systems offer only individual items to individual users and are not able to provide aggregated recommendations.

- **Effectiveness** – The problem of developing good evaluation metrics for measuring recommendation effectiveness has been extensively studied in the literature. The most commonly used metrics are coverage (i.e. the percentage of items for which a recommender system can generate predictions) and accuracy (i.e. how well a recommender system can make predictions of high-relevance items). These metrics are limited in the sense that they are typically applied on a test data that users chose to rate. Although further controlled experiments are expensive and time consuming, high-quality experiments are needed in order to understand how well a recommendation method works.

2.2.1.5. Evaluation methods

As we previously stated, there is a vast amount of recommendation methods which can be employed and choosing between a set of candidate approaches can be sometimes a very difficult task. According to [65, 140], a first step towards selecting the appropriate algorithm is to decide which properties of the application to focus upon when making this choice.

With the growing field of recommender systems focused on designing new algorithms, most researchers suggest new methods by comparing their prediction power to a set of existing approaches. However, in [140] it is argued that accurate predictions are crucial but insufficient, due to other existing user needs: discovering new items, exploring diverse items, privacy preservation, etc.

In the same work [140] a few basic guidelines for experimental studies are identified:

- **hypothesis** – important to formulate before running an experiment (e.g. algorithm A predicts better than algorithm B);

- ***controlling variables*** – fix the values of all variables that are not being tested (e.g. train two different algorithms on the same data set); and
- ***generalization power*** – draw conclusions that generalize beyond the immediate context of the experiments.

There are three types of experiment settings for making choices between algorithms [140]:

- ***Offline*** – performed by using a pre-collected data set of user ratings (or selections). The disadvantage of this approach is that it can answer a very narrow set of questions, typically questions related to the prediction power. Also, such a setting will not allow us to directly measure the recommender's influence on user behavior. Usually, such experiments are used to filter out inappropriate approaches.
- ***User studies*** – are conducted by recruiting a set of users and asking them to perform several tasks of interaction with the recommender system. Compared to offline experiments, this setting allows researchers to test user behavior and the collection of other quantitative measurements. However, user studies are very expensive to conduct and are prone to the risk of having a weak representativeness of real system users.
- ***Online*** – the system is used by real users performing real tasks. Such experiments allow multiple algorithms to be compared and overall system goals to be directly measured. Nevertheless, it can also be risky, in the sense that a test system providing irrelevant recommendations may discourage the test users from using the real system again. Therefore, it is best to run such an evaluation last, after an extensive offline study has been done.

2.2.2. Query recommendation

After reviewing the main concepts, methods and the most recent approaches in the field of recommender systems, this subsection will give an overview of a more specific area within this vast research field, namely, *query recommendation engines*. Such approaches were mainly developed to address the recommendation needs of search engines.

Despite of the simple interaction mechanism and success of search engines on the Web, a list of keywords does not always represent the information needs of users [14]. One of the reasons behind this statement is that it is not always easy for users to formulate effective queries:

- ambiguous terms within queries may retrieve documents which are not what users are searching for;
- users typically submit very short queries which are more likely to be ambiguous; and

2.2 Recommender systems

- users phrase their queries differently, depending on how familiar they are with the terminology in a knowledge domain.

Many advancements have been made towards improving query recommendation and query-based information retrieval. These approaches can be roughly classified into the following categories:

- based on clustering [14, 133, 152],
- based on classification [42],
- based on association rules [57],
- based on query expansion,
- based on graphs [13, 16, 29, 30, 31, 32, 33, 35, 34, 51],
- based on probabilistic models [43, 68], and
- based on query templates [144].

In the following, we will review the related work in the field of graph-based query recommendation and information retrieval.

2.2.3. Graph-based query recommendation

The first attempt to model the users' sequential search behavior is presented by Zhang and Nasraoui in [162], where edges between consecutive queries in the same session are weighted by a dumping factor, while the similarity between non-consecutive queries in the same session is calculated by multiplying the values of the edges that join them.

Among the advances made in the area of graph-based query recommendation, we mention here two popular approaches:

- *graphs from search engine queries* [13, 15] and
- *the query-flow graph* [16, 29, 30, 31, 32, 33, 35, 51].

2.2.3.1. Graphs from search engine queries

If we assume that most of the time the queries submitted to a search engine are meaningful, we could safely assume that this information contains implicit knowledge related to user's intent or goal. Therefore, we face the challenge of *extracting interesting relations* from user query logs [13]. The most popular approach adopted towards solving this problem is inferring graphs from search queries. In [13], relations between queries are explored and categorized based on different sources of information: words in a query, clicked URLs, links between their answers. For each source they define different sets and conditions on these sets that generate a query graph (see Figure 2.2).

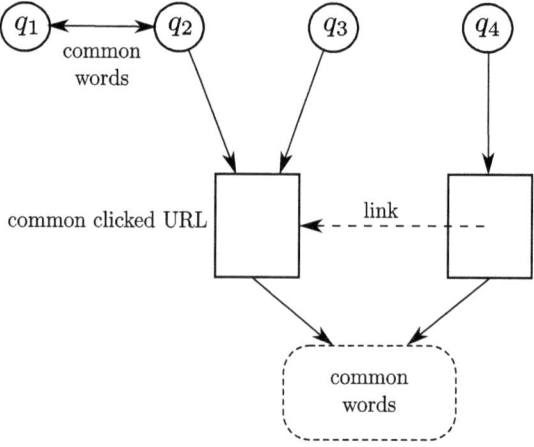

Figure 2.2.: Different relations among queries [13].

Figure 2.3 shows the relationships between the different entities that participate in the process induced by the use of a search engine. In order to formally define the relations within the query graph, the authors [13] introduce the following concepts:

- **Query instance** – defined as the combination of a query (a set of words or a sentence) plus zero or more clicks related to that query:

$$QI = (q, p, t, c^*),$$

where $q = \{words\}$ and $c = (u, t)$, q being the query, p a user profile, u a clicked URL and t a timestamp. QI_i will be used to define the elements of an instance, i.e. $i \in \{q, p, t, c(u), c(t)\}$.

- **Query session** is one or more query instances with the same user profile with an ordered sequence on the timestamps:

$$QS = QI^+.$$

- **URL cover** is a set of all URLs clicked by a query instance:

$$UC_p = \bigcup_{QI_q = p} QI_{c(u)}.$$

Based on these concepts they define the following induced weighted graphs:

2.2 Recommender systems

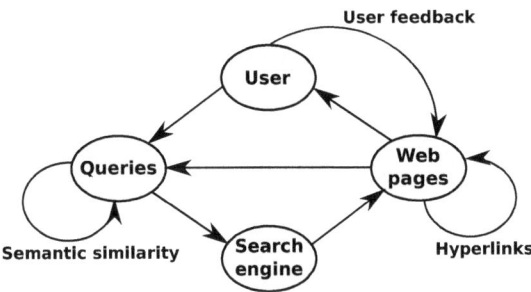

Figure 2.3.: Search engine interaction cycle [13].

1. **Word graph**

   Each vertex v in this graph is a question instance QI and its weight is the number of occurrences of QI. There is an edge between two vertices v_1 and v_2 if $v_{1_q} \cap v_{2_q} \neq \emptyset$. The weight of such an edge is the number of cases where this condition is true.

2. **Session graph**

   Each vertex v in this graph is a question instance QI and its weight is the number of sessions that have this query. There is a directed edge from v_1 to v_2 if both QIs are in the same session and v_1 happened before v_2. The weight of such an edge is the number of such cases.

3. **URL cover graph**

   Each vertex v is a question instance QI and its weight is the number of occurrences of the query. There are different types of edges between v_1 and v_2 depending on whether we have a

   - complete cover: $UC_{v_{1_q}} \subset UC_{v_{2_q}}$ determines a directed edge from v_1 to v_2;
   - identical cover: $UC_{v_{1_q}} = UC_{v_{2_q}}$ determines an undirected edge between v_1 and v_2; or
   - partial cover: $UC_{v_{1_q}} \cap UC_{v_{2_q}} \neq \emptyset$ determines an undirected edge between v_1 and v_2, but could be directed from v_1 to v_2 if $|UC_{v_{1_q}}| > |UC_{v_{2_q}}|$.

   The weight of any of these edges is then the size of the smallest set covered.

4. **URL link graph**

   Each vertex v in this graph is a question instance QI and its weight is the number of occurrences of the query. There is a directed edge from v_1 to v_2 if there is at least a link from a URL in $UC_{v_{1_q}}$ to a URL in $UC_{v_{2_q}}$. The weight of the edge is then the number of such links.

5. **URL terms graph**

From every clicked URL we can extract a set of terms to represent it: either the full text of the page (without HTML tags and stop-words), a text snippet generated by the search engine (sentences or passages containing the query), a subset of the text content of the URL, the anchor text in the links that point to the URL or a combination of these. Then, a URL is represented by a set of terms and the frequency of each term. The induced graph is similar to the previous: each vertex v is a question instance QI and its weight is the number of occurrences of the query. There is a directed edge from v_1 to v_2 if there is at least l common terms in the intersection of the representations of at least one URL in $UC_{v_{1_q}}$ to a URL in $UC_{v_{2_q}}$. The weight of the edge is the sum of the frequencies of the common terms in such URLs.

The previously mentioned graphs have been presented as independent graphs, although one can have a single graph which aggregates all the above ones with different labels for each edge type (see Figure 2.2). Such graphs can be used for a various number of applications, such as:

- polysemy recognition,
- query similarity,
- query relatedness,
- query clustering, and
- pseudo-taxonomy of queries.

In [15], a weighted version of the cover graph is studied, which provides information not only about how people query but also about how they behave after a query and the content distribution of what they look at. The studied framework was used to infer semantic relations between queries and to detect "multi-topical" URLs.

2.2.3.2. The query-flow graph

Based on the important observation that query logs contain valuable information about how web users interact with search engines as well as knowledge about the interests, preferences and behavior of those users, [29] introduces a graph representation of knowledge about latent querying behavior. This approach, called the **query-flow graph**, has become very popular in the IR field and many advances have been made based on this graph representation [16, 30, 33, 35, 51].

The query-flow graph is based on the intuitive idea that two queries q_1 and q_2 which are part of the same "search mission" should be connected through an edge. Therefore, any path over this graph may be regarded as a search behavior, whose likelihood is given by the "strength" of the edges along the path. The query-flow graph is basically a Markov chain-based representation of a query log.

This graph has as nodes all queries contained in the log and a directed edge between two queries q_1 and q_2 has a weight $w(q_1, q_2)$ which represents the probability that

2.2 Recommender systems

two queries appear in the given order and part of the same search goal. One might explain a high $w(q_1, q_2)$ value as q_2 being a reformulation of q_1.

Before going further to discuss the detailed representation of this graph, let us define some basic concepts related to this approach.

Let $\mathcal{U}$ be the set of all users and $\mathcal{D}$ the set of all documents indexed by the search engine.

A **query log** records information about the search actions of the users while using the search engine. Such information includes:

- submitted queries,
- viewed documents, and
- clicked documents.

A query log $\mathcal{L}$ is defined as a set of records $< q_i, u_i, t_i, V_i, C_i >$, where q_i is the submitted query, $u_i \in \mathcal{U}$ is a unique identifier for the user who submitted the query, t_i is a timestamp, V_i is the set of the returned result documents, and C_i is the set of documents clicked by the user ($C_i \subseteq V_i \subseteq \mathcal{D}$). For the purposes of the query-flow graph, the authors reduced the definition of query logs to $\mathcal{L} = \{< q_i, u_i, t_i >\}$.

A **user query session** is defined as a sequence of queries of one user within a fixed time limit t_θ:

$$S = << q_{i_1}, u_{i_1}, t_{i_1} >, \ldots, < q_{i_k}, u_{i_k}, t_{i_k} >>,$$

where $u_{i_1} = \cdots = u_{i_k} = u \in \mathcal{U}$, $t_{i_1} \leq \cdots \leq t_{i_k}$ and $t_{i_{j+1}} - t_{i_j} \leq t_\theta$, for all $j \in \{1, 2, \ldots, k-1\}$.

A **super-session** is the sequence of all queries of a particular user in the query log, ordered by timestamp. A super-session, therefore, allows time differences larger than t_θ.

A **chain** is a topically coherent sequence of queries of a particular user, which in [124] is also defined as "a sequence of queries with a similar information need." This requires relating queries based on the user information need, which is not a trivial problem. Also, for the formal definition of chains, no timeout constraint is imposed.

The **query-flow graph** is a directed graph $G_{qf} = (V, E, w)$, where $V = Q \cup \{s, t\}$ is the set of all queries Q submitted to the search engine together with s a starting state and t a terminal state. $E \subseteq V \times V$ is the set of directed edges and $w : E \to (0, 1]$ is a weighting function that assigns to every pair of queries $(q_1, q_2) \in E$ a weight $w(q_1, q_2)$ representing the probability that q_1 and q_2 are part of the same chain. The two special nodes s and t represent the beginning and the end of query chains. Therefore, an edge (s, q_i) means that q_i is a potential starting query in a chain and $w(s, q_i)$ quantifies the probability of having this event. In a similar way, the edge (q_i, t) implies the probability of q_i being a terminal query in a chain.

In [29], a machine learning algorithm is used to obtain the edge weights in the query-flow graph from the query log. The algorithm takes as input a set of sessions $\mathcal{S}(\mathcal{L}) = \{S_1, S_2, \ldots, S_m\}$ and for each query pair $(q, q'), q, q' \in Q$ it creates an edge if there is at least one session in $\mathcal{S}(\mathcal{L})$ in which q and q' are consecutive:

$$T = \{(q, q') | \exists S_j \in \mathcal{S}(\mathcal{L}) \ s.t. \ q = q_i \in S_j \text{ and } q' = q_{i+1} \in S_j\}.$$

For each edge (q, q'), a probability $w(q, q')$ and a set of features (e.g. textual, session and time-related) are assigned using a machine learning model. The learning of the weighting function is performed using a manually labeled training data. In [29], Boldi et al. describe two weighting schemes: the *chaining probability* and the *relative frequencies*. In the case of arc weighting, it has been shown that the chaining probability is the most effective scheme.

Using the query-flow graph, the authors introduce a method that exploits the information in the graph for segmenting the user sessions into logically coherent query chains. For the problem of query recommendation, [29] proposes an algorithm using random walks that builds on the concept of the query-flow graph and allows leveraging query similarity and the overall complexity of the graph.

Boldi et al. [30] perform further experiments with this approach and show that it can improve the recommendations based on query-click graphs without using the user clicks. Their work also suggests that it is important to consider adding transition-type labels on edges for having good quality recommendations.

However, there are several problems with directly using the query-flow graph for recommendation:

- **Graph sparsity** – recommendation for many dangling queries (with no out-links) are not well handled;
- **Ambiguous intents** – queries are often ambiguous and reflect different search intents.

In [16], the authors propose to model the query-flow graph for better recommendation results, avoiding these drawbacks. They introduce a novel mixture model for the query-flow graph. The model employs a probabilistic approach to interpret the generation of the graph: how the queries and the transitions between queries are generated under the hidden search intents. Further on, the learned user intents are used to obtain better query recommendation with an intent-biased random walk.

2.2.3.3. The term-query graph

Bonchi et al. [34] introduce a recommendation method based on the concept of *center-piece subgraphs* [145] that allows time/space efficient generation of suggestions also for rare (i.e. long-tail) queries.

This technique relates terms contained in queries with highly correlated queries in a query-flow graph. It is based on a graph called *TQGraph (Term-Query Graph)* having *term* nodes, *query* nodes, and two kinds of connections: *term-query* and *query-query*. Arcs connect a term node to all the query nodes containing it, while arcs between query nodes express the likelihood that a user submits the second query after having issued the first one.

According to [34], the TQGraph, being term-centric, does not suffer from the problem of sparsity of queries and it is able to generate recommendations for previously unseen queries, to the extent of the previously recorded terms. To overcome the limitation of computing the center-piece subgraph from query terms, an *inverted list-based data structure* was used to store precomputed vectors. This data structure is compressed using a lossy compression method able to reduce by an average of 80% the space needed for the uncompressed data. The loss of the compression method was evaluated through a user study and found to be negligible.

The TQGraph model

Let $Q = <q_q, q_2, \ldots, q_n>$ be a query log composed of queries annotated with a *userID* and *timestamp*. The TQGraph is a tuple $G = (V, E)$, where V is the set of vertices and E is the set of edges. If T is the set of all terms occurring in Q, then $V = V_T \cup V_Q$, where V_T is the set of term nodes and V_Q is the set of query nodes. Similarly, $E = E_Q \cup E_{TQ}$. Arcs in E_Q are defined as in the query-flow graph and E_{TQ} contains arcs of the type (t, q), where $t \in T$ is a term contained in the query $q \in Q$. Finally, a weighting function $w : E \to (0, 1]$ is defined, which assigns to each arc $(u, v) \in E$ a value $w(u, v)$. For $(t, q) \in E_{TQ}$, $w(t, q) = \frac{1}{d}$, where d is the number of distinct queries in which t occurs (i.e. the number of outlinks of t). The arcs in E_Q are weighted using the query-flow graph weighting scheme, namely the *chaining probability* which is computed using logistic regression.

In [34], the suggestions for a given query q are generated based on a TQGraph by performing a procedure called *Random Walk with Restart* (RWR) starting from the nodes associated with the query terms. The proposed technique computes efficiently and on-the-fly suggestions by exploiting a pruned and approximated index. An experimental evaluation was conducted to assess the effectiveness and efficiency of this method. Bonchi et al. [34] show that the TQGraph-based technique can provide suggestions for about 99% of the questions and also the quality of the recommendations were judged higher than using the query-flow graph.

2.2.4. Query recommendation using probabilistic models

Within the area of query recommendation based on probabilistic models, we mention here two approaches (see [43, 68]) that use variable length Markov models to generate query recommendations. The motivation behind the development of these techniques is two-fold. First, the pair-wise approach (i.e. predicting the probability of the next query based only on a single preceding query) is not sufficient to capture the contextual information and the user's search goal. Second, many query sessions can only be correctly modeled by treating the previous queries sequentially. The work behind these methods is inspired by search engines, where the task of query recommendation is to help users formulate queries that better represent their search intent, but also for other purposes: search relevance enhancement, online advertisement, search result presentation and personalized search.

Sequential query prediction using a MVMM model

The work presented in [68] is based on an empirical study with 20,000 randomly picked query sessions which were manually classified by 30 labelers to seven common types of search patterns: spelling change, parallel movement, generalization, specification, synonym substitution, repeated queries and others. At least three of these categories, including *spelling change*, *generalization* and *specialization* are directly related to the order of queries in sessions. Therefore, modeling query sessions as sequences instead of bags or pair of queries is crucial.

The proposed sequence-based query recommendation approach consists of two main phases:

1. *Offline model learning phase* - each session from the log is treated as a query sequence based upon which a probabilistic prediction model is constructed.

2. *Online query recommendation phase* - where the observed query context of a user is fed to the prediction model and the top N queries with the highest prediction scores are returned as suggestions.

The second phase is straightforward. Therefore, the key idea of this technique lies within the choice of the prediction model in the first phase. A wide range of statistical models were surveyed and the choice was narrowed down to the family of Markov models and their extensions. Markov models are parametric approaches that accurately estimate sequence distributions and have been proven to be successful in modeling complex sequences in the field of natural language processing and biological gene sequence analysis.

One of the fundamental Markov models is the N-gram. The naive N-gram model relies on a maximum length context which causes low-coverage and over-fitting problems. For example, consider a sequence of user input series $< q_1, \ldots, q_{i-1} >$. The goal would be to predict the user's next query q_i. For this, we would need to search the training evidence of $< q_1, \ldots, q_{i-1} >$ from the fixed i-gram model, where i varies over user inputs. In order to avoid this, the Variable Memory Markov (VMM) model was considered, which allows backtracking along uncovered suffix contexts. Additionally, the VMM models also aim at determining a bound D on the maximum context length.

Although both the naive N-gram and the VMM have proved to be more effective than the traditional pair-wise approaches, neither of the two models can adapt to the

2.2 Recommender systems

user input on the fly and dynamically determine the optimal length of the context used for query prediction. To address this problem, He et al. propose a sequential probabilistic model called *Mixture Variable Memory Markov* (MVMM) model [68].

This approach consists of two steps:

1. *Training* - multiple VMM models with different context bounds are learned.
2. *Testing* - a mixture model is constructed to adapt to the test query sequence on-the-fly.

The technique was evaluated on a large dataset using various data and user-centric metrics. The authors discovered that ordered queries within the same sessions are highly correlated and, therefore, the order within a sequence should be used to understand the user information needs. Also, it has been shown, that the proposed MVMM model achieved the best balance between accuracy and coverage both in terms of data (objective) and user (subjective) centric evaluation metrics. A thorough time and memory complexity analysis of the MVMM approach was conducted and it was found to be practical and effective for real-time deployment and, therefore, suitable for real-time search engine recommendation.

Context-aware search using vlHMM

In [43], the authors propose a general approach to context-aware search using a *variable length hidden Markov model* (vlHMM). This work is motivated by the belief that the context of a user's query, i.e. the past queries and clicks in the same session, may help understand the user's information need and improve the search experience substantially.

Cao et al. [43] develop a strategy for parameter initialization within the vlHMM learning, which can reduce the number of parameters to be estimated in practice. Additionally, they devise a method for distributed vlHMM learning under the map-reduce model.

Within this context, the authors also argue that by considering only correlations between query pairs, the model cannot capture well the user's search context. In order to achieve general context-aware search, a comprehensive model is needed that can be used simultaneously for multiple applications (e.g. query suggestion, URL recommendation, document re-ranking).

Consider q_t to be the current query. The vlHMM can rank search results by the posterior probability distribution $P(s_t|q_t, O_{1...t-1})$, where s_t is the current search intent and $O_{1...t-1}$ is the context of q_t given by the past queries $q_1, \ldots, q_{t-1}$ and the URL clicks of these queries $u_1, \ldots, u_{t-1}$ (see Figure 2.4). Additionally, the vlHMM can also predict the user's next search intent s_{t+1} by $P(s_{t+1}|q_t, O_{1...t-1})$ and generate query suggestions.

Although hidden Markov models have been adopted in many applications, their use for context-aware search is far from trivial. Due to the extremely large search session data, it is impractical to apply the existing algorithms [43].

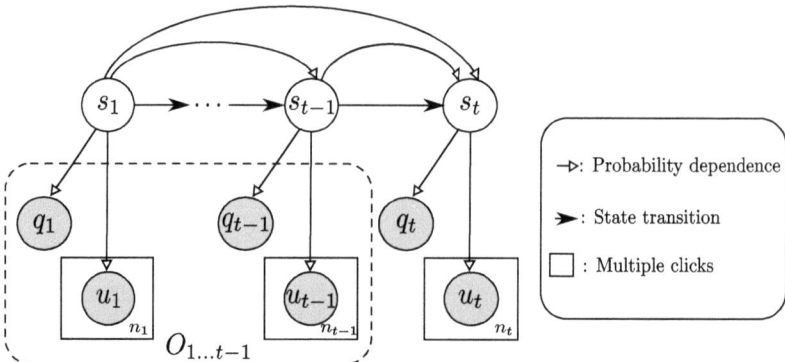

Figure 2.4.: Graphical structure of the vlHMM [43].

Cao et al. propose a novel model to support context-aware search and develop efficient algorithms and strategies for learning a very large vlHMM from big log data [43]. The experimental results show that this vlHMM-based context-aware approach is effective and efficient.

2.2.5. Summary

In this section, we have reviewed the state-of-the-art within the field of recommender systems, emphasizing the query recommendation techniques. We have seen that existing recommender systems employ one or more of the following basic techniques: content-based, collaborative, demographic, utility-based and knowledge-based. All of them being subject to advantages and disadvantages.

Hybrid recommender systems were adopted in order to avoid the downsides of these methods and to obtain an improved performance. A significant amount of recent research has been dedicated to the exploration of various hybrids, but [41] indicates that less than a half of the possible recommender hybrids have not been explored yet. Burke introduces a hybrid recommender system, called EntreeC, that combines knowledge-base and collaborative techniques using a cascade hybrid [41]. Experiments show that collaborative filtering improves the performance of the knowledge-based component. Additionally, the semantic ratings of the knowledge-based component delivered more accurate predictions with respect to the user preferences.

Advances in the area of query recommendation are based on one or a combination of the following methods: clustering, classification, association rules, query expansion, query graphs, probabilistic models and query templates. One of the most prominent results is based on the query-flow graph [29]. Starting from this graph structure, much progress has been made towards segmenting user sessions into logically-coherent query chains and towards generating useful query sugges-

2.3. Semantic text similarity

Although the concept of *similarity* is well formalized in psychology, *text similarity* is less well-defined and, according to [17], is often used *"as an umbrella term covering quite different phenomena."* Therefore, it is important to define a formal model that indicates the *properties* based on which the similarity between two texts is evaluated.

In [17], text similarity is formalized based on the geometric model of *conceptual spaces* along three dimensions: *structure*, *style* and *content*. *Structure* refers to the internal developments of a given text (e.g. order of sections), *style* addresses grammar, usage, mechanics and lexical complexity and *content* refers to all topics and their relationships within the text. The experiments conducted in this work show that humans indeed judge similarity along different dimensions and that is important for text similarity measures to address and explicitly state the conceptual dimensions they target. It was also demonstrated that the datasets used for their experiments encode only the content dimension of text similarity, concluding that further datasets are necessary to inspire the development of measures along the other two dimensions.

In contrast, [76] classifies related work in the field of text similarity measures into four major categories: *word co-occurrance* or *vector-based* documents model methods (e.g. cosine measure), *corpus-based* methods (LSA [82], HAL [39]), *hybrid* methods [90] and *descriptive feature-based* methods using a trained classifier. All these categories cover only the content and some also the structural dimensions mentioned above. Moreover, it was demonstrated that, by taking the structural dimension into account, the similarity measure obtains a lower accuracy and correlation with human ratings.

Since this work focuses on short text similarity (see chapter 3), more specifically question similarity, the structure and style dimensions are more or less fixed. Therefore, our further investigations will concentrate on similarity measures which describe the content dimension.

In this regard, we distinguish two main branches of text similarity measures: the ones that focus on the *object's parts* (e.g. letters, words, concepts, etc.) and the ones that use the *location of the objects or their parts* within an ontology [23]. From the first group, which in some sources are referred to as *syntactic* measures, we briefly mention here the popular edit (Levenstein) distance, Euclidean vector distance, Jaccard, Dice and cosine similarity measures.

In the following, we will mainly focus on the state-of-the-art within the second group, the ontology-based *semantic* text similarity measures, but we will also mention some fundamental syntactic similarity measures.

Chapter 2 State of the Art

Semantic similarity is a heavily researched subject in computer science, in particular, text similarity plays an important role in information retrieval (IR) and natural language processing (NLP) applications. Measuring similarity between documents has a long tradition in IR. These approaches rely on comparisons between vectors of document features [39, 82, 83, 114]. The most commonly used feature is the frequency of single words or word stems.

There is extensive literature on measuring similarity between documents [82, 83, 86] or between concepts within a taxonomy [8, 25, 36, 46, 52, 66, 77, 84, 85, 87, 89, 91, 123, 127, 128, 136, 151, 157], while there are few methods that aim at computing short text semantic similarity [76, 90, 115, 112, 146] or semantic similarity between sets of concepts [36, 46, 66]. In [90], the authors argue that existing long text similarity measures have some limitations and drawbacks and that their performance is unsatisfactory when applied to short sentences.

Therefore, in the following, we will briefly present in the order of their evolution the related research in the area of semantic similarity between concepts, sets of concepts and documents, and short text similarity.

2.3.1. Concept similarity

There are basically two ways of using an ontology or taxonomy to determine the semantic similarity between concepts: the *edge-based approach* and the *information content-based approach*. The following two sections presents these two methodologies, concluding with a comparison and discussion on the benefits of each of these approaches based on related literature findings.

2.3.1.1. Edge-based concept similarity

Intuitively, the similarity of different concepts in an ontology is measured by computing the distance between the concepts within the ontology. Namely, if two concepts reside closer in the ontology, then we can conclude that they are more similar. When computing the ontology distance we actually use the specialization graph of objects and we define it as being the shortest path between the two concepts [85, 123]. The specialization graph is a hierarchical representation of concepts within an ontology, where concepts are represented by nodes and edges between these nodes represent specialization/generalization (or IS-A) relationships. Usually, these hierarchical graphs are trees (each node can have at most one parent), but in some cases nodes can have several parents, i.e. some concepts can be sub-classes of several parent classes (like *cat* is a specialization of *mammal* and *pet*).

Rada et al. [123] defined the conceptual distance measure as

$$sim(c_1, c_2) = \text{ the minimum number of edges separating } c_1 \text{ and } c_2,$$

2.3 Semantic text similarity

where c_1 and c_2 are the node representations of the two concepts in the ontology. Wu and Palmer [157] redefined the edge-based similarity measure taking into account the depth of the nodes in the hierarchical graph:

$$sim(c_1, c_2) = \frac{2 \cdot N_3}{N_1 + N_2 + 2 \cdot N_3}, \qquad (2.2)$$

where N_1 and N_2 are the number of nodes from c_1 and c_2 to c_3, which is known as *the least common super-concept* (LCS) of c_1 and c_2. N_3 is the number of nodes on the path from c_3 to the root node.

Similarly, Li et al. [89] introduced the similarity between two concepts as:

$$sim(c_1, c_2) = \begin{cases} e^{-\alpha l} \cdot \frac{e^{\beta h} - e^{-\beta h}}{e^{\beta h} + e^{-\beta h}} & \text{, if } c_1 \neq c_2 \\ 1 & \text{, otherwise} \end{cases} \qquad (2.3)$$

where, the parameters α and β scale the contribution of the two values: l, the shortest path length between c_1 and c_2, and h, the depth of the LCS of c_1 and c_2. Based on the benchmark data set, they obtained the optimal parameters $\alpha = 0.2$ and $\beta = 0.6$.

Al-Mubaid and Nguyen [8] formulated a combined semantic similarity measure which achieves a better correlation with human ratings than the ones defined in [84, 123, 157]:

$$sim(c_1, c_2) = log((Path(c_1, c_2))^\alpha \cdot (CSpec(c_1, c_2))^\beta + k),$$

where $Path(c_1, c_2)$ is the length of the shortest path between c_1 and c_2 in the graph. $CSpec(c_1, c_2)$ is the *common specificity* of c_1 and c_2, which is determined by the LCS of the two nodes. The parameters α and β scale the contribution of the two functions. In [8], the similarity measure was based on clusters. Therefore, the computation of the two above mentioned functions would differ depending on the clusters that the two nodes belong to.

The above reviewed edge-based similarity measures are limited by the assumption that links in the taxonomy represent uniform distances, whereas such an assumption does not reflect the real semantic connections between concepts [127, 151].

2.3.1.2. Information content-based concept similarity

The second type of concept similarity is the information content (IC)-based similarity, which was introduced by Resnik in [127]. The information content-based approach assumes that the frequency of two co-occurring terms within a given ontology represents the similarity of the two terms. Resnik shows that by associating probabilities with concepts in the taxonomy it is possible to capture the same idea of edge-based similarity, but avoid the unreliability of uniform edges.

In order to do this, the ontology is augmented with a function $p : C \to [0, 1]$, such that

$$\forall c \in C, \quad p(c) = \text{the probability of encountering an instance of concept } c.$$

According to the standard argumentation of information theory, the information content of concept c is defined as the negative log likelihood:

$$IC(c) = -log[p(c)]. \qquad (2.4)$$

Intuitively, this means that as probability increases, informativeness decreases, so the more abstract a concept, the lower its information content.

Following this argumentation, Resnik defined the similarity of two concepts as

$$sim(c_1, c_2) = \max_{c_3 \in S(c_1, c_2)} [-log(p(c_3))], \qquad (2.5)$$

where $S(c_1, c_2)$ is the set of concepts that subsume both c_1 and c_2.

In this context, Resnik also considers word similarity and formulates it as

$$wsim(w_1, w_2) = \max_{c_1 \in s(w_1), c_2 \in s(w_2)} [sim(c_1, c_2)], \qquad (2.6)$$

where $s(w)$ represents the set of concepts in the taxonomy that are senses of word w.

Compared to the edge-counting method, the similarity measure introduced by Resnik is conceptually quite simple. However, it is not sensitive to the problem of varying link distances. In addition, by combining an ontological structure with empirical probability estimates, it provides a way of adapting a static knowledge structure to multiple contexts.

This similarity measure was further improved by Lin [91], when he introduced the information-theoretic definition of similarity. Based on it, he formulated the semantic similarity in a taxonomy as:

$$sim(c_1, c_2) = \frac{2 \cdot log[p(c_3)]}{log[p(c_1)] + log[p(c_2)]}, \qquad (2.7)$$

2.3 Semantic text similarity

where c_3 is the LCS of c_1 and c_2. One can notice here the similarities to the measure defined by Wu and Palmer (see Equation 2.2).

Additionally, Jiang and Conrath introduced in [77] a similarity measure that combines the edge-based and IC-based measure and also takes edge weights into account. The edge weight is determined by several factors: local density, node depth, and connection type. Wang considers both edge-based and IC-based measures when formulating in [151] a similarity criterion based on hierarchy information content and attribute information content. In [25], a similar concept was used taking into account the PART-OF relations. Concurrently, a hybrid semantic similarity measure was defined that can be directly applied to a semantic-rich ontology environment [52]. It computes concept similarity based on the content of pseudo-concepts (Latent Semantic Indexing) and based on the structure of a lightweight ontology graph.

2.3.2. Concept-set similarity

The next step towards determining text similarity was defining a relatedness measure between *sets of concepts*. Let us consider two objects $\mathcal{O}_1$ and $\mathcal{O}_2$, which could either represent textual questions, answers, documents, image descriptions, etc. Then, $\mathcal{C}_1$ and $\mathcal{C}_2$ are the corresponding sets of simple concepts, assigned to the two objects, and represent attributes of $\mathcal{O}_1$ and $\mathcal{O}_2$, respectively (e.g. extracted words, word stems). The goal of defining a semantic similarity measure between $\mathcal{C}_1$ and $\mathcal{C}_2$ is to find a way of evaluating the *relatedness* of $\mathcal{O}_1$ and $\mathcal{O}_2$. Hence, the similarity measure will depend on how we define the mapping between objects and corresponding sets of concepts.

In [36], the ontological distance between sets of concepts is computed by summing up the distances between every pair (c_1, c_2), where $c_1 \in \mathcal{C}_1$ and $c_2 \in \mathcal{C}_2$. Haase et al. [66] used the edge-based measure defined by Li et al. [89] and formulated the similarity between sets of concepts as:

$$Sim(\mathcal{C}_1, \mathcal{C}_2) = \frac{1}{|\mathcal{C}_1|} \cdot \sum_{c_1 \in \mathcal{C}_1} \max_{c_2 \in \mathcal{C}_2} sim(c_1, c_2), \qquad (2.8)$$

which computes an average of distances between $c_1 \in \mathcal{C}_1$ and the most similar corresponding concept in $\mathcal{C}_2$.

Following this work, a new similarity measure between sets of concepts was introduced in [46] as:

$$Sim(\mathcal{C}_1, \mathcal{C}_2) = \sqrt[m]{\frac{\sum_{c_1 \in \mathcal{C}_1}[sim(c_1, \mathcal{C}_2)]^m}{|\mathcal{C}_1|}}, \quad m \in \{1, 2, \ldots\}, \qquad (2.9)$$

which is calculated using a similarity measure between a single concept and a set of concepts: $sim(c, \mathcal{C})$. This is obtained by determining the similarity from the source concept c_1 to all concepts in $\mathcal{C}_2$, ordering these values and then combining them using the following function:

$$f(x_i) = \begin{cases} x_i + (1 - x_i) \cdot f(x_{i+1}) & \text{, if } i < n \\ x_i & \text{, if } i = n \end{cases},$$

In this context, $(x_1, \cdots, x_n)$ is the ordered sequence of similarity values between c_1 and $c_2 \in \mathcal{C}_2$, where $n = |\mathcal{C}_2|$. This function gives more weight to the higher values, but still allowing lower values to contribute to the final outcome. Then

$$sim(c_1, \mathcal{C}_2) = f(x_1).$$

It is important to notice here that the two measures defined in (Equation 2.8) and (Equation 2.9) are asymmetric, i.e. they compute the similarity based on the source object $\mathcal{O}_1$ and how its features relate to the other object's features.

2.3.3. Document similarity

Modeling text similarity between text documents has been a heavily researched subject in the IR field and it still represents a great theoretical and practical challenge for the cognitive science [86]. A variety of different methods were developed for measuring document similarity: word-based, keyword-based and n-gram measures [134], etc.

One of the most prominent findings in the field of document similarity is Latent Semantic Analysis (LSA) and its variations. In this section we give an overview of the theory behind this popular method and other similar corpus-based text document similarity measures.

These approaches do not make use of an ontology structure, but instead use a rather simple technique to extract semantic relatedness between text documents.

2.3.3.1. Latent semantic analysis

Latent semantic analysis (LSA) [82, 83] is a popular technique in the field of natural language processing (NLP) that analyzes the relationships between a corpus of texts and the words (in this context, often referred to as *terms*) they contain by producing a set of concepts related to the documents and terms. LSA assumes that words that are close in meaning will occur in similar fragments of text.

LSA uses a high dimensional association model, analyzes a large corpus of natural language text and generates a matrix that captures the similarity of words and textual compositions (sentences, paragraphs, documents, etc.). The underlying idea

2.3 Semantic text similarity

is that the aggregation of all word contexts, which contain or not a given word, provides a set of constraints that determines the similarity between words or between sets of words [82].

This technique constructs a matrix from a corpus of texts containing word frequencies per textual fragment (e.g. paragraph, document) and uses *singular value decomposition* (SVD) to find semantic relationships between words by analyzing the statistical interplay among words within the analyzed text corpus. LSA takes the vector space representation of the documents and applies a dimension reducing linear projection. The claim of this technique is that similarities between textual fragments can be better estimated in the reduced latent space representation than in the original, initial representation. The rationale behind this approach is that textual fragments which share frequently co-occurring terms will have a similar representation in the latent space, even if they have no words in common.

To compute sentence similarity using LSA, for each sentence a vector in the reduced-dimensional space is formed. Then, the similarity is measured by the cosine of the angle (see Equation 2.13) between their corresponding vectors.

Due to the computational limitations of SVD, the size of the word by context matrix is fixed to several hundreds and, therefore, we might obtain a very sparse representation of short texts (e.g. sentences). Also, LSA does not take into account the syntactic information. Consequently, this method is more appropriate for longer texts, such as documents [76, 90].

Although LSA has been applied with great success in various IR and NLP applications, it has some deficits, mainly due to its unsatisfactory statistical foundation [70].

2.3.3.2. Probabilistic latent semantic analysis

Probabilistic latent semantic analysis (PLSA) is a statistical technique for the analysis of two-mode and co-occurrence data, which has applications in many fields, including IR, NLP and machine learning (ML) from text [69, 70].

PLSA was mainly conceived to overcome the deficits of LSA and factor analysis. It is based on the likelihood principle and defines a proper generative model of the data, therefore having a solid statistical foundation.

Compared to standard LSA, which stems from linear algebra and reduces the occurrence tables using SVD, PLSA is based on a mixture decomposition derived from a latent class model and uses a widely applicable generalization of maximum likelihood model fitting by tempered expectation maximization (EM).

The PLSI approach models each word in a textual fragment as a sample from a mixture model, where the mixture components are multinomial random variables that can be viewed as *topic* representations. Therefore, each word is generated from a single topic, and different words in a document may be generated from different topics. Additionally, each document is represented as a list of mixing proportions of these components and, thereby, reduced to a probability distribution on a fixed set of topics. This distribution is called the *reduced description* associated with the document.

The factor representation obtained by PLSA can deal with polysemous words and is able to explicitly distinguish between different meanings and different word usage types [70]. According to [69], this approach yields substantial and consistent improvements over LSA in a number of experiments.

Although the PLSA method shows an improved performance over LSA, it is incomplete according to [27], in the sense that it provides no probabilistic model at the level of documents. In PLSI, each document is represented as a list of numbers (the mixing proportions for topics), for which no generative probabilistic model is defined. This leads to several problems:

- the number of parameters in the model grows linearly with the size of the corpus, which leads to overfitting, and
- it is not a clear approach for assigning a probability to a document outside of the training set.

2.3.3.3. Hyperspace analogues to language

Like LSA and PLSA, *hyperspace analogues to language* (HAL) [39] is a corpus-based method that uses lexical co-occurrence to produce a high-dimensional semantic space in which words are represented as points and the position of each word along the axes is related to the word's meaning.

This high-dimensional semantic space is constructed by moving a window over a large corpus and recording weighted lexical co-occurrences in an $n \times n$ matrix with one row and one column for each unique word appearing in the textual corpus.

Each word is then represented by a $2n$ dimensional vector obtained by concatenating the transpose of that word's column to its row. Similarly, a textual fragment will be represented by a vector formed by adding together the previously obtained word vectors, for all words in the fragment.

The similarity between sentences can then be calculated using a vector-space metric (e.g. Euclidean, cosine, etc.). However, according to the experiments conducted in [39], when computing similarity between short texts, HAL didn't show as promising results as LSA did. The reason behind this behavior might be that the word-by-word matrix does not capture sentence meaning as well and that the sentence meaning becomes diluted as many of words are added to it [90].

2.3.3.4. Latent Dirichlet allocation

Latent Dirichlet allocation (LDA) [27] is a generative probabilistic model for collections of discrete data such as text corpora, which overcomes the inconsistent

2.3 Semantic text similarity

generative semantics of PLSA. LDA is a three-level hierarchical Bayesian model, in which each item of a collection is modeled as a finite mixture over an underlying set of topics. Each topic is, in turn, modeled as an infinite mixture over an underlying set of topic probabilities. In the context of text modeling, the topic probabilities provide an explicit representation of a document.

In LDA, each document may be viewed as a mixture of various topics. This is similar to PLSA, except that in LDA the topic distribution is assumed to have a Dirichlet prior distribution. In practice, this results in more reasonable topic mixtures within a document. However, it has been noted that the PLSA model is equivalent to the LDA model under a uniform Dirichlet prior distribution and, therefore, the perceived shortcomings of PLSA can be resolved and elucidated within the LDA framework [63].

As a probabilistic module, LDA can be readily embedded in a more complex model – a property that is not possessed by LSI. Moreover, LDA is highly modular and can be extended in numerous ways. For example, LDA can be extended to continuous data or other non-multinomial data.

One of its extensions is the hierarchical LDA (hLDA) [26], where topics are joined together in a hierarchy by using the nested Chinese restaurant process. LDA can also be extended to a corpus in which a document includes two types of information (e.g. words and names), as in the LDA-dual model [141]. Supervised versions of LDA include L-LDA, which has been found to perform under certain conditions better than support vector machines [120].

2.3.4. Short-text similarity

Until now, we have reviewed some of the main developments within the area of concept and document similarity. In the following, we will focus on three *short text* similarity measures.

The STASIS method

The method proposed in [90] derives text similarity from semantic and syntactic information contained in the two compared texts. The semantic similarity of two sentences was obtained using information from a structured lexical database and from a corpus statistics. They first introduced a word similarity measure [89] (see Equation 2.3) and then, based on it, defined a semantic similarity measure between short text fragments:

$$S_s = \frac{s_1 \cdot s_2}{\|s_1\| \cdot \|s_2\|} \tag{2.10}$$

where s_1 and s_2 are the corresponding semantic vectors derived using the lexical database and the corpus. Unlike other methods that use a fixed vocabulary, the method proposed by Li et al. dynamically forms a joint word set using all distinct words in the pair of compared texts. The significance of a word is weighted by using information content derived from the corpus, which is an indication of how each word contributes to the meaning of the whole sentence.

The order similarity is calculated using the two order vectors:

$$S_r = \frac{r_1 \cdot r_2}{\|r_1\| \cdot \|r_2\|}. \tag{2.11}$$

The order vectors r_1 and r_2 are formed based on the joint word set, like in the case of the semantic vectors. Each entry in the order vector represents an index number: the position of the word, if it appears in the text, otherwise the index of the most similar word. The order dissimilarity of two texts is the result of a different word ordering.

Finally, the two measures (Equation 2.10) and (Equation 2.11) are combined into an overall sentence similarity as follows:

$$S = \delta S_s + (1-\delta) S_r \tag{2.12}$$

where $0 \leq \delta \leq 1$ decides the relative contributions of semantic and word order information to the overall similarity computation.

Their experiments show that a lower accuracy and correlation with human ratings is obtained when considering the order similarity (i.e. $0 < \delta \leq 1$). One of the possible reasons might be that the same meaning is expressed by different word order. A similar conclusion is drawn in [76] with the STS method, which is also based on a syntactic word order similarity measure.

The Semantic Text Similarity (STS) method

In [76], a new method is introduced for measuring the semantic similarity of texts using a corpus-based measure of semantic word similarity and a normalized and modified version of the *longest common subsequence* (LCS) string matching algorithm [9]. The proposed method can be used in a variety of applications involving textual knowledge representation and discovery.

To derive the final STS measure, three similarity functions are considered:

- string similarity,
- semantic word similarity and
- common-word order similarity (optional).

2.3 Semantic text similarity

For measuring *string similarity between words*, three different modified versions of LCS are used, and then a weighted sum of these is calculated. The *normalized longest common subsequence* (NLCS) is defined in a way to account for the length of both the shorter and the longer strings. Consider two strings s_1 and s_2. Then

$$NLCS(s_1, s_2) = \frac{length(LCS(s_1, s_2))^2}{length(s_1) \cdot length(s_2)}$$

Further on, they define a *normalized maximal consecutive longest common subsequence* (NMCLCS) function, starting from the first character and then starting from any character n:

$$NMCLCS_1(s_1, s_2) = \frac{length(MCLCS_1(s_1, s_2))^2}{length(s_1) \cdot length(s_2)}$$

and

$$NMCLCS_n(s_1, s_2) = \frac{length(MCLCS_n(s_1, s_2))^2}{length(s_1) \cdot length(s_2)},$$

where $MCLCS_k$ is the *maximal consecutive longest common subsequence* starting at character k.

Finally, a weighted sum of these individual values is computed to determine the **string similarity score**:

$$\alpha = w_1 \cdot NLCS(s_1, s_2) + w_2 \cdot NMCLCS_1(s_1, s_2) + w_3 \cdot NMCLCS_n(s_1, s_2),$$

where $w_1 + w_2 + w_3 = 1$.

The **semantic PMI similarity** function between two words w_1 and w_2 is defined as

$$Sim(w_1, w_2) = \frac{f(w_1, w_2, \beta_1)}{\beta_1} + \frac{f(w_2, w_1, \beta_2)}{\beta_2},$$

where

$$f(w_1, w_2, \beta) = \sum_{i=1}^{\beta} (f^{pmi}(X_i^{w_1}, w_2))^\gamma$$

is the β-PMI summation of word w_1 with respect to word w_2 [75].

The **common-word order similarity** is defined as

$$S_o = \begin{cases} 1 - \frac{2\sum_{i=1}^{\delta}|x_i-y_i|}{\delta^2} & \text{if } \delta \text{ is even} \\ 1 - \frac{2\sum_{i=1}^{\delta}|x_i-y_i|}{\delta^2-1} & \text{if } \delta \text{ is odd and } \delta > 1 \\ 1 & \text{if } \delta \text{ is odd and } \delta = 1 \end{cases}$$

where

$X = \{x_1, x_2, \ldots, x_\delta\}$ and $Y = \{y_1, y_2, \ldots, y_\delta\}$ are the common δ words in a pair of sentences P and R, arranged in the order they appear in these sentences.

Finally, the **overall semantic sentence similarity** is introduced using a six step method. Due to space limitations, we won't go into further details. The main idea is to find for each word in the sentence the most similar matching one in the second sentence. A detailed explanation of this procedure can be found in [76].

The OMIOTIS method

Omiotis is a measure of semantic relatedness between texts introduced in [146] and it is based on the construction of semantic links between individual words (e.g. WordNet [55]).

Omiotis was the first measure of semantic relatedness between texts that considered all three factors of measuring the pairwise word-to-word semantic relatedness scores:

1. the semantic path length,
2. the intermediate nodes' specificity denoted by the node depth in the thesaurus hierarchy, and
3. the types of the semantic edges that compose the path.

The **semantic relatedness** between a pair of senses $S = (s_1, s_2)$, given a word thesaurus O and a path $P = <p_1, p_2, \ldots, p_l>$ of length l, where either $s_1 = p_1$ and $s_2 = p_l$ or $s_1 = p_l$ and $s_2 = p_1$, is defined as

$$SR(S, O) = \max_P \{SCM(S, O, P) \cdot SPE(S, O, P)\}$$

where SCM is the *semantic compactness* and SPE is the *semantic path elaboration* of S. These two parameters capture two of the most important parameters of measuring semantic relatedness between terms: *path length* and *senses depth*.

2.3 Semantic text similarity

In a word thesaurus there can be more than one semantic path connecting two senses. In this case, the path that maximizes the semantic relatedness is computed based on a modification of Dijakstra's algorithm.

The **semantic relatedness** between a pair of terms $T = (t_1, t_2)$ is

$$SR(T, S, O) = \max_{S_k}\{\max_{P}\{SCM(S_k, O, P) \cdot SPE(S_k, O, P)\}\}$$

where S is a set of pair of senses $S_k = (s_1, s_2)$, corresponding to the terms t_1 and t_2, respectively.

Consider now two texts A an B. The lexical relevance $\lambda_{a,b}$ between terms $a \in A$ and $b \in B$ is given by

$$\lambda_{a,b} = \frac{2 \cdot \text{TF-IDF}(a, A) \cdot \text{TF-IDF}(b, B)}{\text{TF-IDF}(a, A) + \text{TF-IDF}(b, B)}.$$

For every word $a \in A$, a corresponding word $b^* \in B$ is selected so it that maximizes the product of semantic relatedness and lexical similarity:

$$b^* = \arg\max_{b \in B}(\lambda_{a,b} \cdot SR(a, b)).$$

Aggregating the lexical and semantic relevance scores for all terms in A with reference to their best match in B, we obtain the score

$$\zeta(A, B) = \frac{1}{|A|}(\sum_{a \in A} \lambda_{a,b^*} \cdot SR(a, b^*)).$$

Finally, the degree of relevance between texts A and B is given by combining the estimate of their maximum lexical and semantic relevance to one another:

$$Omiotis(A, B) = \frac{\zeta(A, B) + \zeta(B, A)}{2}.$$

Experimental evaluation showed that this measure approximates human understanding of semantic relatedness between words better than previous measures. The Omiotis and SR measures were successfully applied to various different tasks, including sentence similarity, paraphrase recognition, synonym identification and word similarity.

2.3.5. Syntactic similarity measures

In the IR field, it is common to represent documents and queries in the so-called *bag of words* (BOW) format. A BOW format is a set of pairs (t_i, w_i), where $t_i \in \mathcal{T}$ is a term or a word that describes an object $o \in \mathcal{O}$ (in our case, the document or the query) and w_i is the weight of the term t_i, which denotes the *importance* of the respective term for describing the object o. $\mathcal{T}$ is the set of all terms, whereas $\mathcal{O}$ is the set of all objects. The weights w_i can be defined in several ways, but we will mention here the most commonly used definitions:

- **binary:** $w_i = 1$ if the term t_i is part of o, otherwise $w_i = 0$;
- **term frequency (tf):**

$$w_i = tf(t_i, o) = \frac{frequency(t_i, o)}{max\{frequency(t, o) | t \in o, t \in \mathcal{T}\}}$$

where

$frequency(t, o)$ is the number of occurrences of term t in the textual object o;

- **term frequency - inverse document frequency (tf-idf):**

$$w_i = tfidf(t, o, \mathcal{O}) = tf(t_i, o) \cdot idf(t_i, \mathcal{O})$$

where

$$idf(t, O) = \frac{|\mathcal{O}|}{|\{o \in \mathcal{O} | t \in o\}|}.$$

The main idea behind BOW-based similarity measures is that the relatedness of two objects can be determined by computing the similarity between their BOW representations.

The *cosine similarity* between two objects is defined by the cosine angle between their corresponding BOW vectors. Consider the vector representation of an object o_j to be $v(o_j) = (w_1, w_2, \ldots, w_n)$, where $n = |\mathcal{T}|$. Then, the Euclidean norm of the object o_j is $\|v(o_j)\| = \sqrt{\sum_{i=1}^{n} w_i^2}$. Based on this, the cosine similarity between o_j and o_k is defined to be

$$Sim_{cos}(o_j, o_k) = \frac{v(o_j) \cdot v(o_k)}{\|v(o_j)\| \|v(o_k)\|}. \tag{2.13}$$

The *Jaccard similarity coefficient* is computed by considering only the set of terms mapped to each object. Consider again two objects o_j and o_k, and their binary

2.3 Semantic text similarity

BOW representations. The set of terms corresponding to an object o is defined as $terms(o) = \{t_i \in \mathcal{T} | w_i = 1\}$. Then, the Jaccard similarity coefficient is

$$Sim_{Jaccard}(o_j, o_k) = \frac{|terms(o_j) \cap terms(o_k)|}{|terms(o_j) \cup terms(o_k)|}. \tag{2.14}$$

Finally, *Dice's coefficient* is defined as

$$Sim_{Dice}(o_j, o_k) = \frac{2 \cdot |terms(o_j) \cap terms(o_k)|}{|terms(o_j)| + |terms(o_k)|}. \tag{2.15}$$

Recent work has been recorded in [59] towards extending the cosine similarity metric to include semantics by computing the cosine similarity on ontology concepts instead of words or terms. This new description of the objects is called the *bag of concepts* (BOC) representation. Studies show that, by pre-processing the documents into the BOC representation before computing the cosine similarity, higher accuracy is obtained than the term vector similarity measure.

2.3.6. Summary

Research in the field of text similarity evolved in the past decades from two perspectives:

- the complexity of the considered text, i.e. from concepts to words, entire documents and, finally, to short text or sentences;
- the adopted approach: based on the object's parts or based on the object's location within an ontology.

In [23], a catalogue of ontology-based similarity measures were experimentally compared with a "similarity gold standard" obtained by surveying 50 persons. The result of this experiment was quite interesting. The following points were concluded:

- The tested similarity measures correlated with the subjects' assessment only as much as the subjects did among themselves.
- Although human predictions had a large variance, both the algorithmic measures and the human assessment results could be grouped into cohesive clusters. The first group of measures, which focused on the object's parts (i.e. attributes, relationships), consists of two edit distances and the vector model. The second group, as mentioned at the beginning of this section, is formed by the measures which use the object's location within an ontology (e.g. information theory, ontology distance, tf-idf). Bernstein et al. argue that if we could predict a subject's cluster membership, then we could choose the best performing similarity measure in that cluster and use it further as an automated similarity measure.

- Some measures were contradicting previous findings using WordNet by unexpectedly outperforming other measures. This raised the question whether the use of a similarity measure is ontology and domain dependent.

The findings presented in [23] support an important observation: the obtained clusters are the result of different human similarity judgment processes. With this idea in mind, they constructed a personalized similarity assessment algorithm that predicts a person's cluster membership using a machine learning technique. Surprisingly, it provided highly accurate similarity assessments. Therefore, knowing more about human understanding and ontologies could help us develop appropriate similarity measures.

These results address only a fraction of the current needs within the field of semantic similarity. According to [23], further investigation is required on better, ontology-adapting and personalized similarity assessment measures, as well as exploring the human understanding of similarity.

2.4. Predictive models for sequential data

Sequential data can appear in two main forms: *temporal* or *time series data* (e.g. financial, meteorological data), generated sequentially by a causal process, and *sequence data* (e.g. bio-sequences, market-basket data). For modeling time-series data, one is naturally inclined to use directed graphical models: it captures the time flow aspect. As for modeling atemporal sequence data, it is common to use both directed or undirected graphical models, but there are other classes of predictive models that can be learned with this type of data.

The rest of this section will give an overview of the related work within the field of predictive models for sequential data, both temporal and atemporal.

2.4.1. Sequential event prediction

Sequential event prediction refers to a wide class of problems in which a set of initially hidden events are sequentially revealed [88, 100, 101, 131, 132]. The motivation behind this approach is to use the set of revealed events, but *not necessarily their order*, to predict the future (hidden) events in the sequence. The problems that can be solved using this method are different from time-series prediction problems, which can be handled by using Markov chains.

Recommender systems are a particularly interesting example of sequential event prediction, due to the fact that predictions are expected to influence the sequence [138]. Recent work in this area shows that measurements of user behavior can be used to improve search engine rankings [5].

Consider the online grocery store problem (see Figure 2.5), where items are added to the basket one at a time. The customer may add items in any order, even in an order

2.4 Predictive models for sequential data

provided by a recommender system. This means that the predictions actually alter the sequence of events. The approach proposed in [88, 131, 132] allows for models of user behavior to be incorporated while the recommender system is learned.

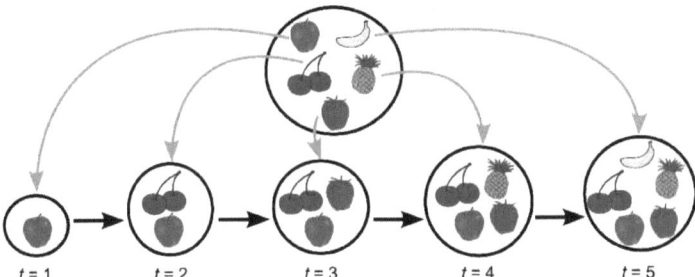

Figure 2.5.: An example of the online grocery store problem. Items from an unordered shopping list are sequentially added to the user's basket [88].

Another application example of such an approach is to predict each next symptom of a sick patient, given the patient's past sequence of symptoms and treatments, and a database of the timeline of symptoms and treatments of other patients. In this case, a subset of past events can be useful to predict the next event.

In order to make predictions using subsets of data, Rudin et al. [131, 132] employ association rules [6, 7] for a supervised learning problem. They argue about the efficiency of the strict minimum support threshold used for association rule mining and introduce a new, adjusted confidence measure that provides a weaker minimum support condition and has several advantages over the common minimum support threshold.

An association rule is an implication of the form

$$A \to b,$$

where A is a subset of items and b is a single item. For example, for the grocery store problem, $\{lettuce, carrots\} \to tomatoes$ is an association rule that has the following meaning: "most people who buy lettuce and carrots also buy tomatoes" or "there is a high probability that those who purchase lettuce and carrots will also get tomatoes".

Although association rule mining has proven to be successful for market basket applications and has the advantage of being able to model underlying conditional probabilities $P(b|a)$, it is generally used as an exploratory method, rather than a predictive tool. In their work, Rudin et al. synthesize tools from several fields to analyze the use of association rules in a supervised learning environment [131, 132]. The introduced adjusted confidence allows rare rules to be pointed out while still encouraging generalization and, additionally, when there are several rules with similar confidence, it prefers those with a larger support.

As previously stated, association rule discovery can be successfully employed to predict the next item in a sequence of events, but in some application areas it fails to emphasize an important aspect. The *temporal dimension* or the *order of events* can be a crucial information when analyzing processes (e.g. chain of thoughts, evolution or growth progress, financial time series or learning processes etc.). Therefore, given the problem of predicting a user's next question within a QA system under the assumption that his actions are driven by a well defined **learning goal**, our next analysis target will be methods and techniques that rely on the temporal aspect.

2.4.2. Temporal probabilistic models

In this section, an overview of the current state-of-the-art in the field of *temporal probabilistic models*, also commonly referred to as *time series modeling*, will be presented. Temporal or dynamic probabilistic models refer to probabilistic models that use and leverage the temporal dimension. When using these models we are interested in reasoning about the state of the world as it evolves and changes over time [78]. To do this, we model the considered reality at a certain time as a *system state*, whose value at time t is a snapshot of the relevant (hidden or observed) attributes of the system at time t.

Example *Consider a vehicle localization task, where a moving car tries to track its current location using the information obtained from a sensor (possibly faulty). The system state can be encoded using the Location (the car's current position), Velocity (the car's current) velocity, Weather (the current weather state), Failure (the failure status of the sensor) and Observation (the current observation). For each t, we have an instantiation of this set of variables. The joint distribution over all of these instantiations defines a probability distribution over the car trajectories. This distribution can help us answer various queries, for example: Given a sequence of observations, where is the current location of the car? Where is it likely to be in ten minutes?* [78].

Consider the system state represented as a value assignment to some set of random variables $\mathcal{X}$. Therefore, $X_i^{(t)}$ represents the instantiation of the variable X_i at time t. Variable X_i is instantiated at various points in time and each $X_i^{(t)}$ is a variable that takes a value in $Val(X_i)$.

Each of these assignments represents a "possible world" which is considered a *trajectory* in the probability space. Therefore, the goal of temporal probabilistic models is to represent a joint distribution over such trajectories. Since such a probability space can be clearly very complex, we need to make certain simplifying assumptions to allow a lighter distribution representation.

2.4 Predictive models for sequential data

Simplifying assumptions

1. Timeline discretization

    The first simplification is the discretization of the timeline into a set of time slices. This means that system state measurements are taken at intervals that are regularly spaced with a predefined interval Δ. Consider a distribution sampled over $t \in \{0, 1, \ldots, T\}$: $P(\mathcal{X}^{(0)}, \mathcal{X}^{(1)}, \ldots, \mathcal{X}^{(T)}) = P(\mathcal{X}^{(0:T)})$. Using the chain rule for probabilities, we can reparametrize the distribution in the following way:

    $$P(\mathcal{X}^{(0:T)}) = P(\mathcal{X}^{(0)}) \prod_{t=0}^{T-1} P(\mathcal{X}^{(t+1)} | \mathcal{X}^{(0:t)})$$

2. Markov assumption

    A dynamic system over a set of variables $\mathcal{X}$ satisfies the Markov assumption if, for every $t \geq 0$, the following holds:

    $$\mathcal{X}^{(t+1)} \perp \mathcal{X}^{(0:(t-1))} | \mathcal{X}^{(t)}, \tag{2.16}$$

    where $a \perp b \mid c$ means "a is conditionally independent of b given c".

    Given the Markov assumption we can define a more compact representation of the distribution:

    $$P(\mathcal{X}^{(0:T)}) = P(\mathcal{X}^{(0)}) \prod_{t=0}^{T-1} P(\mathcal{X}^{(t+1)} | \mathcal{X}^{(t)}). \tag{2.17}$$

One might argue whether the Markov assumption is a reasonable approximation of the dependencies in the given distribution. Koller and Friedman [78] argue that in most cases, when reasonably rich state descriptions are used, this approximation is appropriate.

2.4.2.1. Dynamic Bayesian networks (DBNs)

Before introducing two of the most popular temporal probabilistic models, let us briefly review the theory behind dynamic Bayesian networks. Bayesian networks (BN) [79] are directed acyclic graphs that encompass dependencies between variables in a probabilistic model. There are two important aspects related to BN:

1. Conditional independence (from basic probability theory):

    A variable (or set of variables) A is conditionally independent from B given C if $P(A, B|C) = P(A|C)P(B|C)$, for all A, B and C, with $P(C) \neq 0$. We can also write $A \perp B|C$.

Chapter 2 — State of the Art

2. Semantics of a Bayesian network:

   Each node is conditionally independent from its non-descendants given its parents. Let $\mathcal{G}$ be a Bayesian network structure represented as a directed graph whose nodes $X_1, \ldots, X_n$ are random variables. Then:

   $$\forall X_i : (X_i \perp NonDesc(X_i) | Parents(X_i)),$$

   where $NonDesc(X)$ is the set of all nodes in the graph $\mathcal{G}$ that are not descendants of node X and $Parents(X)$ is the set of all parents of X.

In time series modeling, the values of certain variables are observed at various points in time [62, 104, 78]. An important assumption that simplifies the design of DBN is that an event can cause another event in the future, but not the other way around. The first-order Markov model is the simplest causal model for sequential data. Hidden Markov models, extensively used in speech recognition, and Kalman filter models, used in filtering and control applications, are also considered as examples of dynamic Bayesian networks. However, general DBNs can capture much richer structures.

In the following, we will only focus on different variations of Markovian temporal models that will later be used for learning user question sequences. Then, based on the output model, we can generate useful, meaningful recommendations.

2.4.2.2. Mixed transition distribution models (MTDs)

The mixture transition distribution model (MTD) was introduced in 1985 by Raftery [21, 125] for the modeling of high-order Markov chains with a finite state space in order to avoid the estimation of a large number of parameters of the transition probability. The MTD model is a mixture of first-order Markov chains which, on one hand, significantly reduces the number of parameters that need to be estimated and, on the other hand, maintains a flexible structure to model the high-order temporal dependence in Markov chains.

Markov chains

A Markov chain is a probabilistic model used to represent the dependencies between successive observations of a random variable (see Figure 2.6). It was introduced by Andrey Andreevic Markov in 1906 and it is used in various fields: biology, chemistry, geography, meteorology, physics, social sciences, music, etc.

Consider a discrete-time random variable $X^{(t)}$ taking values in the finite set $\{1, 2, \ldots, m\}$. The goal is to predict (or to explain) the value taken by $X^{(t)}$ as a function of the values taken by previous observations of this variable: $X^{(t-1)}, X^{(t-2)}, \ldots, X^{(0)}$. Given the Markov hypothesis, we can write:

2.4 Predictive models for sequential data

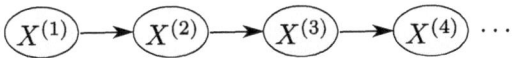

Figure 2.6.: Graphical structure for a first-order Markov chain.

$$P(X^{(t)} = x_t | X^{(0)} = x_0, \ldots, X^{(t-1)} = x_{t-1}) = P(X^{(t)} = x_t | X^{(t-1)} = x_{t-1}) = q_{x_{t-1}x_t}(t),$$

where $x_0, \ldots, x_t \in \{1, \ldots, m\}$. Suppose that the probability $q_{x_{t-1}x_t}(t)$ is time-invariant. Therefore, we have a homogeneous Markov chain and we can replace $q_{x_{t-1}x_t}(t)$ with $q_{x_{t-1}x_t}$. Given all the combinations of x_t and x_{t-1}, the following transition matrix Q is constructed:

$$Q = \begin{array}{c} \\ X^{(t-1)} \\ 1 \\ \vdots \\ \vdots \\ m \end{array} \begin{array}{c} X^{(t)} \\ \begin{array}{cccc} 1 & \cdots & \cdots & m \end{array} \\ \left(\begin{array}{cccc} q_{11} & \cdots & \cdots & q_{1m} \\ \vdots & \ddots & & \vdots \\ \vdots & & \ddots & \vdots \\ q_{m1} & \cdots & \cdots & q_{mm} \end{array} \right) \end{array},$$

where each of the rows sums to 1.

Let $\mathbf{X}_t = (c_t(1), \ldots, c_t(m))'$ be a vector, such that

$$c_t(i) = \begin{cases} 1, & \text{if } X^{(t)} = i \\ 0, & \text{otherwise} \end{cases},$$

and let $\hat{\mathbf{X}}_t = (P(X^{(t)} = 1), \ldots, P(X^{(t)} = m))'$ be the probability vector.

Then, the following two relationships hold:

$$\hat{\mathbf{X}}'_t = \mathbf{X}'_{t-1} Q, \tag{2.18}$$
$$\hat{\mathbf{X}}'_t = \mathbf{X}'_0 Q^t, \tag{2.19}$$

where X' represents the transpose of matrix X. Once the initial vector $\mathbf{X}_0$ and the transition matrix Q are known, the process is fully defined.

An l-th order Markov chain is a probabilistic model that represents situations when the present depends not only on the first lag, but on the last l observations (see Figure 2.7). Its transitions probabilities are defined as

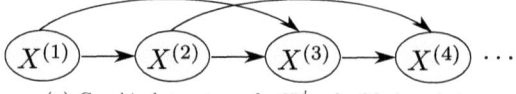
(a) Graphical structure of a 2nd order Markov chain.

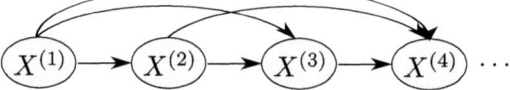
(b) Graphical structure of a 3rd order Markov chain.

Figure 2.7.: Examples of l-th order Markov chains.

$$P(X^{(t)} = x_t | X^{(0)} = x_0, \ldots, X^{(t-1)} = x_{t-1})$$
$$= P(X^{(t)} = x_t | X^{(t-l)} = x_{t-l}, \ldots, X^{(t-1)} = x_{t-1})$$
$$= q_{x_{t-l}\ldots x_t}.$$

Each possible combination of l successive observations of X is called a *state* of the model and the number all possible states is equal to m^l. There are $(m-1)$ independent probabilities in each row of the matrix Q, therefore, the total number of independent parameters to be estimated is equal to $m^l(m-1)$.

As the order l and the number m of possible values increase, the number of independent parameters increases exponentially and it becomes too large to be estimated efficiently (see Table A.1).

In order to approximate high-order Markov chains with fewer parameters than the fully parametrized model, the mixture transition distribution model was introduced. Its transition matrix contains the probabilities of observing an event at time t given the events observed at times $(t-l)$ to $(t-1)$. In contrast to the full high-order Markov chain, in the MTD model, the effect of each lag upon the present is considered separately and the conditional probability is given by

$$P(X^{(t)} = x_t | X^{(t-l)} = x_{t-l}, \ldots, X^{(t-1)} = x_{t-1}) = \sum_{g=1}^{l} \lambda_g q_{x_{t-g} x_t}, \quad (2.20)$$

where $q_{x_{t-g} x_t}$ are the probabilities of the $m \times m$ transition matrix Q and λ_g is the weight parameter associated with the lag g for which the following conditions hold:

2.4 Predictive models for sequential data

$$0 \leq \sum_{g=1}^{l} \lambda_g q_{x_{t-g} x_t} \leq 1,$$

$$\sum_{g=1}^{l} \lambda_g = 1 \text{ and}$$

$$\lambda_g \geq 0.$$

The MTD model is composed of a small transition matrix $Q(m \times m)$ and a vector of lag parameters $\lambda = (\lambda_1, \ldots, \lambda_l)$ which are easier to interpret and estimate. The model has only $m(m-1) + (l-1)$ independent parameters. Table A.1 shows that the MTD model is far more parsimonious than the corresponding fully parametrized Markov chain.

2.4.2.3. Variable length Markov models (VLMMs)

Consider a stationary process $(X^{(t)})_{t \in \mathbb{Z}}$, where X_t takes values in a finite categorical space $\mathcal{H}$. Assuming no particular underlying mechanistic system, the most general model for such a process is a full Markov chain of high, but finite order.

Although, theoretically, the full Markov chain is a nice model, practically, such models are most of the time inefficient and impossible to estimate. Bühlman and Wyner [38] identify two main problems concerning the full Markov chain:

1. The class of all finite-order full Markov chains is **structurally poor**, in the sense that there are not many members in this class. This aspect is due to the fact that not any kind of parsimonious representation of the state space can be modeled by a full Markov chain. As an example, consider a state space $\mathcal{H}$ with 4 states, i.e. $|\mathcal{H}| = 4$. Table 2.1 below shows the dimension of a full Markov chain over $\mathcal{H}$ in terms of its order k: $(|\mathcal{H}| - 1)|\mathcal{H}|^k$.

k	0	1	2	3	4	5	10
Dimension	3	12	48	192	768	3072	$\approx 3.1 \cdot 10^6$

Table 2.1.: Dimensionality of a full Markov chain over a state space with 4 states.

As formulated in [38], there are "no models in between" and this "discontinuous" increase in dimensionality of the model does not allow a good trade-off between bias (many parameters) and variance (few parameters). For example, having a state space with 4 states, it is impossible to fit a full Markov chain with 72 parameters.

2. Since the dimensionality of full Markov chains increases exponentially with the order k, we face the **curse of dimensionality**.

To address these two problems, Bühlmann and Wyner introduced the *variable length Markov chain (VLMC)* [38, 94] which follows a very simple idea: the memory of a stationary Markov chain can have a variable length, as a function of the values in the past. Formally described,

$$P(X^{(t)} = x_t | X^{(0)} = x_0, \ldots, X^{(t-1)} = x_{t-1})$$
$$= P(X^{(t)} = x_t | X^{(t-l)} = x_{t-l}, \ldots, X^{(t-1)} = x_{t-1}),$$

where $x_0, \ldots, x_t \in \mathcal{H}$ and $l = l(x_{t-1}, x_{t-2}, \ldots)$ is a function of the past. Therefore, VLMCs provide the means for capturing both large and small order Markov dependencies.

When $\sup_{x_{t-1}, x_{t-2}, \ldots} l(x_{t-1}, x_{t-2}, \ldots) = k$, we have an embedding full Markov chain of order k with a well-interpretable structure of a variable length memory, namely: some transition probabilities are lumped together.

Prediction In [19], Begleiter et al. considered a number of VLMC model learning methods and compared their performance according to various prediction tasks (e.g. average log-loss, classification error, compression rate, etc.). Six prominent VLMC algorithms were selected and applied to several types of sequential data from three different domains (molecular biology, text and music):

- Lempel-Ziv 78 (LZ78) [20, 163],
- Prediction by Partial Match (PPM) [44],
- Context Tree Weighting method (CTW) [155, 156],
- Decomposed Context Tree Weighting method (DE-CTW) [149],
- Probabilistic Suffix Tree (PST) [130] and
- Improved Lempel-Ziv algorithm (LZ-MS) [110].

Consider $\mathcal{H}$ a finite categorical state space and a training sequence $q_1^n = q_1 q_2 \cdots q_n$, $q_i \in \mathcal{H}$. Based on q_1^n, the goal is to learn a model $\hat{P}$ that provides a probability assignment for any new future state, given some past sequence. More specifically, for any *context* $s \in \mathcal{H}^*$ and state $\sigma \in \mathcal{H}$, the learner should generate a conditional probability distribution $\hat{P}(\sigma|s)$.

Then, the prediction performance of such a model is computed using the **average log-loss**:

$$l(\hat{P}, x_1^T) = -\frac{1}{T} \sum_{t=1}^{T} \log \hat{P}(x_t | x_1 \cdots x_{t-1}), \tag{2.21}$$

where $x_1^T = x_1 \cdots x_T$ is a test sequence and $\hat{P}(x_t | x_1 \cdots x_{t-1}) = \hat{P}(X^{(t)} = x_t | X^{(1)} = x_1, \ldots, X^{(t-1)} = x_{t-1})$. The average log-loss is directly related to the likelihood

2.4 Predictive models for sequential data

$\hat{P}(x_1^T) = \prod_{t=1}^T \hat{P}(x_t|x_1 \cdots x_{t-1})$ and, therefore, minimizing the average log-loss is equivalent to maximizing the likelihood.

Most of the existing VLMC learning algorithms base their probability estimates $\hat{P}(\sigma|s)$ on the number of occurrences of the state value σ after contexts s in the training sequence.

The log-loss has various meanings. On one hand, $-\log \hat{P}(x_t|x_1 \cdots x_{t-1})$ is the ideal compression or "code length" of x_t with respect to the conditional distribution $\hat{P}(X|x_1 \cdots x_{t-1})$, also known as "self-information" in the field of loss-less compression. In this setting, the average log-loss measures the average compression rate of the test sequence, meaning that a small average log-loss over a test sequence implies a good compression rate.

On the other hand, within a probabilistic setting, when the true distribution P is unknown and a model $\hat{P}$ is learned using the training sequence, the extra loss is called *redundancy* and is given by

$$D_T(P||\hat{P}) = \mathbf{E}_P \left\{ -\log \hat{P}(x_1^T) - (-log P(x_1^T)) \right\}.$$

In this probabilistic setting, the goal of a general-purpose prediction algorithm would be to minimize the redundancy uniformly, with respect to all possible distributions.

The extensive empirical evaluations over the tree domains (biology, text and music) presented in [19] shows that there are some prominent algorithms that tend to generate more accurate predictions than the rest of the considered algorithms. These algorithms were the *prediction by partial match* (PPM) and the *decomposed context tree weighting* (DE-CTW).

2.4.2.4. Hidden Markov models (HMMs)

The literature on prediction methods for discrete sequences is extensive and various. The most commonly used techniques in this field are based on Hidden Markov Models (HMMs) [121, 122].

Although HMMs provide flexible structures that can be used to model complex sources of sequential data, they require a deep understanding and insight into the problem domain. Another consequence of their flexibility is the need for large training datasets, if a successful training of such a model is desired.

A HMM can be considered as the simplest DBN. In a HMM we have a hidden state $Y^{(t)}$ taking values in $\mathcal{H}_Y$, not directly "visible" or "measurable", and an observed output $X^{(t)} \in \mathcal{H}_X$, "visible" or "measurable", which is dependent on the state $Y^{(t)}$. The hidden state space $\mathcal{H}_Y$ is discrete and assumed to contain N possible values, whereas the observation state $\mathcal{H}_X$ can be either discrete or continuous, typically generated from a categorical or Gaussian distribution.

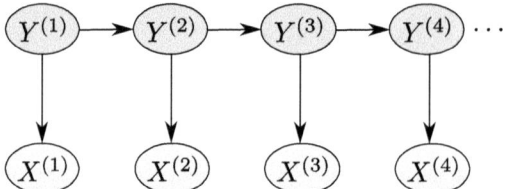

Figure 2.8.: Graphical structure of a hidden Markov model.

Figure 2.8 shows the structure of a HMM, where $Y^{(t)}$ is the hidden state at time t and $X^{(t)}$ is the observation at time t. The arrows denote conditional dependencies. From the diagram, we can conclude that $Y^{(t-1)}$ and $Y^{(t+1)}$ are independent given $Y^{(t)}$ and $X^{(t)}$ is dependent only on the hidden variable $Y^{(t)}$. Then, the joint probability distribution of the hidden Markov model is given by

$$P(X^{(1:T)}, Y^{(1:T)}) = P(Y^{(1)}) \prod_{t=2}^{T} P(Y^{(t)}|Y^{(t-1)}) \prod_{t=1}^{T} P(X^{(t)}|Y^{(t)}), \qquad (2.22)$$

where $P(Y^{(t)}|Y^{(t-1)})$ is the state *transition probability*, $P(X^{(t)}|Y^{(t)})$ is the *observation probability*, $T \in \mathbb{N}$ and $P(Y^{(1)})$ is the initial state distribution.

Given a set of output sequences, the learning goal of HMM is to find the best set of state transition probabilities and observation probabilities, as well as the initial state distribution. This task is usually achieved by deriving the *maximum likelihood estimation* using the *Baum-Welch algorithm* [18, 50], which is based on the *forward-backward algorithm* [121].

Another interesting and sometimes necessary task is, given the parameters of a HMM and a particular sequence of observations, to compute the most likely sequence of states that could have generated the observed sequence. This problem can be efficiently solved using the *Viterbi algorithm*.

HMMs have been successfully applied to a variety of problems in information extraction and natural language processing.

2.4.3. Summary

In this section, we have reviewed a variety of predictive models for sequential data. The above studied models revealed some important aspects regarding the type of input data (e.g. temporal or atemporal) and output data supported by such methods. The majority of the mentioned related work argues about the suitability of specific models for any class of sequential data or, in other words, about the existence of a general purpose temporal model that can be successfully applied to any domain.

Extensive empirical studies showed in several cases that such a model or learning method does not exist and the performance of a particular learning method is greatly related to the application field. Therefore, in order to choose a suitable model, one should first analyze and evaluate the domain-specific data and the expected results. A thorough understanding of the problem state space and the dependencies between different states can direct one towards an appropriate model and learning method.

The work presented in this thesis focuses on textual data and aims at finding an adequate model for generating useful and meaningful recommendations within a QA system setting and, subsequently, at predicting user learning behavior. Besides the predictive mechanism, there are various text mining tasks that need to be performed in order to allow this functionality. An overview of probabilistic models for various text mining operations can be found in [143].

2.5. The learning taxonomy

2.5.1. Overview

This section gives an overview of the theory behind Bloom's taxonomy – a *classification of learning objectives* within education –, proposed in 1956 by a committee of educators chaired by Benjamin Bloom [28] and revised in 2000 [10, 81]. These series of conferences were driven by the desire of finding a theoretical framework that could facilitate the communication among examiners for sharing test materials and ideas about testing.

Later, they have come to the agreement that such a theoretical framework might best be obtained through a system that classifies the goals of an educational process, given that educational objectives provide the basis for building curricula and tests, and represent the starting point for the educational research [11]. As a result, a learning taxonomy was developed (see Figure 2.9), which was named after Bloom. Bloom's Taxonomy is considered to be a basic and essential element within the education community. In 2001, the taxonomy was revised and improved by Anderson et al. [10]. Table B.1, Table B.2 and Table B.3 give an overview of the revised taxonomical structure.

One of the goals of Bloom's taxonomy was to motivate educators to focus on all three domains: cognitive (knowing), affective (feeling) and psycho-motor (doing), creating a more holistic form of education.

Why was the categorization of learning objectives so important in order to develop such a framework? According to [10], in life, objectives indicate "what we want to accomplish" and help us focus our attention and efforts, while in education, objectives describe "what we want our students to learn". Additionally, such a classification enables us to assess the learning process and even identify learning patterns.

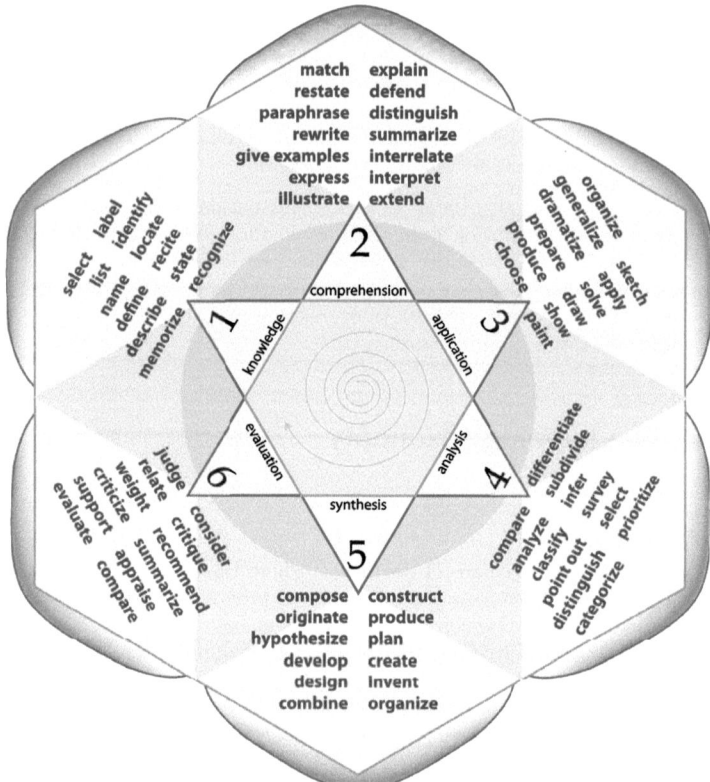

Figure 2.9.: Bloom's taxonomy (adapted after[1]).

Current conceptions about learning assume learners as active agents and not passive recipients or simple recorders of information. This shift away from a passive perspective on learning towards more cognitive and constructionist perspectives emphasizes what learners **know** (knowledge) and **how they think** (cognitive processes) about what they know [10].

After examining the historical and motivational background, let us turn to a detailed review of the *two dimensions* that make up the taxonomy: the *knowledge* and the *cognitive process*.

2.5.2. The knowledge dimension

The problem of how to characterize knowledge and, more importantly, how individuals represent knowledge is a well-known and enduring question in the educational psychology.

There are many types of knowledge and even more terms used to describe them: conceptual knowledge, conditional knowledge, domain knowledge, factual knowledge, procedural knowledge, semantic knowledge, metacognitive knowledge, strategic knowledge, disciplinary knowledge, content knowledge, etc. Some of them refer to important differences among the various knowledge types, but others are just different labels for the same knowledge category.

The revised Bloom's taxonomy identifies four general classes of knowledge:

1. *Factual Knowledge,*
2. *Conceptual Knowledge,*
3. *Procedural Knowledge,* and
4. *Metacognitive Knowledge.*

Factual knowledge represents discrete, isolated "bits of information" [10], while conceptual knowledge denotes more complex, organized knowledge forms. Factual knowledge contains the basic elements that experts use in communicating about their academic discipline, in order to understand and organize it systematically. Its two subtypes are *knowledge of terminology* and *knowledge of specific details and elements*.

Conceptual knowledge includes knowledge of categories, their classification and the relationships between them. It refers to deeper, more organized, integrated and systematic knowledge forms. The three subtypes of this class are: *knowledge of classification and categories*, *knowledge of principles and generalizations*, and *knowledge of theories, models and structures*.

Procedural knowledge is the knowledge of "how to do something", whereas factual and conceptual knowledge represent the "what" of knowledge. In other words, procedural knowledge reflects knowledge of various processes. Similarly, we can distinguish three subtypes of this class: *knowledge of subject-specific skills and algorithms*, *knowledge of subject-specific techniques and methods*, and *knowledge of criteria for determining when to use appropriate procedures*.

Metacognitive knowledge encompasses knowledge about cognition in general, about awareness of and knowledge about one's own cognition. It includes knowledge of more general strategies that cut across subject matters or academic disciplines, whereas procedural knowledge is specific to particular subject matters or academic disciplines. The different subtypes of metacognitive knowledge are: *strategic knowledge, knowledge about cognitive tasks*, including contextual and conditional knowledge, and *self-knowledge*.

Table B.1 presents a more detailed description and characterization of the knowledge dimension.

2.5.3. The cognitive process dimension

Early views on learning suggest that instruction and assessment commonly emphasize only one kind of cognitive processing: *remembering,* but actually schooling can be expanded to include a broader range of cognitive processes. According to [10], **meaningful learning** provides students with the knowledge and cognitive process needed for successful problem solving.

The cognitive process dimension shows the *degree* to which students learned some subject matter content, retained and transferred it over a period of time.

The revised learning framework includes six categories of processes, the first, most closely related to retention and the next five increasingly related to knowledge transfer:

1. *Remember,*
2. *Understand,*
3. *Apply,*
4. *Analyze,*
5. *Evaluate,* and
6. *Create.*

Remembering involves retrieving relevant knowledge from long-term memory. Its associated cognitive processes are *recognizing* and *recalling.*

Understanding refers to situations where students are able to construct meaning from instructional messages. According to [10], students understand, when they build connections between the "new" knowledge to be gained and their prior knowledge. Cognitive processes within this category are: *interpreting, exemplifying, classifying, summarizing, inferring, comparing,* and *explaining.*

Applying involves using procedures or methods to perform exercises and solve problems. Therefore, there is a close connection between procedural knowledge and this cognitive process category. Is consists of two cognitive processes: *executing* – when the task is an exercise (familiar) – and *implementing* – when the task is a problem (unfamiliar).

Analyzing refers to breaking material into its constituent parts and determining how these parts are related to one another and to the overall structure. Objectives classified as *analyze* include *differentiating, organizing,* and *attributing.*

Evaluate is defined as making judgments based on criteria and standards. The most often used criteria is quality, effectiveness, efficiency and consistency. This category includes the cognitive processes of *checking* (judgments about internal consistencies) and *critiquing* (judgments based on external criteria). An important observation that needs to be emphasized here is that not all judgments are evaluative.

Create involves putting elements or knowledge together to form a coherent or functional whole. Objectives classified as *create* engage students to produce something

2.5 The learning taxonomy

by mentally reorganizing some parts into a pattern or structure not explicitly presented before. This class consists of the following cognitive processes: *generating*, *planning* and *producing*.

Table B.2 and Table B.3 offer a more detailed description and characterization of the cognitive process dimension.

2.5.4. Summary

This section has reviewed the modern conception about learning objectives within the educational psychology, mainly pioneered by the revised framework of Bloom's taxonomy. The two guiding dimensions within this taxonomy enables us to characterize and classify learning objectives, i.e. "*what*" students are expected to know about a particular domain/topic/element and "*how*" this knowledge is retained or transferred.

According to [10], each learning task can be categorized based on the knowledge and cognitive process dimensions. Imagine a two-dimensional space, one dimension for the knowledge domain $\mathcal{K}$, the other dimension for the cognitive process domain $\mathcal{CP}$. Any learning task can be projected onto this two-dimensional space, obtaining therefore a "point" with coordinates (k, cp), where $k \in \mathcal{K}$ and $cp \in \mathcal{CP}$.

From the IR and information processing point of view, Bloom's taxonomy allows us to classify, organize and label information subject to or influenced by learning objectives. Moreover, it adds new knowledge to our understanding of the world and helps us automatically construct patterns and models for various learning purposes.

3. Semantic Short-Text Similarity

3.1. Overview

This chapter introduces a novel technique for measuring semantic similarity between short fragments of text using a domain specific taxonomy. First, the concept of *semantic short text similarity* and its use is defined, then an overview of the underlying knowledge-base is presented and, finally, the *four-layered semantic short text similarity* measure is formally described.

In order to understand the role and use of the semantic text similarity, let us start by mentioning some of its applications within the text mining field.

Consider a question answering (QA) web application, where users have the possibility both to view the answers for previously asked questions and to post new questions. For reasons concerning effectiveness and redundancy avoidance, we might find useful having a method that could deliver the most appropriate existing answers for a new question. This problem could be solved by measuring the relatedness between the new question and the existing ones. Under the same setting, another application of this measure could be the implementation of a semantic auto-complete search engine that looks up the entire question database for semantically similar questions.

3.2. Definition

The semantic short text similarity is defined as a function which describes how "related" or "similar" two short segments of text (e.g., sentence, expression, phrase) are. *Relatedness* or similarity, in this particular context, implies a domain-specific association and it is related to the shared commonality and differences.

According to Lin[91], there are three main intuitions about similarity that help us formally define it.

Intuition 1: The similarity between two objects from the same class is related to their ***commonality***. The more commonality they share, the more similar they are.

Intuition 2: The similarity between two objects from the same class is related to the ***differences*** between them. The more differences they have, the less similar they are.

Intuition 3: The maximum similarity between two objects from the same class is reached when they are identical, no matter how much commonality they share.

There are many alternative ways to formally define a similarity measure and it is highly dependent on the domain it is intended for. In our case, when measuring text similarity, we might consider the following aspects: *concepts, words, synonymy, polysemy, part-of-speech tags, word taxonomies, word order*, etc. For example, two sentences might be compared based on the common words they share either on a purely syntactic level, or on a semantic level. Clearly, the syntactic approach might not identify subtle dependencies between words, for example, synonyms or polysemic words.

In order to obtain more accurate results, a semantic similarity is needed, which makes full use of the available domain-specific information and, ideally, identifies successfully subtle or hidden meanings.

Moving towards this goal, this section introduces new semantic short-text similarity measures that try to elevate such subtle dependencies by using domain-specific taxonomies. The rationale behind choosing a domain-specific taxonomy, instead of a general-purpose one like WordNet [55, 103, 119], is that certain concepts might have different meanings and relationships to other concepts, depending on the domain under study.

Therefore, the four-layered semantic similarity measure defined in this chapter is based on a domain-specific taxonomy, enriched with corresponding keywords that enable a better coverage of the respective field of study. In the following, we present in detail the knowledge-base used for the formalization of the semantic short-text similarity measure.

3.3. Knowledge-base description

3.3.1. General overview

Under the intuitions and assumptions highlighted at the beginning of this chapter, we introduce the building blocks and structure of the knowledge-base: the *topic taxonomy*, the *topic mappings* and the *database of textual objects* for which the semantic similarity measure is defined.

Figure 3.1 shows the relationship between these three main building blocks in the case of a QA system. The **topic taxonomy** contains *topics* organized as a hierarchical tree to reflect IS-A dependencies – *generalization* and *specialization* – between its elements and keywords (see subsection 3.3.2). The **topic mappings** are basically connections between the elements of the topic taxonomy (i.e. topics and keywords) and the textual objects (e.g. questions, answers). The **database of textual objects** can contain any textual objects (e.g. questions, answers, sentences), for which a semantic similarity measure is to be defined.

3.3 Knowledge-base description

The only condition needed to allow the application of this measure and guarantee meaningful results is the possibility to map these objects to the topic taxonomy. This aspect is on its own a challenging research subject, especially when considering more abstract objects that do not provide explicitly the means to create such connections to the topic taxonomy. For example, textual fragments, like sentences or questions, are composed of words that can be extracted using NLP methods (e.g. parsing, tokenization, part-of-speech tagging, stop-word filtering, etc.) [97].

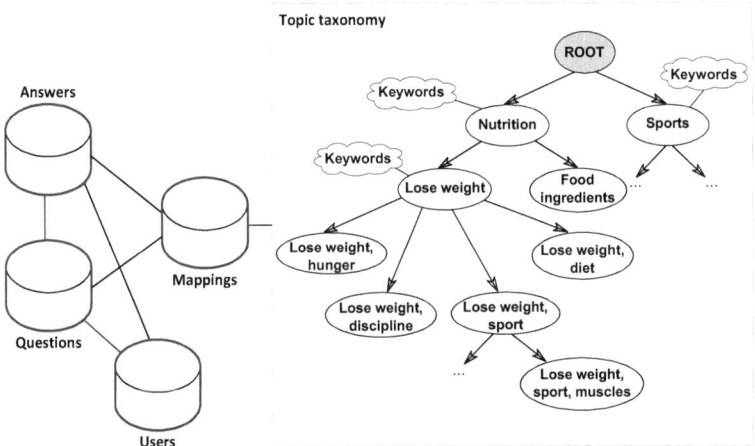

Figure 3.1.: Knowledge-base structure of a QA system.

3.3.2. The topic taxonomy

Before we formally define the semantic short-text similarity measure, it is important to understand the structure of the underlying domain-specific taxonomy. While most of the previously described similarity measures (see section 2.3) make use of the English lexical taxonomy WordNet [55, 103, 119], the proposed similarity measure is based on a new domain-specific taxonomy with a tree-like structure, where links between nodes represent IS-A relationships.

The reason for adopting a new taxonomy emerged from the need of having a language-independent and domain-specific structure that can be used as a foundation for building efficient retrieval and mining methods in a QA system. For the rest of this thesis, we will refer to this structure as *topic-tree*. The topic-tree can integrate several domains of interest (e.g. nutrition, sports, business & management, etc.). However, the experiments and tests presented here are based only on a nutrition topic-tree and a set of corresponding questions from the nutrition domain.

The topic-tree is defined by a set of *topics* $\mathcal{T} = \{\tau_1, \tau_2, ..., \tau_n\}$ and *an IS-A relationship* between topics:

$$\mathcal{L} \subseteq \mathcal{T} \times \mathcal{T}, (\tau_i, \tau_j) \in \mathcal{L} \iff \tau_i \text{ parent of } \tau_j.$$

Additionally, a set of *keywords* $\mathcal{K} = \{k_1, k_2, ..., k_m\}$ is considered to enrich the topic-tree taxonomy using a *mapping* relationship between topics and keywords:

$$\mathcal{M} \subseteq \mathcal{T} \times \mathcal{K}, (\tau_i, k_j) \in \mathcal{M} \iff \text{ keyword } k_j \text{ mapped to topic } \tau_i.$$

Moreover, to each pair $(\tau_i, k_j) \in \mathcal{M}$, a *mapping weight* is assigned by

$$w : \mathcal{M} \to (0, 1],$$

where the value $w(\tau_i, k_j)$ represents how relevant is keyword k_j for topic τ_i.

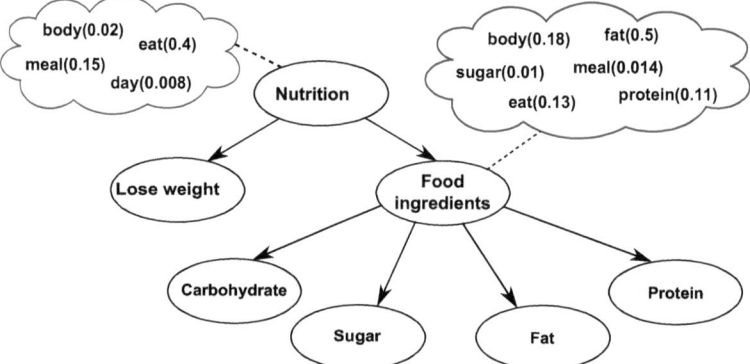

Figure 3.2.: Snapshot of the topic-tree with assigned keywords and corresponding weights.

Figure 3.2 shows a partial snapshot of the above defined taxonomy. The *topics* represent selected categories and sub-categories in the specified nutrition domain, the mapped keywords are frequent relevant words occurring within these topics, which can be extracted from relevant sources (e.g. websites or documents). The corresponding weights were calculated using their term frequency - inverse document frequency (see subsection 2.3.5) within these sources .

The idea of introducing a "cloud" of keywords to each topic emerged from the need of an efficient mapping of textual fragments to topics. In fact, as humans, we also tend to group and categorize certain words as belonging to a specific topic. It is important to notice here that one keyword can belong to several topics with different meanings and/or weights. This aspect reflects the *diversity of word meanings* and *usage frequency* within different contexts. Examples of such taxonomies can be found in Appendix C, Figure C.1, Figure C.2 and Figure C.3.

3.3.3. Topic mappings

As mentioned before, *topic mappings* are introduced as *connections* between the database of objects and the topic taxonomy, more specifically, the topics within the taxonomy. It is important to distinguish here between mappings *within* the topic-tree, i.e. between keywords and topics (see subsection 3.3.2), and mappings between objects and topics. In this subsection, we only refer to the latter kind.

The role of the object-topic mappings is two-fold. On one hand, they are used to *identify the "meaning"* of the object and, on the other hand, they *reflect the source* of the keywords within a particular topic. Identifying the "meaning" of the object is important for the calculation of the semantic similarity value; section 3.4 gives a more detailed overview of how semantic meaning is extracted and used for comparison.

Initially, in the case of the QA system used for our experiments, the topic-tree was constructed manually with the help of domain experts. Similarly, questions and answers formulated by experts were assigned to topics. Next, the keywords were automatically extracted from the available questions and answers, and semi-automatically filtered. Finally, the corresponding weights were identified and added to the keyword-topic assignments. Questions are, therefore, also seen as a source for keyword generation.

Since a topic, in general, can contain far more keywords than what the available questions and answers can provide, a different source was needed to acquire a larger amount. If the topic-tree is not rich enough, the system might not be able to deal with new questions that contain unknown keywords. To avoid this, the initial topic-tree was extended using Wikipedia [158]. The technique behind this approach will not be presented here, since it is beyond the scope of this thesis.

3.4. The four-layered semantic short-text similarity

Consider a QA system with a finite set of questions $\mathcal{Q}$ from a particular domain. Our objective is to define a semantic similarity measure between questions

$$sim_q : \mathcal{Q} \times \mathcal{Q} \to [0, 1]$$

using the topic-tree defined in subsection 3.3.2. Assume that, to each question $q \in \mathcal{Q}$, a set of keywords $\mathcal{K}_q \subset \mathcal{K}$ can be assigned, where $\mathcal{K}_q$ is extracted from q using NLP methods [67, 147, 74, 58]. For example, for

$q = $ "What type of food can I eat and at what time in order to lose weight?",

$\mathcal{K}_q = \{$food, eat, time, weight loss$\}$.

In the following, the semantic question similarity sim_q is defined using three other similarity measures: between topics, between keywords and between sets of keywords, each incorporating the one before.

3.4.1. Topic similarity

Let $sim_\tau : \mathcal{T} \times \mathcal{T} \to [0,1]$ be the *topic similarity* function where $sim_\tau(\tau_i, \tau_j)$ represents the semantic similarity between two topics $\tau_i, \tau_j \in \mathcal{T}$ using the structure of the topic-tree. For our experiments, we define sim_τ using the well-known semantic similarity measures from Equation 2.2 and Equation 2.3, although, we could consider any other similarity measure between concepts in an ontology.

3.4.2. Keyword similarity

Let $sim_k : \mathcal{K} \times \mathcal{K} \to [0,1]$ be the *keyword similarity* measure, where $sim_k(k_i, k_j)$ represents the semantic similarity between two keywords $k_i, k_j \in \mathcal{K}$. The function sim_k is defined in the following way:

$$sim_k(k_i, k_j) = \frac{w_i + w_j}{2} sim_\tau(\tau_i, \tau_j), \qquad (3.1)$$

where

$$w_p = \max_{\substack{\tau \in \mathcal{T} \\ (\tau, k_p) \in \mathcal{M}}} w(\tau, k_p), \quad p \in \{i, j\}$$

and

$$\tau_p = \arg\max_{\substack{\tau \in \mathcal{T} \\ (\tau, k_p) \in \mathcal{M}}} w(\tau, k_p), \quad p \in \{i, j\}.$$

In our experiments, several definitions of sim_k were tested, but the measure defined above obtained the highest correlation with human intuition when integrated into the final question similarity [80].

3.4 The four-layered semantic short-text similarity

3.4.3. Keyword-set similarity

Let $sim_{ks} : \mathcal{P}(\mathcal{K}) \times \mathcal{P}(\mathcal{K}) \to [0,1]$ be the *keyword-set similarity* function where $sim_{ks}(\mathcal{S}_i, \mathcal{S}_j)$ represents the semantic similarity between two sets of keywords $\mathcal{S}_i, \mathcal{S}_j \subset \mathcal{K}$ and $\mathcal{P}(\mathcal{K})$ contains all subsets of $\mathcal{K}$. In the following, several definitions of sim_{ks} are defined using well-known set distance measures.

The Sum of Maximum Similarities

The sum of minimum distances measure was originally defined by Niiniluoto [109] to measure truth-likeness in belief revision theory. We apply the same concept to define the similarity measure sim_{ks} between sets of keywords, which will further be referred to as *sum of maximum similarities*:

$$sim_{ks}(\mathcal{S}_i, \mathcal{S}_j) = \tfrac{1}{2}\left(\tfrac{1}{|\mathcal{S}_i|} \sum_{k \in \mathcal{S}_i} Sim(k, \mathcal{S}_j) + \tfrac{1}{|\mathcal{S}_j|} \sum_{k \in \mathcal{S}_j} Sim(k, \mathcal{S}_i) \right), \quad (3.2)$$

where

$$Sim : \mathcal{K} \times \mathcal{P}(\mathcal{K}) \to [0,1], \quad Sim(k, \mathcal{S}) = \max_{k' \in \mathcal{S}} sim_k(k, k').$$

is the semantic similarity between a keyword $k \in \mathcal{K}$ and a set of keywords $\mathcal{S} \subset \mathcal{K}$. This similarity measure sim_{ks} takes into account the similarities between each concept and the other set.

The Surjection Measure

The surjection measure was introduced by Oddie [111], who suggested defining the distance between two sets by considering surjections that map the larger set to the smaller one. Applying this concept to measure similarity between sets of keywords, we obtain the *surjection similarity measure* sim_{ks}, defined as

$$sim_{ks}(\mathcal{S}_i, \mathcal{S}_j) = \max_{\eta} \frac{1}{|\eta|} \sum_{(k_i, k_j) \in \eta} sim_k(k_i, k_j), \quad (3.3)$$

where the maximum is taken over all surjections η that map the larger set to the smaller one. This similarity measure tries to find for each concept in the larger set the most similar one in the smaller set, such that all concepts from the smaller set are mapped.

The Maximum Link Similarity Measure

The minimum link distance measure was proposed in [53] as an alternative to the previously mentioned distance measures between point sets. First, let us define the *link* between $\mathcal{S}_i$ and $\mathcal{S}_j$ as a relation $\mathcal{R} \subseteq \mathcal{S}_i \times \mathcal{S}_j$ satisfying

(a) for all $k_i \in \mathcal{S}_i$, there exists $k_j \in \mathcal{S}_j$, such that $(k_i, k_j) \in \mathcal{R}$; and

(b) for all $k_j \in \mathcal{S}_j$, there exists $k_i \in \mathcal{S}_i$, such that $(k_i, k_j) \in \mathcal{R}$.

Now we can apply this concept to define the *maximum link similarity* between sets of keywords as

$$sim_{ks}(\mathcal{S}_i, \mathcal{S}_j) = \max_{\mathcal{R}} \frac{1}{|\mathcal{R}|} \sum_{(k_i,k_j) \in \mathcal{R}} sim_k(k_i, k_j), \qquad (3.4)$$

taking the maximum over all relations $\mathcal{R}$.

3.4.4. Short-text similarity

Finally, the *short-text* or *question similarity* measure $sim_q : \mathcal{Q} \times \mathcal{Q} \to [0,1]$ is defined as

$$sim_q(q_a, q_b) = sim_{ks}(\mathcal{S}_{q_a}, \mathcal{S}_{q_b}) \qquad (3.5)$$

where $\mathcal{S}_{q_a}, \mathcal{S}_{q_b} \subset \mathcal{K}$ are the corresponding set of keywords extracted from q_a and q_b, respectively.

3.5. Example

Consider the following two questions and the corresponding set of keywords:

$q_a = $ "What should I eat and at what time in order to lose weight?",
$\mathcal{S}_{q_a} = \{$eat, time, weight loss, meal, fat, $\ldots\}$
and
$q_b = $ "What food has few calories?",
$\mathcal{S}_{q_b} = \{$eat, food, calories, $\ldots\}$.

In the first step, for the extracted keywords, the best matching topics are identified. Then, for each pair of topics, the similarity is computed according to sim_τ. Based on this, we can now calculate the keyword similarities and, subsequently, the keyword-set similarity, depending on the chosen method. Figure 3.3 sketches this computation process.

3.5 Example

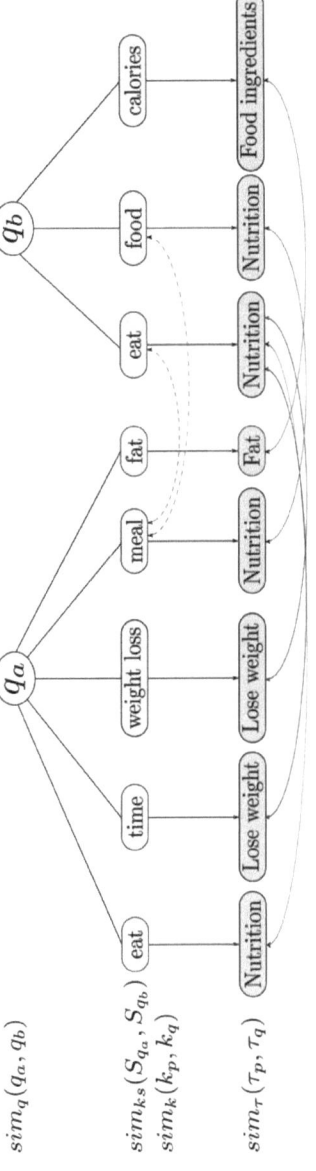

Figure 3.3.: Example of question similarity calculation.

3.6. Summary

In this chapter, a new technique based on a domain-specific taxonomy is introduced for measuring short text semantic similarity. The idea behind these measures is to discover interrelationships between concepts or keywords and use them to compute the semantic relatedness between questions.

The four-layered semantic similarity measure was adopted and successfully used for measuring semantic text similarity between questions in a particular QA system. The usage of such measures is vast and diverse within the IR and NLP fields. We mention here only a few: searching for existing answers for a particular new question, searching for questions similar to a set of keywords provided by the user, avoiding redundant questions or answers, recommending questions to users [105].

The proposed measures were evaluated against other popular similarity measures [80] using different taxonomies and application areas [105, 106]. Further results can be found in chapter 6, section 6.2.

4. Short-term Recommendation

4.1. Overview

The following two chapters focus on two recommendation techniques designed for QA systems, addressing two different user needs. The first one refers to generalized, semantic question suggestions, whereas the second type uses the history log to generate personalized, learning-oriented recommendations. This chapter introduces the first category.

Consider the following scenario. A user is in search for the answer for a particular question and types in the search field of the system either the full question or the keywords relevant to this question. In return, the system queries the existing database of questions for semantically similar questions and recommends the users the first N most related ones. We call this **short-term recommendation**, because it uses only the user's current search intent to provide recommendations. Based on the classification of recommender systems (see section 2.2), the technique presented in this chapter is a *content-based recommendation* method.

In contrast, the second recommendation technique suggests questions based on the user's entire question history. We will introduce this approach in detail in the next chapter.

In the following, the short-term recommendation concept will be formally defined and a particular implementation of this approach is introduced, which is referred to as *conversation recommender*. This technique can produce relevant recommendations corresponding to the user's last search intent by employing the semantic similarity measure presented in chapter 3.

4.2. Definition

Consider $\mathcal{Q}$ to be the set of all questions of a QA system.

For any user $c \in \mathcal{C}$ and a **search query** S, we define a **utility function** $u(S,q) \in [0,1]$ that measures the usefulness or relatedness of question $q \in \mathcal{Q}$ to search query S. S is defined to be either a set of keywords $\{k_{i_1}, \ldots, k_{i_{|S|}}\} \subseteq \mathcal{K}$ or a new question $q_{new} \notin \mathcal{Q}$. If S is a question, it is parsed, tokenized and a corresponding set of keywords $\{k_{i_1}, \ldots, k_{i_p}\} \subseteq \mathcal{K}$ is extracted. For simplicity, consider $S = \{k_{i_1}, \ldots, k_{i_p}\} \subseteq \mathcal{K}$, where p is the number of relevant keywords corresponding to the user's search query S.

Then $u : \mathcal{P}(\mathcal{K}) \times \mathcal{Q} \to [0,1]$, where $\mathcal{P}(\mathcal{K})$ is the power-set of $\mathcal{K}$.

Consider a search query $S \in \mathcal{P}(\mathcal{K})$. Our goal is to find the first N questions from $\mathcal{Q}$ with the highest utility values.

Then

$$R = \arg\max_{q \in \mathcal{Q}}^{N} u(S, q).$$

is the set of N best question recommendations for any user that provides the search query S.

4.3. Semantic utility

The semantic utility function u is defined based on the semantic similarity measure sim_{ks} between keyword sets introduced in subsection 3.4.3.

Let $S = \{k_{i_1}, \ldots, k_{i_p}\} \subset \mathcal{K}$ be a search query. For $q \in \mathcal{Q}$, the **semantic utility** of S with respect to q is formalized as

$$u(S, q) = sim_{ks}(S, \mathcal{S}_q),$$

where $\mathcal{S}_q \subset \mathcal{K}$ is the set of keywords extracted from q.

4.4. Recommendation generation

Having defined the semantic utility function, it is now straightforward to apply this measure to generate recommendations. In the following, a general framework for using this technique, as well as two scenarios that highlight the capabilities of this type of recommender are presented.

Search suggestions

Consider a user is in search for the answer for a particular question and types in the search field of the system either the full question or the keywords relevant to this question.

For every user input, the text is parsed and corresponding keywords from $\mathcal{K}$ are extracted to S. Then, for each question $q \in \mathcal{Q}$ in the database, the system retrieves the corresponding set of keywords $\mathcal{S}_q$ and calculates the semantic similarity

4.5 The conversation recommender

$sim_{ks}(S, S_q)$ between the search query keywords and the respective question in the database.

For a more efficient similar question retrieval, we adopted the indexing services provided by Lucene[99]. This enabled us to introduce the short-term recommendation as an auto-complete search engine.

Semantic recommendations

In a different context, the user has recently learned about the answer for a question within a particular topic, but there are still open questions related to the same topic. In this case, the user might be interested to understand more about it.

For this purpose, the semantic utility function can be applied to the most recent question q_t: the similarity between q_t and every $q \in Q$ is computed, then the first N most relevant questions are returned as recommendations.

In the next section, a specific short-term recommender is introduced that, additionally, also uses the hierarchical structure of the domain-specific taxonomy to produce more useful recommendations. This recommender is called *conversation recommender,* because it tries to generate recommendations in a way that it gives the user the impression of being in a conversation with another person.

On one hand, the technique presented in this chapter has the advantages of avoiding redundancy in the question database and being immune to some typical recommender system problems: the cold-start, new item or new user problems.

On the other hand, it is not capable of learning user search patterns and use them to improve recommendation results or to avoid recommending familiar questions to the user. To avoid this, the *long-term* or *learning-oriented recommendation* concept is introduced in chapter 5.

4.5. The conversation recommender

Using the semantic similarity measure defined in chapter 3, various short-term recommendation methods were constructed. Our goal was to add semantics to a typical content-based RS in order to improve the quality of the recommendations by mapping relevant keywords from the existing taxonomy (see subsection 3.3.2) to the available questions. Therefore, six different short-term recommendation methods were implemented that extensively used the hierarchical structure of the topic taxonomy.

The combined recommender is content-based, but context independent, i.e. it does not take the user history into consideration. It tries to simulate a "conversation" between the user and a fictitious expert that guides him through a specific subject. We call it *conversation recommender*, because it tries to generate recommendations in a way that gives the user the feeling of being in a conversation with another person.

The conversation recommender consists of six particular short-term recommendation approaches: *Similar in Topic, Similar over Topic, More General, More Specific, Most relevant in Similar Topic* and *Latest relevant in Similar Topic*. The following methods are based on the topic-tree and the correct assignment of keywords and questions to topics.

Similar in Topic (SiT) This recommender type searches for similar questions which are assigned to the same topic as the recently visited one. For rating questions, it uses a semantic query similarity measure. It compares the last question with all other questions assigned to the current topic. This will provide the user with similar questions to the one he/she recently visited. The returned queries are rated by their similarity score.

Similar over Topic (SoT)

In this case, the recently viewed question will be compared to all questions that are assigned to topics which don't contain this question. The resulting questions are also rated by their semantic similarity score. This allows the user to find the most realistic next question in a conversation guiding to a different topic.

More General (MG)

This recommender type will look on higher levels of the topic-tree for questions. This algorithm provides more general recommendations and, therefore, avoids the situation of a user getting stuck in a certain topic or its sub-topics. Using these recommendations the user can navigate to other relevant topics. The questions are rated by their semantic similarity to the current question.

More Specific (MS)

This algorithm searches for more specific questions. It works like the MG algorithm, but searches for questions in lower levels.

Most relevant in Similar Topic (MrST)

The MrST algorithm scans the database for the most similar topics in the topic-tree. In contrast to the SoT technique, it also considers a rating of the topics. The questions will still be rated by their similarity to the initial question.

Latest relevant in Similar Topic (LrST)

This algorithm is a special form of MrST. It also takes into account the novelty of questions (i.e. the timestamp when the question was added to the database). Only questions not older than M days (e.g. questions added in the last 30 days) will be used in the similarity calculation. This algorithm ensures that also new questions will be recommended. On one hand, this avoids the new item problem, very common among recommender systems. On the other hand, it serves marketing purposes.

By combining the six recommendation techniques, we give the user the opportunity to explore a broad horizon of questions related by similarity to his/her current choice. This combination should provide the user enough possibilities to navigate through all relevant topics and explore the whole question knowledge base.

4.6. Summary

In this chapter, the short-term recommendation concept is formalized and defined based on a semantic utility function, introduced with the purpose of retrieving semantically related questions to the user's last search intent.

Based on this semantic utility function, we can generate recommendations that are suitable for two variations of the same user need, as mentioned before: the user is searching for the answer for a particular question, which might be already available in the database, possibly under a different formulation. We call this recommendation type "short-term", because it generates recommendations based only on the user's current search intent.

The advantages of such a technique are:

- it avoids redundant questions and answers;
- it provides the user with a range of concrete questions, when the user does not know how to formulate it;
- avoids the cold-start, new item and new user problems, given that a considerable amount of questions are already available.

One of the disadvantages of using this recommendation approach on its own is that it cannot take into consideration the user's question browsing history in order to avoid recommending questions that were already visited or that are too similar to the user's last choice.

The conversation recommender presented in this chapter was adopted by an existing QA system [93] and its effectiveness was evaluated against human ratings [105]. Further experimental results are presented in section 6.3.

5. Learning-oriented Recommendation

5.1. Overview

Consider again a QA system designed to *guide* the user through a particular topic, learning with each question new information. The typical user is driven by a specific learning goal or motivation which can be different or similar to other users' learning objective. In order to accompany the user on a meaningful and helpful learning journey, the system should be able to *detect* the user's objective and *provide suitable suggestions* based on previous experiences.

Learning is a process along which a person can acquire new knowledge, can apply or use this knowledge to analyze, evaluate or create. Current conceptions about learning assume learners as active agents and not passive recipients or simple recorders of information. Therefore, the past learning path, as well as the order in which knowledge is assimilated, is of high importance. It can reveal the end goal(s), the learning pace and interests of a particular user.

Most of the existing recommender systems use a collaborative filtering or association rule mining approach to discover common patterns among users (see subsection 2.2.2 and subsection 2.4.1). The order in which items are selected has no influence on the generated recommendations. Although such methods might work well for a learning-oriented QA system, they do not leverage fully the available information about user browsing behavior and the complexity of items.

Other content-based approaches provide too "similar" recommendations and the user might find himself "stuck" within the same topic, not advancing his/her learning experience (see section 6.3). One might be tempted to consider, in this particular situation, to employ a learning curriculum to help guide the user. This is a feasible and reliable source, since it might be well established by experts, therefore less error-prone. However, generally, QA systems also deal with novel topics for which a learning curriculum has not yet been developed. Creating such a curriculum is not an easy task. It requires time, experience, a rich knowledge of the domain and experts ready to invest their effort into it.

In order to constructively exploit the user's past learning path to produce useful recommendations, a new technique is needed that goes beyond the generalism of existing methods and tries to leverage the particular aspects of a learning-oriented QA system.

Chapter 5 Learning-oriented Recommendation

In this chapter, a new probabilistic model-based recommender system is introduced using VLMCs, a domain-specific taxonomy and Bloom's revised learning framework. We will further refer to this recommender technique as *learning-oriented recommender* (LoR).

5.2. Knowledge-base description

Let $\mathcal{Q}$ be a set of questions and $\mathcal{T}$ be the set of predefined topics from a particular domain. Usually, $|\mathcal{Q}| \gg |\mathcal{T}|$, i.e. the QA system's database contains much more questions than topics in the topic-tree. The structure of the corresponding topic taxonomy is given by a *generalization-specification relationship* between topics:

$$\mathcal{L} \subset \mathcal{T} \times \mathcal{T}, (\tau_i, \tau_j) \in \mathcal{L} \iff \tau_i \text{ parent of } \tau_j, \qquad (5.1)$$

where $\tau_i, \tau_j \in \mathcal{T}$.

Examples of such taxonomies can be found in Appendix C, Figure C.1, Figure C.2 and Figure C.3.

Consider also a mapping relationship between $\mathcal{Q}$ and $\mathcal{T}$ which maps to each question in $\mathcal{Q}$ one or more topics in $\mathcal{T}$. We will further refer to this relationship as **topic mapping** (see subsection 3.3.3) and it is defined in the following way:

$$\mathcal{M}_\tau \subset \mathcal{Q} \times \mathcal{T}, (q, \tau) \in \mathcal{M}_\tau \iff \text{question } q \text{ is mapped to topic } \tau.$$

The topic mapping $\mathcal{M}_\tau$ is a surjection with respect to $\mathcal{Q}$ (i.e. all questions are mapped to at least one topic). Moreover, one question can be mapped to several topics and one topic can map several questions (see Figure 5.1).

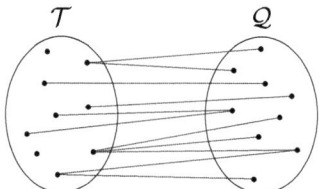

Figure 5.1.: Question-topic mapping.

A mapping tuple $(q, \tau) \in \mathcal{M}_\tau$ has the following meaning: "question q refers to or is about topic τ". For example, consider the question from section 3.5 :

5.2 Knowledge-base description

q = "What should I eat and at what time in order to lose weight?"

This question could be mapped to the following topics: τ_1 = "Nutrition", τ_2 = "Lose weight".

Additionally, we enrich the knowledge-base with Bloom's learning taxonomy (see section 2.5). Therefore, consider the following sets:

- the **knowledge dimension**

$$\mathcal{KD} = \{\ \kappa_1 = \text{"factual"}, \kappa_2 = \text{"conceptual"},$$
$$\kappa_3 = \text{"procedural"}, \kappa_4 = \text{"metacognitive"}\ \}$$

and

- the **cognitive process dimension**

$$\mathcal{CD} = \{\ \rho_1 = \text{"remember"}, \rho_2 = \text{"understand"}, \rho_3 = \text{"apply"},$$
$$\rho_4 = \text{"analyze"}, \rho_5 = \text{"evaluate"}, \rho_6 = \text{"create"}\ \}.$$

To each question $q \in \mathcal{Q}$, a unique pair $(\kappa, \rho) \in \mathcal{KD} \times \mathcal{CD}$ is assigned, which will further be referred to as **learning objective**. The logic behind this assignment is given by the actual learning goal of question q and can be identified by the two features. According to Bloom's revised taxonomy [10], each learning objective is defined by the knowledge and cognitive process dimensions. For more details on the structure and role of Bloom's taxonomy within the learning process, see section 2.5. Table B.1, Table B.2 and Table B.3 also contain some intuitive examples which reveal the usage context of these values.

Opposed to the topic-tree, which can evolve, change and grow over time, the learning taxonomy defined by the two dimensions is fixed. Therefore, we have an exact number of $4 \times 6 = 24$ learning objectives:

$$\mathcal{LO} = \{\ \phi_1 = \text{"list"}, \phi_2 = \text{"summarize"}, \phi_3 = \text{"respond"}, \phi_4 = \text{"select"},$$
$$\phi_5 = \text{"check"}, \phi_6 = \text{"generate"}, \phi_7 = \text{"recognize"}, \phi_8 = \text{"classify"},$$
$$\phi_9 = \text{"provide"}, \phi_{10} = \text{"differentiate"}, \phi_{11} = \text{"determine"}, \phi_{12} = \text{"assemble"},$$
$$\phi_{13} = \text{"recall"}, \phi_{14} = \text{"clarify"}, \phi_{15} = \text{"carry out"}, \phi_{16} = \text{"integrate"},$$
$$\phi_{17} = \text{"judge"}, \phi_{18} = \text{"design"}, \phi_{19} = \text{"identify"}, \phi_{20} = \text{"predict"},$$
$$\phi_{21} = \text{"use"}, \phi_{22} = \text{"deconstruct"}, \phi_{23} = \text{"reflect"}, \phi_{24} = \text{"create"}\ \},$$

where each $\phi_i \in \mathcal{LO}$ corresponds to a pair $(\kappa_j, \rho_l) \in \mathcal{KD} \times \mathcal{CD}$, such that $i = (j-1)*6+l$.

The names assigned to each of the learning objectives $\phi \in \mathcal{LO}$ are possible examples that generally correspond to the various combinations of $\kappa \in \mathcal{KD}$ and $\rho \in \mathcal{CD}$. A detailed list can be found in Table B.1, Table B.2 and Table B.3.

As previously mentioned, to each question $q \in \mathcal{Q}$, a unique pair $(\kappa, \rho) \in \mathcal{KD} \times \mathcal{CD}$ or a single learning objective $\phi \in \mathcal{LO}$ is assigned.

Therefore, the following mapping relationships are introduced:

1. The **knowledge mapping** – maps each question to an element in the knowledge dimension:

$$\mathcal{M}_\kappa \subset \mathcal{Q} \times \mathcal{KD},$$
$$(q, \kappa) \in \mathcal{M}_\kappa \iff \text{question } q \text{ is mapped to the knowledge } \kappa.$$

2. The **cognitive process mapping** – maps each question to an element in the cognitive process dimension:

$$\mathcal{M}_\rho \subset \mathcal{Q} \times \mathcal{CD},$$
$$(q, \rho) \in \mathcal{M}_\rho \iff \text{question } q \text{ is mapped to the cognitive process } \rho.$$

3. The **learning objective mapping** – maps each question to a learning objective:

$$\mathcal{M}_\phi \subset \mathcal{Q} \times \mathcal{LO},$$
$$(q, \phi) \in \mathcal{M}_\phi \iff \text{question } q \text{ is mapped to the learning objective } \phi.$$

For every $q \in \mathcal{Q}$, the following holds:

- $\exists! \, \kappa \in \mathcal{KD}$ s.t. $(q, \kappa) \in \mathcal{M}_\kappa$,
- $\exists! \, \rho \in \mathcal{CD}$ s.t. $(q, \rho) \in \mathcal{M}_\rho$, and
- $\exists! \, \phi \in \mathcal{LO}$ s.t. $(q, \phi) \in \mathcal{M}_\phi$.

In contrast to the topic mapping $\mathcal{M}_\tau$, a question can be mapped to a single learning objective. Intuitively, this means that a question can refer to several topics, but a single learning goal. In general, questions contain also only one topic. In our experiments, we have only dealt with single topic assignments (see section 6.4). For simplicity, consider in the following $\mathcal{M}_\tau$ to map each question to a single topic.

5.3. Learning-oriented recommendation

5.3.1. Preliminaries

Let Q, T, K, C and L be random variables taking values in the question set $\mathcal{Q}$, the topic space $\mathcal{T}$, the knowledge dimension $\mathcal{KD}$, the cognitive process dimension $\mathcal{CD}$ and the set of learning objectives $\mathcal{LO}$, respectively.

Consider $\mathcal{H}$ to be the history database which contains, for each user, an ordered sequence of questions representing the user's history log.

A learner is given a training set (usually a subset of the history database $\mathcal{H}$) of question sequences $q_1^n = q_1 q_2 \cdots q_n$, where $q_i \in \mathcal{Q}$ and $q_i q_{i+1}$ means that question q_i was asked before question q_{i+1}. The sequence q_1^n, therefore, represents the history log of a particular user and its length can be different for each user.

Given this training set, our goal is to learn a model $\hat{P}$ that provides a probability assignment for any future outcome given some past. More specifically, given a "context" of previously asked questions $s \in \mathcal{Q}^*$ and a question $q \in \mathcal{Q}$, the learner should generate a conditional probability distribution $\hat{P}(q|s)$.

Prediction performance

We measure *prediction performance* using the *average log-loss* $l(\hat{P}, x_1^t)$ of $\hat{P}(\cdot|\cdot)$ with respect to a test sequence $x_1^t = x_1 x_2 \cdots x_t$:

$$l(\hat{P}, x_1^t) = -\frac{1}{t} \sum_{i=1}^{t} \log \hat{P}(x_i | x_1 \cdots x_{i-1}). \tag{5.2}$$

The average log-loss [19] is directly related to the likelihood

$$\hat{P}(x_1^t) = \prod_{i=1}^{t} \hat{P}(x_i | x_1 \cdots x_{i-1}) \tag{5.3}$$

and, therefore, minimizing the average log-loss is equivalent to maximizing the likelihood.

Question projections

Let $q \in \mathcal{Q}$ be a question. We define the following projection functions:

1. The **topic projection** – a function that projects a question on the topic space using the mapping $\mathcal{M}_\tau$:

$$p_\tau : \mathcal{Q} \to \mathcal{T}, \; p_\tau(q) = \tau \iff \exists (q, \tau) \in \mathcal{M}_\tau. \tag{5.4}$$

2. The **knowledge projection** – a function that projects a question on the knowledge dimension using the mapping $\mathcal{M}_\kappa$:

$$p_\kappa : \mathcal{Q} \to \mathcal{KD},\ p_\kappa(q) = \kappa \iff \exists (q, \kappa) \in \mathcal{M}_\kappa. \tag{5.5}$$

3. The **cognitive process projection** – a function that projects a question on the cognitive process dimension using the mapping $\mathcal{M}_\rho$:

$$p_\rho : \mathcal{Q} \to \mathcal{CD},\ p_\rho(q) = \rho \iff \exists (q, \rho) \in \mathcal{M}_\rho. \tag{5.6}$$

4. The **learning objective projection** – a function that projects a question on the learning objective space using the mapping $\mathcal{M}_\phi$:

$$p_\phi : \mathcal{Q} \to \mathcal{LO},\ p_\phi(q) = \phi \iff \exists (q, \phi) \in \mathcal{M}_\phi. \tag{5.7}$$

Consider now the question sequence $q_1^n = q_1 q_2 \cdots q_n$ with $q_i \in \mathcal{Q}$. The projection of this sequence on the topic space is

$$proj_\tau(q_1^n) = p_\tau(q_1) p_\tau(q_2) \cdots p_\tau(q_n) = \tau_1 \tau_2 \cdots \tau_n = \tau_1^n,$$

where $proj_\tau : \mathcal{Q}^* \to \mathcal{T}^*$.

Similarly, we define $proj_\kappa : \mathcal{Q}^* \to \mathcal{KD}^*$, $proj_\rho : \mathcal{Q}^* \to \mathcal{CD}^*$ and $proj_\phi : \mathcal{Q}^* \to \mathcal{LO}^*$, functions that project a question sequence on the knowledge, cognitive process and learning objective dimensions, respectively.

Therefore, the projection of question sequence q_1^n on the knowledge dimension is

$$proj_\kappa(q_1^n) = p_\kappa(q_1) p_\kappa(q_2) \cdots p_\kappa(q_n) = \kappa_1 \kappa_2 \cdots \kappa_n = \kappa_1^n,$$

its projection on the cognitive process dimension is

$$proj_\rho(q_1^n) = p_\rho(q_1) p_\rho(q_2) \cdots p_\rho(q_n) = \rho_1 \rho_2 \cdots \rho_n = \rho_1^n,$$

and its projection on the dimension of learning objectives is

$$proj_\phi(q_1^n) = p_\phi(q_1) p_\phi(q_2) \cdots p_\phi(q_n) = \phi_1 \phi_2 \cdots \phi_n = \phi_1^n.$$

5.3 Learning-oriented recommendation

The learning-oriented recommender

Based on the learned model $\hat{P}$, we define the ***learning-oriented recommender*** (LoR). For each user with history log s, we want to recommend a set $R(s) \subset \mathcal{Q}$ of N questions that satisfies the following:

$$R(s) = \underset{q \in \mathcal{Q} \text{ and } q \notin s}{\arg\max^{N}} \hat{P}(q|s), \tag{5.8}$$

where $\arg\max^N$ returns the first N maximal arguments with respect to the given function. In other words, the learning oriented recommender tries to recommend the first N "best" questions that maximize the user's utility.

This utility is given by the learned model $\hat{P}$.

In the next subsection, eleven different models based on VLMCs are introduced, with the goal to leverage the users' learning behavior. The various models were defined in order to identify which of them "mimic" better a general learning process pattern.

5.3.2. Models

Simple recommender

The simple recommender is defined using a VLMC with random variable Q over the question space $\mathcal{Q}$. Consider $P(Q^{(t+1)}|Q^{(1:t)})$ to be the transition model of the VLMC trained over a subset of the history database $\mathcal{H}$. In order to learn a VLMC model, the algorithms presented in [19] were employed.

Then, for a given context of questions $x_1^t = x_1 x_2 \cdots x_t$ with $x_i \in \mathcal{Q}$ and a new question $x_{t+1} \in \mathcal{Q}$, the probability of observing x_{t+1} after x_1^t is given by:

$$\begin{aligned} \hat{P}(x_{t+1}|x_1^t) &= P(Q^{(t+1)} = x_{t+1}|Q^{(1)} = x_1, \ldots, Q^{(t)} = x_t) \\ &= P(Q^{(t+1)} = x_{t+1}|Q^{(t-\lambda+1)} = x_{t-\lambda+1}, \ldots, Q^{(t)} = x_t), \end{aligned}$$

where $\lambda = \lambda(x_t, x_{t-1}, \ldots)$ is a function of the past determined during the learning process of the VLMC. Let $D = \max_{x_t, x_{t-1}, \ldots} \lambda(x_t, x_{t-1}, \ldots)$ be the maximal memory length of the VLMC.

Figure 5.2 represents a simple recommender model with $D = 3$.

Intuitively, the simple recommender tries to learn the order in which users ask questions by considering questions as any other object. We could replace the questions with a unique identification number, which has no meaning at all, and the result

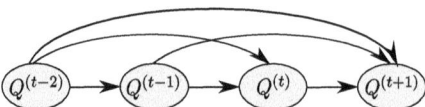

Figure 5.2.: Simple question recommender based on a VLMC.

would be the same. There is no feature or question aspect used to learn such a model.

The following recommender models try to leverage hidden information within questions and use this to return "better" recommendations and extract intuitive patterns from the user logs.

Topic-based recommender

The topic-based recommender is defined using a vlHMM with hidden states T over the topic space $\mathcal{T}$ and observations Q over the question space $\mathcal{Q}$. Consider $P(T^{(t+1)}|T^{(1:t)})$ to be the state transition model and $P(Q^{(t+1)}|T^{(t+1)}, Q^{(1:t)})$ to be the observation model of the vlHMM, trained over a subset of the history database $\mathcal{H}$.

To learn such a model, we project the question sequences on the topic space using $proj_\tau(\cdot)$ and learn a VLMC over these projections. As a result, we obtain the state transition model $P(T^{(t+1)}|T^{(1:t)})$.

We define the observation probability

$$P(Q^{(t+1)} = q_{t+1}|T^{(t+1)} = \tau_{t+1}, Q^{(1:t)} = q_1^t)$$

of observing question q_{t+1}, given the topic τ_{t+1} and the context q_1^t, as the probability of randomly selecting a question from topic τ_{t+1} which has not yet been visited:

$$P(q_{t+1}|\tau_{t+1}, q_1^t) = \begin{cases} 0 & \text{, if } \nexists(q_{t+1}, \tau_{t+1}) \in \mathcal{M}_\tau \\ \frac{1}{|\mathcal{S}|} & \text{, otherwise} \end{cases},$$

where $\mathcal{S} = \{q' \in \mathcal{Q}\backslash\{q_1, \ldots, q_t\} | (q', \tau_{t+1}) \in \mathcal{M}_\tau\}$ is the set of all unvisited questions in topic τ_{t+1}.

Then, for a test context of questions $x_1^t = x_1 x_2 \cdots x_t$ with $x_i \in \mathcal{Q}$ and a question $x_{t+1} \in \mathcal{Q}$, the probability of observing x_{t+1} after x_1^t is given by:

$$\hat{P}(x_{t+1}|x_1^t) = P(\tau_{t+1}|\tau_1^t) \cdot P(x_{t+1}|\tau_{t+1}, x_1^t),$$

5.3 Learning-oriented recommendation

where $\tau_{t+1} = p_\tau(x_{t+1})$, $\tau_1^t = proj_\tau(x_1^t)$ and

$$\begin{aligned}\hat{P}(\tau_{t+1}|\tau_1^t) &= P(T^{(t+1)} = \tau_{t+1}|T^{(1)} = \tau_1, \ldots, T^{(t)} = \tau_t) \\ &= P(T^{(t+1)} = \tau_{t+1}|T^{(t-\lambda+1)} = \tau_{t-\lambda+1}, \ldots, T^{(t)} = \tau_t).\end{aligned}$$

Here, $\lambda = \lambda(\tau_t, \tau_{t-1}, \ldots)$ is a function of the past determined during the learning process of the VLMC. Let $D = \max_{\tau_t, \tau_{t-1}, \ldots} \lambda(\tau_t, \tau_{t-1}, \ldots)$ be the maximal memory length of the VLMC.

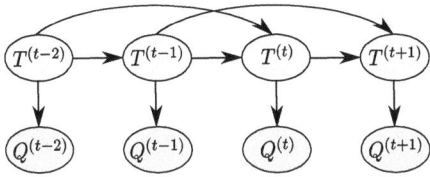

Figure 5.3.: Topic-based question recommender based on a vlHMM.

Figure 5.3 represents a topic-based recommender model with $D = 2$.

Knowledge- and cognitive process-based recommender

The knowledge- and cognitive process-based recommender is similar to the topic-based one, but in this case we use a factorial vlHMM with two hidden states: K over the knowledge dimension $\mathcal{KD}$ and C over the cognitive process dimension $\mathcal{CD}$. The observations are the same: Q over the question space $\mathcal{Q}$. Then, our model would have to learn two transition models $P(K^{(t+1)}|K^{(1:t)})$ and $P(C^{(t+1)}|C^{(1:t)})$, and the observation model $P(Q^{(t+1)}|K^{(t+1)}, C^{(t+1)}, Q^{(1:t)})$.

Notice that for this particular recommender we identify and use the learning objectives defined as a tuple $(kd, cd) \in \mathcal{KD} \times \mathcal{CD}$.

To learn such a model, we project the question sequences on the knowledge dimension using $proj_\kappa(\cdot)$ and on the cognitive process dimension using $proj_\rho(\cdot)$, then learn a VLMC over each of these projections. As a result, we obtain the two corresponding state transition models mentioned above.

We define the observation probability

$$P(Q^{(t+1)} = q_{t+1}|K^{(t+1)} = \kappa_{t+1}, C^{(t+1)} = \rho_{t+1}, Q^{(1:t)} = q_1^t)$$

of observing question q_{t+1}, given the knowledge κ_{t+1}, the cognitive process ρ_{t+1} and the context q_1^t, as the probability of randomly selecting a question having as learning objective $(\kappa_{t+1}, \rho_{t+1})$ and which has not yet been visited:

$$P(q_{t+1}|\kappa_{t+1},\rho_{t+1},q_1^t) = \begin{cases} 0 & \text{, if } \not\exists (q_{t+1},\kappa_{t+1}) \in \mathcal{M}_\kappa \\ & \text{or } \not\exists (q_{t+1},\rho_{t+1}) \in \mathcal{M}_\rho, \\ \frac{1}{|\mathcal{S}|} & \text{, otherwise} \end{cases}$$

where $\mathcal{S} = \{q' \in \mathcal{Q}\backslash\{q_1,\ldots,q_t\}|(q',\kappa_{t+1}) \in \mathcal{M}_\kappa \text{ and } (q',\rho_{t+1}) \in \mathcal{M}_\rho\}$ is the set of all unvisited questions within the learning objective $(\kappa_{t+1}, \rho_{t+1})$.

Then, for a test context of questions $x_1^t = x_1 x_2 \cdots x_t$ with $x_i \in \mathcal{Q}$ and a question $x_{t+1} \in \mathcal{Q}$, the probability of observing question x_{t+1} after x_1^t is given by:

$$\hat{P}(x_{t+1}|x_1^t) = P(\kappa_{t+1}|\kappa_1^t) \cdot P(\rho_{t+1}|\rho_1^t) \cdot P(x_{t+1}|\kappa_{t+1},\rho_{t+1},x_1^t),$$

where $\kappa_{t+1} = p_\kappa(x_{t+1})$, $\rho_{t+1} = p_\rho(x_{t+1})$, $\kappa_1^t = proj_\kappa(x_1^t)$, $\rho_1^t = proj_\rho(x_1^t)$ and

$$\begin{aligned} \hat{P}(\kappa_{t+1}|\kappa_1^t) &= P(T^{(t+1)} = \kappa_{t+1}|T^{(1)} = \kappa_1,\ldots,T^{(t)} = \kappa_t) \\ &= P(T^{(t+1)} = \kappa_{t+1}|T^{(t-\lambda_1+1)} = \kappa_{t-\lambda_1+1},\ldots,T^{(t)} = \kappa_t), \\ \hat{P}(\rho_{t+1}|\rho_1^t) &= P(T^{(t+1)} = \rho_{t+1}|T^{(1)} = \rho_1,\ldots,T^{(t)} = \rho_t) \\ &= P(T^{(t+1)} = \rho_{t+1}|T^{(t-\lambda_2+1)} = \rho_{t-\lambda_2+1},\ldots,T^{(t)} = \rho_t). \end{aligned}$$

In this context, $\lambda_1 = \lambda_1(\kappa_t, \kappa_{t-1}, \ldots)$ and $\lambda_2 = \lambda_2(\rho_t, \rho_{t-1}, \ldots)$ are functions of the past determined during the learning process of the corresponding VLMCs. Let $D_1 = \max_{\kappa_t,\kappa_{t-1},\ldots} \lambda_1(\kappa_t, \kappa_{t-1}, \ldots)$ be the maximal memory length of the knowledge-based VLMC and $D_2 = \max_{\rho_t,\rho_{t-1},\ldots} \lambda_2(\rho_t, \rho_{t-1}, \ldots)$ the maximal memory of the cognitive process-based VLMC.

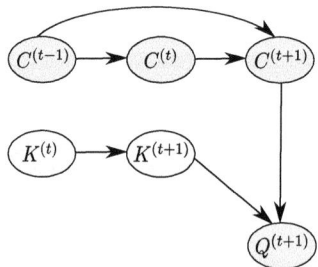

Figure 5.4.: Knowledge- and cognitive process-based question recommender based on two hidden VLMCs.

Then, Figure 5.4 represents a knowledge- and cognitive process-based question recommender model with $D_1 = 1$ and $D_2 = 2$.

5.3 Learning-oriented recommendation

The intuition behind this recommendation model is that if the questions are rather similar with respect to the topic feature, i.e. the questions refer in general to the same topic, then only the knowledge and cognitive process dimensions can be efficiently used to discover patterns. Naturally, this is not always the case. A generalized representation of this idea is introduced below as the hierarchical learning-oriented recommender.

Mixed recommender

For the mixed recommender, a factorial vlHMM is constructed that takes all three features of a question into consideration. Intuitively, if the overall number of questions is high, covering many topics, even from a restricted domain, the previous recommender would fail to generate confident recommendations. Therefore, by adding a new hidden state for the topic variable (see Figure 5.5), we expect to improve the overall performance of the recommender.

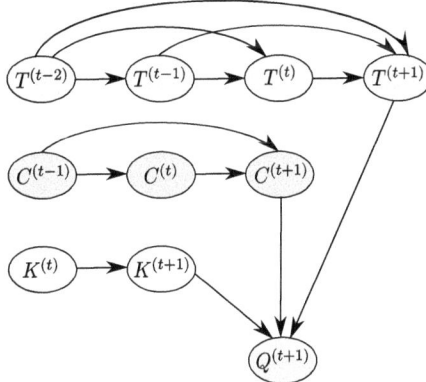

Figure 5.5.: Mixed question recommender based on three hidden VLMCs.

To learn such a model, we project the question sequences on the topic, knowledge and cognitive process dimensions using the projection functions $proj_\tau(\cdot)$, $proj_\kappa(\cdot)$ and $proj_\rho(\cdot)$. Then, a VLMC is trained over each of these projections. As a result, the three corresponding state transition models are obtained:

$$P(T^{(t+1)}|T^{(1:t)}),\ P(K^{(t+1)}|K^{(1:t)}) \text{ and } P(C^{(t+1)}|C^{(1:t)}).$$

We define the observation probability

$$P(Q^{(t+1)} = q_{t+1}|T^{(t+1)} = \tau_{t+1}, K^{(t+1)} = \kappa_{t+1}, C^{(t+1)} = \rho_{t+1}, Q^{(1:t)} = q_1^t)$$

of observing question q_{t+1}, given topic τ_{t+1}, the knowledge κ_{t+1}, the cognitive process ρ_{t+1} and the context q_1^t, as the probability of randomly selecting a question with these features which has not yet been visited:

$$P(q_{t+1}|\tau_{t+1},\kappa_{t+1},\rho_{t+1},q_1^t) = \begin{cases} 0 & \text{, if } \nexists(q_{t+1},\tau_{t+1}) \in \mathcal{M}_\tau \\ & \text{or } \nexists(q_{t+1},\kappa_{t+1}) \in \mathcal{M}_\kappa \\ & \text{or } \nexists(q_{t+1},\rho_{t+1}) \in \mathcal{M}_\rho \\ \frac{1}{|\mathcal{S}|} & \text{, otherwise} \end{cases},$$

where $\mathcal{S} = \{q' \in \mathcal{Q}\setminus\{q_1,\ldots,q_t\}|(q',\tau_{t+1}) \in \mathcal{M}_\tau \text{ and } (q',\kappa_{t+1}) \in \mathcal{M}_\kappa \text{ and } (q',\rho_{t+1}) \in \mathcal{M}_\rho\}$.

Then, for a test context of questions $x_1^t = x_1 x_2 \cdots x_t$ with $x_i \in \mathcal{Q}$ and a question $x_{t+1} \in \mathcal{Q}$, the probability of observing question x_{t+1} after x_1^t is given by:

$$\hat{P}(x_{t+1}|x_1^t) = P(\tau_{t+1}|\tau_1^t) \cdot P(\kappa_{t+1}|\kappa_1^t) \cdot P(\rho_{t+1}|\rho_1^t) \cdot P(x_{t+1}|\tau_{t+1},\kappa_{t+1},\rho_{t+1},x_1^t),$$

where $\tau_{t+1} = p_\tau(x_{t+1})$, $\kappa_{t+1} = p_\kappa(x_{t+1})$, $\rho_{t+1} = p_\rho(x_{t+1})$, $\tau_1^t = proj_\tau(x_1^t)$, $\kappa_1^t = proj_\kappa(x_1^t)$, $\rho_1^t = proj_\rho(x_1^t)$ and

$$\begin{aligned} \hat{P}(\tau_{t+1}|\tau_1^t) &= P(T^{(t+1)} = \tau_{t+1}|T^{(1)} = \tau_1,\ldots,T^{(t)} = \tau_t) \\ &= P(T^{(t+1)} = \tau_{t+1}|T^{(t-\lambda_1+1)} = \tau_{t-\lambda_1+1},\ldots,T^{(t)} = \tau_t), \\ \hat{P}(\kappa_{t+1}|\kappa_1^t) &= P(T^{(t+1)} = \kappa_{t+1}|T^{(1)} = \kappa_1,\ldots,T^{(t)} = \kappa_t) \\ &= P(T^{(t+1)} = \kappa_{t+1}|T^{(t-\lambda_2+1)} = \kappa_{t-\lambda_2+1},\ldots,T^{(t)} = \kappa_t), \\ \hat{P}(\rho_{t+1}|\rho_1^t) &= P(T^{(t+1)} = \rho_{t+1}|T^{(1)} = \rho_1,\ldots,T^{(t)} = \rho_t) \\ &= P(T^{(t+1)} = \rho_{t+1}|T^{(t-\lambda_3+1)} = \rho_{t-\lambda_3+1},\ldots,T^{(t)} = \rho_t). \end{aligned}$$

In this case, $\lambda_1 = \lambda_1(\tau_t,\tau_{t-1},\ldots)$, $\lambda_2 = \lambda_2(\kappa_t,\kappa_{t-1},\ldots)$ and $\lambda_3 = \lambda_3(\rho_t,\rho_{t-1},\ldots)$ are functions of the past determined during the learning process of the corresponding VLMCs.

Let $D_1 = \max_{\tau_t,\tau_{t-1},\ldots} \lambda_1(\tau_t,\tau_{t-1},\ldots)$, $D_2 = \max_{\kappa_t,\kappa_{t-1},\ldots} \lambda_2(\kappa_t,\kappa_{t-1},\ldots)$ and $D_3 = \max_{\rho_t,\rho_{t-1},\ldots} \lambda_3(\rho_t,\rho_{t-1},\ldots)$ be the maximal memory lengths of the VLMCs.

Mixed learning-oriented recommender

Under the same assumption that the topic together with the learning objective determine the order in which questions are selected by users, we construct a more compact recommender. Instead of considering both the knowledge and the cognitive process separately, we combine them and use instead the space of the learning objectives $\mathcal{LO}$.

5.3 Learning-oriented recommendation

The resulting factorial vlHMM has two hidden states: T over the topic space $\mathcal{T}$ and L over the learning objectives space $\mathcal{LO}$ (see Figure 5.6). The observations are the same: Q over the question space $\mathcal{Q}$. Similarly, to obtain such a model, two transition models $P(T^{(t+1)}|T^{(1:t)})$ and $P(L^{(t+1)}|L^{(1:t)})$ and the observation model $P(Q^{(t+1)}|T^{(t+1)}, L^{(t+1)}, Q^{(1:t)})$ are learned.

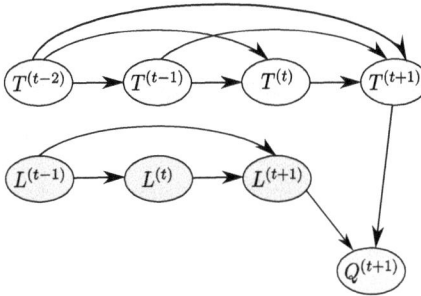

Figure 5.6.: Mixed learning-oriented question recommender based on two hidden VLMCs.

In order to obtain the transition models, we project the training sequences on the topic and on the learning objective dimensions by using the two projection functions $proj_\tau(\cdot)$ and $proj_\phi(\cdot)$.

The observation probabilities are defined as

$$P(q_{t+1}|\tau_{t+1}, \phi_{t+1}, q_1^t) = \begin{cases} 0 & \text{, if } \nexists (q_{t+1}, \tau_{t+1}) \in \mathcal{M}_\tau \\ & \quad \text{or } \nexists (q_{t+1}, \phi_{t+1}) \in \mathcal{M}_\phi \\ \frac{1}{|\mathcal{S}|} & \text{, otherwise} \end{cases}$$

where $\mathcal{S} = \{q' \in \mathcal{Q} \setminus \{q_1, \ldots, q_t\} | (q', \tau_{t+1}) \in \mathcal{M}_\tau \text{ and } (q', \phi_{t+1}) \in \mathcal{M}_\phi\}$.

Consider now an unseen context of questions $x_1^t = x_1 x_2 \cdots x_t$ with $x_i \in \mathcal{Q}$ and a new question $x_{t+1} \in \mathcal{Q}$. The probability of observing question x_{t+1} after x_1^t, according to this model, is given by:

$$\hat{P}(x_{t+1}|x_1^t) = P(\tau_{t+1}|\tau_1^t) \cdot P(\phi_{t+1}|\phi_1^t) \cdot P(x_{t+1}|\tau_{t+1}, \phi_{t+1}, x_1^t),$$

where $\tau_{t+1} = p_\tau(x_{t+1})$, $\phi_{t+1} = p_\phi(x_{t+1})$, $\tau_1^t = proj_\tau(x_1^t)$, $\phi_1^t = proj_\phi(x_1^t)$. Correspondingly, the two VLMCs have variable lengths $\lambda_1 = \lambda_1(\tau_t, \tau_{t-1}, \ldots)$ and $\lambda_2 = \lambda_2(\phi_t, \phi_{t-1}, \ldots)$ as functions of the past.

The following hierarchical models emerged from the idea that, within each topic, the order in which questions are selected by users form a particular pattern, specific to this topic. In other words, question sequences are first influenced by the underlying topic and the order in which these topics are tackled, then, within each topic, a particular question order is observed.

Simple hierarchical recommender

The simple hierarchical recommender model follows this idea by using a hierarchical vlHMM with hidden states T over the topic space $\mathcal{T}$ and observation states Q over the question space $\mathcal{Q}$. The difference between this recommender and the topic-based one is that for each topic a different VLMC of random variable Q is learned (see Figure 5.7).

The transition model $P(T^{(t+1)}|T^{(1:t)})$ is obtained like before, by training on the projection of the question sequences. Then, for each topic $\tau \in \mathcal{T}$, a transition probability $P_\tau(Q^{(t'+1)}|Q^{(1:t')})$ is learned by training on subsequences of questions from topic τ.

For a new context of questions $x_1^t = x_1 x_2 \cdots x_t$, $x_i \in \mathcal{Q}$ and $x_{t+1} \in \mathcal{Q}$, the probability of observing question x_{t+1} after x_1^t, according to this model, is given by:

$$\hat{P}(x_{t+1}|x_1^t) = P(\tau_{t+1}|\tau_1^t) \cdot P_{\tau_{t+1}}(x_{t+1}|x_{t_1}^{t_2}),$$

where $\tau_{t+1} = p_\tau(x_{t+1})$, $\tau_1^t = proj_\tau(x_1^t)$ and $x_{t_1}^{t_2}$ is the last subsequence within topic τ_{t+1}.

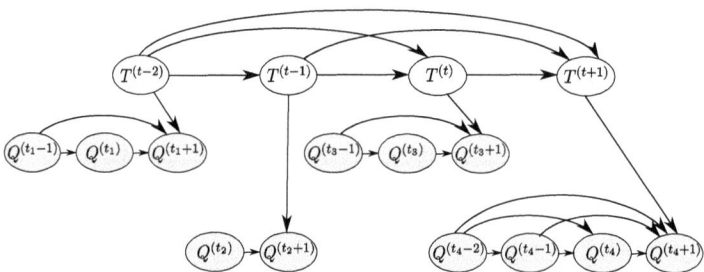

Figure 5.7.: Simple hierarchical question recommender based on a hierarchy of VLMCs.

Hierarchical knowledge-based recommender

The hierarchical knowledge-based recommender follows the previous idea, but instead of learning for each topic a VLMC over the random variable Q, it extracts the corresponding question sequences, projects them on the knowledge dimension and learns instead a VLMC of variable K (see Figure 5.8).

5.3 Learning-oriented recommendation

The transition model $P(T^{(t+1)}|T^{(1:t)})$ is obtained like before, by training on the projection of the question sequences. Then, for each topic $\tau \in \mathcal{T}$, a transition probability $P_\tau(K^{(t'+1)}|K^{(1:t')})$ is learned by training on projections of question subsequences within topic τ.

In contrast to the previous hierarchical recommender, the question variable Q is in this case an observation, therefore we are dealing with vlHMMs, instead of simple VLMCs. As a consequence, we define the observation model as

$$P(q_{t+1}|\tau_{t+1},\kappa_{t+1},q_1^t) = \begin{cases} 0 & \text{, if } \nexists(q_{t+1},\tau_{t+1}) \in \mathcal{M}_\tau \\ & \text{or } \nexists(q_{t+1},\kappa_{t+1}) \in \mathcal{M}_\kappa \text{ ,} \\ \frac{1}{|\mathcal{S}|} & \text{, otherwise} \end{cases}$$

where $\mathcal{S} = \{q' \in \mathcal{Q}\setminus\{q_1,\ldots,q_t\}|(q',\tau_{t+1}) \in \mathcal{M}_\tau \text{ and } (q',\kappa_{t+1}) \in \mathcal{M}_\kappa\}$.

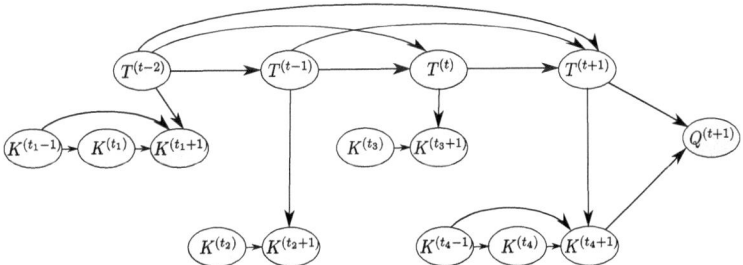

Figure 5.8.: Hierarchical knowledge-based question recommender using a hierarchy of VLMCs.

Once we have the transition and observation models, we can make predictions for unseen data. Let $x_1^t = x_1 x_2 \cdots x_t$ with $x_i \in \mathcal{Q}$ be a context sequence of questions and $x_{t+1} \in \mathcal{Q}$. The probability of observing question x_{t+1} after x_1^t, according to this model, is given by:

$$\hat{P}(x_{t+1}|x_1^t) = P(\tau_{t+1}|\tau_1^t) \cdot P_{\tau_{t+1}}(\kappa_{t+1}|\kappa_{t_1}^{t_2}) \cdot P(q_{t+1}|\tau_{t+1},\kappa_{t+1},q_1^t),$$

where $\tau_{t+1} = p_\tau(x_{t+1})$, $\kappa_{t+1} = p_\kappa(x_{t+1})$, $\tau_1^t = proj_\tau(x_1^t)$ and $\kappa_{t_1}^{t_2} = proj_\kappa(x_{t_1}^{t_2})$, $x_{t_1}^{t_2}$ being the last subsequence within topic τ_{t+1}.

Hierarchical cognitive process-based recommender

The hierarchical cognitive process-based recommender is similar to the previous one, but instead of the knowledge variable K, we use the cognitive process variable C (see Figure 5.9).

As before, we learn the transition models $P(T^{(t+1)}|T^{(1:t)})$ and $P_\tau(C^{(t'+1)}|C^{(1:t')})$ for every $\tau \in \mathcal{T}$.

The observation model is defined as

$$P(q_{t+1}|\tau_{t+1}, \rho_{t+1}, q_1^t) = \begin{cases} 0 & \text{, if } \nexists (q_{t+1}, \tau_{t+1}) \in \mathcal{M}_\tau \\ & \text{ or } \nexists (q_{t+1}, \rho_{t+1}) \in \mathcal{M}_\rho \,, \\ \frac{1}{|\mathcal{S}|} & \text{, otherwise} \end{cases}$$

where $\mathcal{S} = \{q' \in \mathcal{Q} \setminus \{q_1, \ldots, q_t\} | (q', \tau_{t+1}) \in \mathcal{M}_\tau \text{ and } (q', \rho_{t+1}) \in \mathcal{M}_\rho\}$.

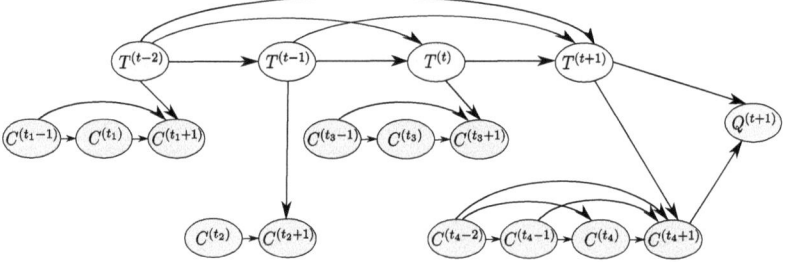

Figure 5.9.: Hierarchical cognitive process-based question recommender using a hierarchy of VLMCs.

Let $x_1^t = x_1 x_2 \cdots x_t$ with $x_i \in \mathcal{Q}$ be a context sequence of questions and $x_{t+1} \in \mathcal{Q}$. Then, the probability of observing question x_{t+1} after x_1^t, according to this model, is given by:

$$\hat{P}(x_{t+1}|x_1^t) = P(\tau_{t+1}|\tau_1^t) \cdot P_{\tau_{t+1}}(\rho_{t+1}|\rho_{t_1}^{t_2}) \cdot P(q_{t+1}|\tau_{t+1}, \rho_{t+1}, q_1^t),$$

where $\tau_{t+1} = p_\tau(x_{t+1})$, $\rho_{t+1} = p_\rho(x_{t+1})$, $\tau_1^t = proj_\tau(x_1^t)$ and $\rho_{t_1}^{t_2} = proj_\rho(x_{t_1}^{t_2})$, $x_{t_1}^{t_2}$ being the last subsequence within topic τ_{t+1}.

Hierarchical knowledge- and cognitive process-based recommender

This hierarchical recommender combines the previous two by considering both the knowledge and the cognitive process features of questions (see Figure 5.10).

There are three types of transition models to be learned: $P(T^{(t+1)}|T^{(1:t)})$ and for every $\tau \in \mathcal{T}$ $P_\tau(K^{(t'+1)}|K^{(1:t')})$ and $P_\tau(C^{(t^*+1)}|C^{(1:t^*)})$. To obtain the topic transition model, we project the question sequences on the topic space and train the model over the resulting topic sequences. As for the knowledge and cognitive process

5.3 Learning-oriented recommendation

transition models, for each $\tau \in \mathcal{T}$ we extract from the training sequences the question subsequences within topic τ and train the models on the resulting set.

For this type of recommender, the observation model $P(Q^{(t+1)}|T^{(t+1)}, K^{(t+1)}, C^{(t+1)}, Q^{(1:t)})$ is defined as

$$P(q_{t+1}|\tau_{t+1}, \kappa_{t+1}, \rho_{t+1}, q_1^t) = \begin{cases} 0 & \text{, if } \not\exists (q_{t+1}, \tau_{t+1}) \in \mathcal{M}_\tau \\ & \text{or } \not\exists (q_{t+1}, \kappa_{t+1}) \in \mathcal{M}_\kappa \\ & \text{or } \not\exists (q_{t+1}, \rho_{t+1}) \in \mathcal{M}_\rho \\ \frac{1}{|\mathcal{S}|} & \text{, otherwise} \end{cases},$$

where $\mathcal{S} = \{q' \in \mathcal{Q} \setminus \{q_1, \ldots, q_t\} | (q', \tau_{t+1}) \in \mathcal{M}_\tau \text{ and } (q', \kappa_{t+1}) \in \mathcal{M}_\kappa \text{ and } (q', \rho_{t+1}) \in \mathcal{M}_\rho\}$.

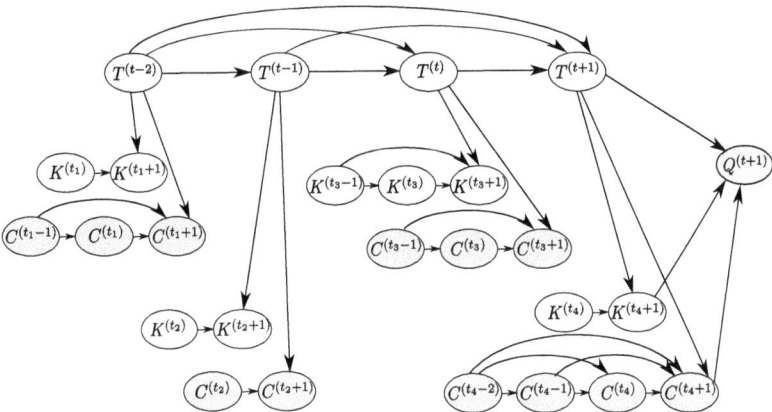

Figure 5.10.: Hierarchical knowledge- and cognitive process-based question recommender using a hierarchy of VLMCs.

Now consider $x_1^t = x_1 x_2 \cdots x_t$ with $x_i \in \mathcal{Q}$ to be a context sequence of questions and $x_{t+1} \in \mathcal{Q}$. Then, according to this model, the probability of observing question x_{t+1} after x_1^t is given by:

$$\hat{P}(x_{t+1}|x_1^t) = P(\tau_{t+1}|\tau_1^t) \cdot P_{\tau_{t+1}}(\kappa_{t+1}|\kappa_{t_1}^{t_2}) \cdot P_{\tau_{t+1}}(\rho_{t+1}|\rho_{t_1}^{t_2}) \cdot P(q_{t+1}|\tau_{t+1}, \kappa_{t+1}, \rho_{t+1}, q_1^t),$$

where $\tau_{t+1} = p_\tau(x_{t+1})$, $\kappa_{t+1} = p_\kappa(x_{t+1})$, $\rho_{t+1} = p_\rho(x_{t+1})$, $\tau_1^t = proj_\tau(x_1^t)$, $\kappa_{t_1}^{t_2} = proj_\kappa(x_{t_1}^{t_2})$ and $\rho_{t_1}^{t_2} = proj_\rho(x_{t_1}^{t_2})$, $x_{t_1}^{t_2}$ being the last subsequence within topic τ_{t+1}.

Hierarchical learning-oriented recommender

This particular hierarchical recommender combines the knowledge and cognitive process dimensions on one hand for a more compact representation, on the other hand for a better prediction performance. The first advantage is straight-forward, while the second one will be demonstrated during the evaluation process (see subsection 6.4.5).

The transition model $P(T^{(t+1)}|T^{(1:t)})$ is obtained like before, by training on the projection of the question sequences. Then, for each topic $\tau \in \mathcal{T}$, a transition probability $P_\tau(L^{(t'+1)}|L^{(1:t')})$ is learned by training on projections of question subsequences within topic τ.

The observation model $P(Q^{(t+1)}|T^{(t+1)}, L^{(t+1)}, Q^{(1:t)})$ in this case is defined as

$$P(q_{t+1}|\tau_{t+1}, \phi_{t+1}, q_1^t) = \begin{cases} 0 & \text{, if } \nexists (q_{t+1}, \tau_{t+1}) \in \mathcal{M}_\tau \\ & \text{or } \nexists (q_{t+1}, \phi_{t+1}) \in \mathcal{M}_\phi \text{ ,} \\ \frac{1}{|\mathcal{S}|} & \text{, otherwise} \end{cases}$$

where $\mathcal{S} = \{q' \in \mathcal{Q}\setminus\{q_1, \ldots, q_t\} | (q', \tau_{t+1}) \in \mathcal{M}_\tau \text{ and } (q', \phi_{t+1}) \in \mathcal{M}_\phi\}$.

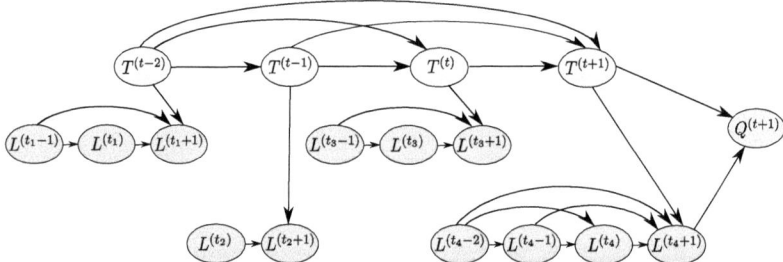

Figure 5.11.: Hierarchical learning-oriented question recommender using a hierarchy of VLMCs.

Let $x_1^t = x_1 x_2 \cdots x_t$ with $x_i \in \mathcal{Q}$, $i \in 1, \ldots, t$ be a context sequence of questions and $x_{t+1} \in \mathcal{Q}$. Then, the probability of observing question x_{t+1} after x_1^t is given by:

$$\hat{P}(x_{t+1}|x_1^t) = P(\tau_{t+1}|\tau_1^t) \cdot P_{\tau_{t+1}}(\phi_{t+1}|\phi_{t_1}^{t_2}) \cdot P(q_{t+1}|\tau_{t+1}, \phi_{t+1}, q_1^t),$$

where $\tau_{t+1} = p_\tau(x_{t+1})$, $\phi_{t+1} = p_\phi(x_{t+1})$, $\tau_1^t = proj_\tau(x_1^t)$ and $\phi_{t_1}^{t_2} = proj_\phi(x_{t_1}^{t_2})$, $x_{t_1}^{t_2}$ being the last subsequence within topic τ_{t+1}.

Figure 5.11 represents such a hierarchical learning oriented recommender. Notice that the VLMCs of L can be of various lengths for the different topic values T.

5.3 Learning-oriented recommendation

Hybrid recommender

The hybrid recommender combines the prediction results of the simple recommender and the hierarchical learning-oriented recommender (see Figure 5.12). The idea of combining the two recommenders emerged from the need of obtaining both a good prediction performance and a better coverage and diversity. More details of these aspects are presented in subsection 6.4.5.

In order to learn a hybrid recommender model, we separately train the corresponding simple and hierarchical learning-oriented recommender models and obtain the transition models $P(Q^{(t+1)}|Q^{(1:t)})$, $P(T^{(t+1)}|T^{(1:t)})$ and, for each topic $\tau \in \mathcal{T}$, $P_\tau(L^{(t'+1)}|L^{(1:t')})$. As for the observation model $P(Q^{(t+1)}|T^{(t+1)}, L^{(t+1)}, Q^{(1:t)})$, we define it as

$$P(q_{t+1}|\tau_{t+1}, \phi_{t+1}, q_1^t) = \max\{P(q_{t+1}|q_1^t), \frac{1}{\mathcal{S}}\},$$

where $\mathcal{S} = \{q' \in \mathcal{Q}\setminus\{q_1, \ldots, q_t\} | (q', \tau_{t+1}) \in \mathcal{M}_\tau \text{ and } (q', \phi_{t+1}) \in \mathcal{M}_\phi\}$.

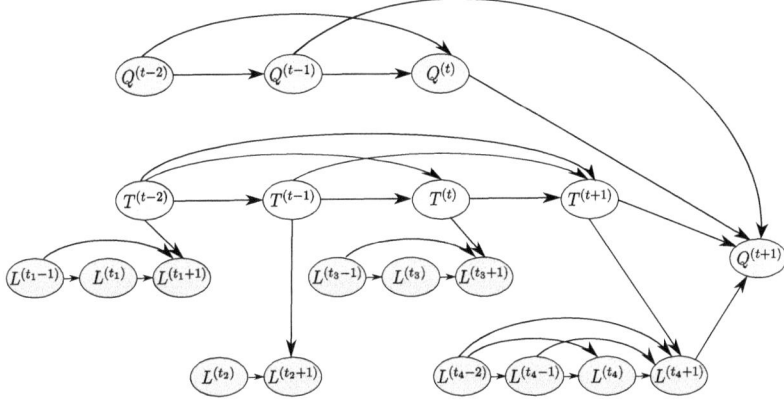

Figure 5.12.: Hybrid recommender using a hierarchy of VLMCs and a simple VLMC.

For an unseen context sequence of questions $x_1^t = x_1 x_2 \cdots x_t$, $x_i \in \mathcal{Q}$ and $x_{t+1} \in \mathcal{Q}$ the probability of observing question x_{t+1} after x_1^t is given by:

$$\hat{P}(x_{t+1}|x_1^t) = \max\{P(x_{t+1}|x_1^t), P(\tau_{t+1}|\tau_1^t) \cdot P_{\tau_{t+1}}(\phi_{t+1}|\phi_{t_1}^{t_2}) \cdot P(q_{t+1}|\tau_{t+1}, \phi_{t+1}, q_1^t)\},$$

where $\tau_{t+1} = p_\tau(x_{t+1})$, $\phi_{t+1} = p_\phi(x_{t+1})$, $\tau_1^t = proj_\tau(x_1^t)$ and $\phi_{t_1}^{t_2} = proj_\phi(x_{t_1}^{t_2})$, $x_{t_1}^{t_2}$ being the last subsequence within topic τ_{t+1}.

In other words, the probability of observing question x_{t+1} after x_1^t is the maximum of the prediction values returned by the two recommenders.

5.4. Summary

In this chapter, a new probabilistic model-based recommender system was introduced using VLMCs, a domain-specific topic taxonomy and Bloom's revised learning framework. Several models were introduced with the goal of identifying which of these can "mimic" better a general learning process pattern in order to leverage the users' learning behavior.

The eleven models can roughly be grouped based on three ***intuitions***:

1. learning patterns within question sequences can be identified based on the unique question identifiers *only* (e.g. simple recommender);
2. learning patterns within question sequences can be discovered based on the co-occurrence of three question aspects or features: the *topic*, the *knowledge* and the *cognitive process* dimension (e.g. topic-based, knowledge- and cognitive process-based, mixed and mixed learning-oriented recommenders);
3. learning patterns within question sequences can be determined by the *order* in which *topics* are tackled and then, *within each of these topics*, by the order in which questions are selected, either based on their unique identifier only or based on their *learning objectives* (e.g. simple hierarchical, hierarchical knowledge-based, hierarchical cognitive process-based, hierarchical knowledge- and cognitive process-based, hierarchical learning-oriented and hybrid recommenders).

Notice, that these intuitions are not formulated in the sense of prediction performance (i.e. capturing and summarizing user logs), but rather towards a higher purpose of **revealing common learning practices** in order to engage the user into a *meaningful* and *useful* knowledge assimilation.

Therefore, the evaluation of such recommendation models should not be based on prediction accuracy alone, but also on other metrics that capture various *desired* aspects of a learning-oriented QA recommender system:

- ***Coverage*** – allow the user to explore as much as possible from the question database (i.e. high catalog coverage[140]) and, in the same time, provide "good" recommendations for a wide range users (i.e. user space coverage[140]).

- ***Diversity*** – presenting the user with a diverse recommendation list, which is an important aspect when we want to guide the user through a learning process. Opposite to this aspect, if we would recommend topics that are too similar to the ones the user already visited, we would defeat the purpose of a learning system. Still, it is important to keep in mind, that diversity comes at the expense of other properties, such as accuracy[160].

- ***Novelty*** – provide recommendations for questions (or on topics) that the user did not yet learn about.

- ***Learning-utility*** – measures the *learning gain* of a user from a recommendation. Capturing learning utility is difficult, since it is unclear how to measure

5.4 Summary

it. Learning gain refers not just to the amount of new information that a user can assimilate by visiting the recommendation, but also to the particular order in which the recommendations are provided over time. One way of measuring learning utility is with user ratings.

- **Robustness** – refers to the stability of the recommendation in the presence of fake information[113] (e.g. a user browsing questions randomly), which are typically inserted on purpose. In general, creating a recommender system that is immune to any attacks is unrealistic[140].

These are some of the many features that a successful learning-oriented recommender should have. In section 6.4 we compare the introduced recommender models against a few of these metrics and present the evaluation results in detail.

6. Results and Evaluation

6.1. Overview

In this chapter we will analyze and evaluate the performance of the four-layered semantic similarity measure defined in chapter 3 and the two recommendation techniques introduced in chapter 4 and chapter 5.

The semantic similarity between questions was introduced not only for the recommendation purpose, but also for its efficiency when it comes to retrieving the best matching answer or for avoiding question redundancy in the database. In order to evaluate this measure, its correlation with human understanding is computed and then compared to other similarity functions.

As for the two recommendation techniques, two offline user experiments were performed, but under different conditions and requirements. While for the short-term recommender we are interested to see how well it meets the user's short-term needs by generating related recommendations, for the learning-oriented approach it is important to evaluate its capability of guiding the user through a meaningful, gradual learning process.

Several metrics are employed to assess the performance of the two recommender types. The analysis of the learning-oriented approach puts great emphasis on the comparison between the different models introduced in subsection 5.3.2 in order to identify the correct intuition behind the users' learning behavior. Subsequently, a brief comparison between the two recommendation categories is performed, not necessarily to prove that one method outperforms the other, but more to stress their different roles in satisfying distinct user needs.

6.2. Semantic short-text similarity measures

In order to evaluate the "goodness" of the semantic similarity measure introduced in chapter 3, we conducted a survey [80] with 15 persons, men and women, age between 25 and 60. We randomly sampled 50 pairs from a dataset of 318 different questions in the nutrition domain and asked the survey participants to compare and measure the relatedness of each pair by rating them with a value between 0 and 4 (0=not related at all, 1=somehow related, 2=related, 3=very related, 4=similar).

Finally, we compared the participants' rating against six different semantic similarity measures: the one defined by Haase et al. (see Equation 2.8), the sum of all similarities [36], the one introduced by Cordì (see Equation 2.9), the cosine similarity (see

Equation 2.10), the sum of maximum similarities (see Equation 3.2), the surjection similarity (see Equation 3.3) and the maximum link similarity (see Equation 3.4).

Before determining the correlation between the participants' intuition and the values delivered by the previously mentioned semantic similarity measures, let us analyze the survey results. While some question pairs were rated almost the same by all participants (low variance), there were some cases where participants answered very differently (high variance). This reflects how *diversely* humans perceive the "relatedness" of two questions.

Table 6.1 contains the mean, maximum and minimum variances calculated by question pairs ratings. The mean variance of 0.93 means that users' rating differed on average with about one point. The minimum variance shows that there was at least one question pair which all users rated equally similar. The third value, the maximum variance shows that the users disagreed with at most 2.14 rating points.

Mean variance	0.93
Maximum variance	2.14
Minimum variance	0

Table 6.1.: User answer variance calculated by question pair ratings.

Method	Correlation
Haase	0.605
Sum of All	0.597
Cordì	0.563
Cosine	0.563
Sum of Maximum	**0.617**
Surjection	**0.634**
Maximum Link	**0.626**

Table 6.2.: Correlation of survey answers with the semantic similarity measures.

Table 6.2 contains the correlation values of each semantic similarity method with the average participant rating values.

Table 6.3 shows the average rating of each participant. Notice that while some participants had a tendency to rate questions pairs with lower values (Participants 5 and 6), others rated them on average with higher values (Participants 10 and 14). Based on our experiments and the above results we make the following observations:

- The semantic similarity measures depend on the structure of the taxonomy. In our case, the topic hierarchy, the keyword-topic mappings and the assigned keyword weights affect the computed similarity. In [23] it is argued that similarity assessment algorithms are ontology dependent. As a future work, we plan to analyze the aspects of taxonomy structure (hierarchy, mappings, weights) that alter the behavior of the semantic similarity measures.

6.2 Semantic short-text similarity measures

Participant 1	Participant 2	Participant 3	Participant 4
1.96	1.36	1.74	1.18
Participant 5	Participant 6	Participant 7	Participant 8
0.94	0.74	1.78	1.36
Participant 9	Participant 10	Participant 11	Participant 12
1.22	2.24	1.44	1.04
Participant 13	Participant 14	Participant 15	
1.96	2.42	1.38	

Table 6.3.: Average rating of survey participants.

- The similarity measure between sets of keywords, and therefore between questions, depends on the chosen topic similarity (edge-based or information content-based) and on the keyword similarity. In our experiments we used the edge-based similarity measures defined by Wu and Palmer [157] and Li et al. [89]. Since both seemed to show a similar "behavior", we presented our analysis results only using one of them, namely the one defined in Equation 2.3. Although the keyword similarity chosen to present our results was the one introduced in subsection 3.4.2 (see Equation 3.1), we also analyzed other measures, which compared to it performed poorly. In the future we plan to integrate information content in our taxonomy and use information content-based topic similarity measures to evaluate the semantic query similarity measures.

Question pair	Var	Avg	SurjSim
Q_1: What is difficult about losing weight? Q_2: How much should I eat in order lose weight?	0.75	0.65	0.74
Q_3: What is low in calories? Q_4: How much protein do I need?	0.85	0.19	0.17
Q_5: How can I eat less? Q_6: Is sushi healthy?	2.14	0.21	0.15
Q_7: Can I eat can vegetables or frozen vegetables? Q_8: How much and what should I drink?	0.07	0.01	0.37
Q_9: Why is losing weight so important? Q_{10}: How can I lose weight quickly and without yo-yo effect?	1.82	0.4	0.84

Table 6.4.: Sample question pairs with their variance and average survey rating and semantic similarity values.

- Although the correlation between the participants' rating and the evaluated measures are rather low (see Table 6.2), this can be explained by the following factors:
  - the queries are selected from a specific and narrow domain (nutrition),

- the concepts that appear in the queries are rather complex (e.g. health, weight loss, nutrition, etc.),
- the participants' rating for some question pairs was very diverse (see table Table 6.1),
- the participants tend to understand the rating values or the question pair "relatedness" differently (see Table 6.3).

- The correlation results (between 0.563 and 0.634) do not contradict the fact that the semantic similarity measures reflect on some level the human perception. Most of the question pairs were evaluated by the participants and the semantic similarity measures almost the same (see Table 6.4).

We distinguish here four types of question pairs:

1. with low rating variance and low difference between rating average and semantic similarity (e.g. question pair 1 and 2),
2. with high rating variance, but low difference between rating average and semantic similarity (e.g. question pair 3),
3. with low rating variance and high difference between rating average and semantic similarity (e.g. question pair 4), and
4. with high rating variance, but high difference between rating average and semantic similarity (e.g. question pair 5).

In our evaluation, compared to the surjection measure, 48% of the question pairs were of type (1), 20% of type (2), 12% of type (3) and 20% of type (4).

The results show that the four-layered similarity measure has a higher correlation with the average survey rating than the other four measures (see Table 6.2). Although these correlation values are relatively low (between 0.563 and 0.634), it does not contradict the fact that the semantic similarity measures reflect on some level the human perception, given the diversity of answers collected during the survey.

Each person understands "similarity" or "relatedness" between two short sentences differently, especially when the sentences contain complex concepts from the same limited domain (e.g. health, weight loss, nutrition, etc.). Evaluations of other semantic similarity measures from the literature use a dataset of simple, short sentences of common understanding.

We believe that measuring semantic similarity between concepts using taxonomies can improve significantly the results retrieved by recommender systems. We also argue that these measures depend on the structure of the underlying taxonomy (hierarchy, keyword-topic mappings, keyword weights, etc.) and on the chosen concept-to-concept similarity measure.

6.3. Short-term recommendation

Using the semantic similarity measure defined in chapter 3, various short-term recommendation methods were constructed. Our goal was to add semantics to a typical content-based RS in order to improve the quality of the recommendations by mapping relevant keywords from the existing taxonomy (see subsection 3.3.2) to the available questions. Therefore, six different short-term recommendation techniques were implemented that extensively used the hierarchical structure of the topic taxonomy.

In order to test and evaluate the effectiveness of these methods, a supervised survey was conducted, where several users were asked to rate the recommendations delivered using these methods [105].

The combined recommender is content-based, but context independent, i.e. it does not take the user history into consideration. It tries to simulate a "conversation" between the user and a fictitious expert that guides him through a specific subject. We call it *conversation recommender*, because it generates recommendations in a way that gives the user the feeling of being in a conversation with another person.

The conversation recommender consists of six particular short-term recommendation approaches: *Similar in Topic, Similar over Topic, More General, More Specific, Most relevant in Similar Topic* and *Latest relevant in Similar Topic* (see section 4.5). These methods are based on the topic-tree and on the correct assignment of keywords and questions to topics.

If the six methods don't generate enough recommendations (e.g. due to design issues), then the "fallback" recommendations are returned. The fallback or default recommendations are a special case. These are predefined recommendations which were manually chosen and generally accepted as suitable for every topic. These recommendations were not used in the evaluation process.

By combining the first six recommendation techniques, we give the user the opportunity to explore a broad horizon of questions related by similarity to his/her current choice.

During the evaluation process, the conversation recommender was designed to recommend up to 16 questions under the following rules: 3 – SiT, 5 – SoT, 1 – LrST, 2 – MS, 2 – MG and 3 – MrST. This combination of recommended questions should provide the user enough possibilities to navigate through all relevant topics and explore the whole question knowledge base.

Results

In order to evaluate the effectivness of the conversation recommender, a survey was conducted to assess the "usefulness" of the generated recommendations. To do this, the following data was used:

- 318 questions about nutrition (specific for the Austrian nutrition expert Sasha Walleczek [150],
- about 13,000 keywords (including synonyms, word forms, word phrases, etc.), which were extracted from the available questions and answers, and
- a topic-tree of the nutrition domain with 38 topics.

The topics where manually selected and the hierarchical structure of the topic-tree was constructed by the nutrition expert Sasha Walleczek [150]. For our evaluation purposes, and in order to reduce as much as possible the variables on which the performance of the conversation recommender depends, the questions were also manually assigned to topics.

Recommendations were generated for all existing questions. According to the previously defined rules, a full conversation recommendation can have at most 16 questions. It is not always possible to generate a full conversation recommender for each question, as it depends on the number of questions assigned to a single topic. The smallest generated recommendation consisted of 9, while the largest had 14 questions. The average number of recommended questions was 12.

From the 318 existing questions, 50 were randomly selected and, based on them, an experiment was conducted. For convenience, 5 surveys were generated, each consisting of 10 questions, for which recommendations were provided. A survey consists of 10 start questions and their corresponding recommendations. The recommendation source (SiT, SoT, MG, MS, MrST or LrST) is undisclosed to the users. Survey participants were asked to rate the recommended questions with a value between 1 and 5 (1 meaning "no match", 5 meaning "best match"). The survey was answered by 38 people, all of which were not directly related to the chosen domain and, therefore, would represent the ideal users. Only a few outliers can be detected in the result of the survey.

The result of the survey showed, that the recommendation types SiT and SoT are more suitable than the recommendations created by MrST or LrST. The first few recommendations of the conversation recommender achieved a higher user satisfaction than the last ones. Taken all the recommendations together, the average rating was 2.66 with an average standard deviation of 1.08. The average standard deviation of the average rating values of each recommendation of the same type was 0.57. Therefore, the rating of the recommendations was stable.

Table 6.5 shows the average rating of the recommendation type and the average standard deviation. The first results of the conversation recommender were better rated than the last ones, although all of them achieved on average good ratings – an average rating greater than 2 means that the recommendations were not completely unrelated to the start-question).

The **item space coverage** of the conversation recommender, for this particular question set, achieved **0.84**, i.e. 84% of the 318 questions. This means that the majority were part of the recommendation set. The **user space coverage** is **100%**, i.e. it can generate recommendations for any user.

6.3 Short-term recommendation

Type	Survey 1		Survey 2		Survey 3		Survey 4		Survey 5	
	avg	sd	avg	sd	avg	sd	avg	sd	avg	sd
SiT	3.85	1.31	3.50	1.34	3.91	0.77	3.92	0.71	4.05	0.93
SoT	3.04	1.20	2.51	1.36	2.22	1.02	2.40	0.95	2.32	0.93
MG	2.98	1.29	2.41	1.29	1.93	0.90	1.94	0.98	2.39	0.98
MS	2.93	1.19	2.98	1.33	2.25	1.07	2.80	0.97	2.56	0.93
MrST	2.67	1.25	2.46	1.37	2.09	1.06	1.82	0.96	2.31	1.09
LrST	2.85	1.07	2.31	1.41	2.23	1.03	2.24	0.82	1.89	1.01

Table 6.5.: Empirical survey results of the conversation recommender.

The recommendation **diversity** was also calculated using the semantic similarity measure defined in chapter 3. The diversity was defined to be the average distance between each question pair within a recommendation:

$$div(R) = \frac{2}{|R|(|R|-1)} \sum_{\substack{q_i,q_j \in R \\ i<j}} [1 - sim_q(q_i, q_j)],$$

where R is the recommendation set for the current question and sim_q is the semantic similarity measure between two questions (see subsection 3.4.4).

The maximum diversity among questions within the same recommendation was 0.98, i.e. the questions were poorly related to each other, while the minimum diversity was 0.28 and the overall **average diversity** achieved **0.68**. Therefore, the conversation recommender can offer the user a wide spectrum of question recommendations, from very similar to less related ones.

It is important to mention here that the quality of the generated recommendations depends on the quality of the topic-topic similarities and the query-query similarities. If these algorithms don't deliver reliable, intuitive results, the quality of the recommendations will also be unsatisfiable. As mentioned in section 6.2, the semantic similarity and, therefore, the conversation recommender depends on the structure of the underlying topic-tree (i.e. its hierarchy, keyword-topic mappings, keyword weights, etc.) and on the chosen concept-to-concept similarity measure. Evaluating the goodness of such structures is beyond the scope of this thesis.

Conclusions

The evaluation results show that the conversation recommender can be successfully adopted by QA systems. Based on the user ratings, the conversation recommender can generate meaningful recommendations without having to know anything about the user's history nor his/her preferences. It also avoids the cold-start, new item and new user problems, which are very common with most recommender techniques.

The system can generate suitable recommendations for new users as well, were no browsing history is available, using the Fallback recommender. Additionally, questions that were recently added can be "pushed" on to the front page by the LrST method.

The catalog and user space coverage, as well as the diversity values, show that this recommender technique is well suited for QA systems. This argument is based on the importance of allowing users, more specifically all users, to have access to a wide spectrum of questions and to navigate through the entire database of questions.

In contrast, the conversation recommender is limited by the features that explicitly describe a question (i.e., topics, keywords). Also, the user is limited to being recommended items that are similar to those already visited. In this case, recommendation serendipity [60] (i.e. attractive and surprising, unexpected and fortuitous) is desired. Although the conversation recommender can handle new users, the fallback method is inflexible and requires expert knowledge to perform changes over time. Additionally, it cannot provide personalized recommendations. We argue that users which faithfully use the services provided by a domain-specific QA system have, in general, a well-defined goal in mind (e.g. find a method to lose weight, interested in better nutrition methods, etc.). The conversation recommender cannot detect these needs and help the user follow his/her learning goal.

From a technical point of view, the bottleneck of the conversation recommender is the calculation of the query similarities. As changes in the database can happen at high frequencies (e.g. queries are added or deleted very often), similarities need to be recalculated repeatedly. This slows down the process of recommendation generation.

In order to improve the quality of the retrieved recommendations, the content-based method needs be extended with collaboration filtering approaches.

The recommendation engine is currently used in the QA system of Lumenz Networks [93], a start-up company located in Linz, Upper Austria. Their system provides domain-specific *channels*, where users can browse and post new questions which in return are answered by renowned experts.

6.4. Learning-oriented recommendation

In this section, we will evaluate the recommendation models introduced in chapter 5. The goal of this evaluation is to show the benefits of the learning-oriented models based on Bloom's taxonomy by using various metrics. In order to show the *overall* advantages of using VLMCs for learning user question sequences, the "random recommender" is introduced, which makes question suggestions randomly, without using any context knowledge. All eleven models will be compared against the random recommender.

In the first part, the experimental data is introduced in detail: the question datasets together with their corresponding domain-specific topic taxonomies, the topic mappings and the knowledge- and cognitive process mappings.

In the second part, the experimental setup, including the experiment type, some statistics of the involved users and the experimental process description is presented, supporting these choices with valid arguments.

In the third part, several metrics are introduced and formally defined, which will further be used for evaluating each of the eleven recommender models and, more importantly, for comparing them among each other.

It is beyond the scope of this thesis to show how a topic taxonomy is constructed or how questions are (semi)-automatically assigned to topics and to the knowledge and cognitive process dimensions. These operations were manually executed in order to maintain the *robustness* of the knowledge-base and reduce as much as possible the variables on which the performance of the recommendation models depend. However, we show some examples and present the logic behind the mapping.

6.4.1. Data

In order to test the recommender models thoroughly, three datasets of questions corresponding to three different domains, extracted from three distinct sources, were collected:

- **Earth sciences** – a selection of questions extracted from Wiki Answers [153] and MadSci [95];

- **Nutrition** – a collection of questions provided by the nutrition expert Sasha Walleczek [150];

- **Homeschooling** – a selected set of questions on homeschooling education, extracted from Wiki Answers [153], also explored in [22] for evaluation purposes.

For reasons of robustness, corresponding to each of these datasets, a topic taxonomy with the structure presented in section 5.2 was manually constructed. Figure C.1 represents a sample taxonomy of the earth sciences domain, which was extracted from Wiki Answers [153], Figure C.2 contains an example nutrition taxonomy manually constructed by the nutrition expert Sasha Walleczek [150], whereas Figure C.3 represents a taxonomy of the homeschooling education domain. None of these taxonomies reflect a unique and complete image of the actual domains. They are merely a snapshot of the domains from a particular perspective. The topic-trees were constructed in a way to cover the question datasets. In this particular case, the structure of the hierarchy does not influence the performance of the recommender models and, therefore, represents no variable in the overall evaluation process. However, the performance of the recommender models does depend on the topic, knowledge and cognitive process mappings.

Dataset	$|\mathcal{Q}|$	$|\mathcal{T}|$	$|\{\tau'|\exists(q,\tau') \in \mathcal{M}_\tau\}|$	$avg_{\tau' \in \mathcal{T}}(|\{(q,\tau') \in \mathcal{M}_\tau\}|)$
Earth sciences	313	49	37	8.46
Nutrition	318	38	24	13.25
Homeschooling	191	42	39	4.89

Table 6.6.: Overview of the question datasets.

Table 6.6 contains a summary of the three datasets. The first column $|\mathcal{Q}|$ represents the total number of questions within the dataset, the second column $|\mathcal{T}|$ contains the total number of topics within the topic taxonomy associated with the dataset, the third column $|\{\tau'|\exists(q,\tau') \in \mathcal{M}_\tau\}|$ represents the number of topics to which questions are assigned and the last column $avg_{\tau' \in \mathcal{T}}(|\{(q,\tau') \in \mathcal{M}_\tau\}|)$ contains the average number of question per topic. This last value is of great importance for those models that make recommendations based on the number of unvisited questions within a topic (e.g. topic-based recommender).

Dataset	$|\mathcal{KD}|$	$\{\kappa'|\exists(q,\kappa') \in \mathcal{M}_\kappa\}$	$avg_{\kappa' \in \mathcal{T}}(|\{(q,\kappa') \in \mathcal{M}_\kappa\}|)$
Earth sciences	4	$\{\kappa_1, \kappa_2, \kappa_3\}$	104.33
Nutrition	4	$\{\kappa_1, \kappa_2, \kappa_3\}$	106
Homeschooling	4	$\{\kappa_1, \kappa_2, \kappa_3\}$	63.67

Table 6.7.: Statistics on the knowledge mapping.

Dataset	$|\mathcal{CD}|$	$\{\rho'|\exists(q,\rho') \in \mathcal{M}_\rho\}$	$avg_{\rho' \in \mathcal{T}}(|\{(q,\rho') \in \mathcal{M}_\rho\}|)$
Earth sciences	6	$\{\rho_1, \rho_2, \rho_4, \rho_5\}$	78.25
Nutrition	6	$\{\rho_1, \rho_2, \rho_4, \rho_5\}$	79.5
Homeschooling	6	$\{\rho_1, \rho_2, \rho_4, \rho_5\}$	47.75

Table 6.8.: Statistics on the cognitive process mapping.

Table 6.7, Table 6.8 and Table 6.9 give an overview of the knowledge, cognitive process and learning objective mappings. The assignment of questions to these

6.4 Learning-oriented recommendation

Dataset	$|\mathcal{LO}|$	$|\{\phi'|\exists(q,\phi')\in\mathcal{M}_\phi\}|$	$avg_{\phi'\in\mathcal{L}}(|\{(q,\phi')\in\mathcal{M}_\phi\}|)$
Earth sciences	24	9	34.78
Nutrition	24	12	26.5
Homeschooling	24	10	19.1

Table 6.9.: Statistics on the learning objective mapping.

three dimensions was performed manually in order to maintain robustness. As the tables show, not all knowledge nor all cognitive process dimensions were identified within the three question sets. The metacognitive knowledge κ_4 was not recognized among the questions. Such questions would refer to self-awareness and knowledge about one's own cognition, which is not common among the chosen domains. Also, questions within the cognitive process dimension $\rho_3 = $ "apply" or $\rho_6 = $ "create" were not discovered. Such questions would demand the user's active participation. However, given the source, questions were meant to be rather reflective.

Table C.2, Table C.3 and Table C.4 give some examples of mapping questions to the topic, knowledge and cognitive process dimensions from each of the three datasets.

6.4.2. Experimental setup

The evaluation of the recommender models introduced in chapter 5 is not an easy task for several reasons. First, to learn such models, a history of user interactions with the QA system is needed. Without any kind of recommendation engine behind the search or browsing functionality, such interactions would not be possible, or even reliable, since the user is not aware of the possible question choices.

Secondly, if suggestions are provided, even in their simplest form, the resulting browsing log would not reflect the user's natural learning process, but rather a learning process influenced by the capabilities of the used recommendation engine. Therefore, the recorded question sequences would still not be suitable to be used for training a new recommender model which relies on the natural learning process of the user.

Assuming that we can acquire the necessary suitable question sequences that reflect the natural learning process of users and use them to train a recommender model, another evaluation step – called *online evaluation* – is needed to test the performance of the model under normal usage conditions, i.e. the user navigates through the question database guided by the recommender engine. Under such conditions, user satisfaction and learning utility needs to be measured.

The second evaluation step requires strict testing conditions, which demand a lot of time and effort. Additionally, such online experiments might turn out to be risky [140]. For these reasons, it is best to run an extensive offline study that provides evidence that the learning-oriented approaches are reasonable. The work presented in this thesis covers only the results of offline experiments.

Offline experiment

In order to test the performance of the various recommender models, a scenario of user interaction with a QA system was simulated, where recommendations were not provided at all. As previously pointed out, having an overview of the available questions is not feasible, given the size of the datasets. Therefore, for each domain, five subsets of 20 questions were randomly generated and users were asked to order each of these 20 question-sets in the sequence that they, *personally*, would want to **ask** them or would want ***learn about***.

Table 6.10 shows, for each of the three domains, the number of collected question sequences, i.e. the total number of user responses, the number of distinct questions within the collected sequences and their percentage with respect to the total number of questions.

Dataset	No. sequences	Distinct questions	Coverage (%)
Earth sciences	61	90	28.75
Nutrition	46	94	29.56
Homeschooling	56	84	43.98

Table 6.10.: Question coverage of survey sequences.

Overall, about 13 male and female users participated in this survey, but not all of them provided an ordering for each of the survey parts. Table 6.11 gives an overview of the number of males and females that answered the 15 survey parts, separately. Notice, that the obtained number of sequences are generally balanced between male and female participants.

To have an overview of the overall "agreement" level between the survey participant on the question ordering, pairwise correlations were computed. Figure C.4, Figure C.5 and Figure C.6 contain the matrix of question sequence correlation between participants for each part, within each domain. Table C.5 summarizes these plots by making an average over the correlations, first for the male participants, then for the female participants and, finally, for all participants. The achieved minimum and maximum correlations are also included.

We notice that, for the nutrition and homeschooling domain, the overall "agreement" was much higher than for the earth sciences domain. However, in some cases, high correlations were also discovered among the answers for the earth sciences survey. The few "disagreements" given by the negative correlations are related to the order in which topics within a domain are selected (e.g. putting the questions about earthquakes before those about tsunamis, or the other way around). However, within specific topics, a general "agreement" was observed for the question orderings. Table C.1 contains an example of two orderings of the same question set.

Observation The various question orderings reflect different perspectives in the human learning process. We all have our unique, personalized way of thinking,

6.4 Learning-oriented recommendation

Dataset	Part	Male ♂	Female ♀
Earth sciences	I	7	6
	II	6	6
	III	6	6
	IV	6	6
	V	6	6
Nutrition	I	5	5
	II	5	4
	III	5	4
	IV	5	4
	V	5	4
Homeschooling	I	6	5
	II	6	5
	III	7	4
	IV	7	6
	V	6	5

Table 6.11.: Survey answer statistics.

but there is still a common backbone, i.e. a general pattern that can be detected within the question sequences. Our goal is to identify such patterns and use them to generate recommendations.

6.4.3. Evaluation metrics

As already mentioned in subsubsection 2.2.1.5, evaluating a recommender system on its prediction power is crucial, but insufficient in order to deploy a good recommendation engine [140]. There are other measures that reflect various aspects. Not all of them are desired to perform well for every recommender. Depending on the application domain, some metrics that seemingly deliver good results might point out a bad feature of the recommender engine. For example, serendipity – a measure of how surprising a successful recommendation is – might not be suitable for users that do not appreciate the deviation from the "natural" predictions, as in the case of a learning system.

Therefore, the evaluation of the recommendation models introduced in chapter 5 should not be based on prediction accuracy alone, but also on other metrics that capture various *desired* aspects of a learning-oriented QA recommender system. Let us briefly define these metrics.

Average log-loss

One way of measuring prediction performance would be using the *average log-loss* [19] $l(\hat{P}, x_1^n)$ of a specific model $\hat{P}$ with respect to a test question sequence $x_1^n =$

$x_1 x_2 \cdots x_n$:

$$l(\hat{P}, x_1^n) = -\frac{1}{n} \sum_{i=1}^{n} \log \hat{P}(x_i | x_1 \cdots x_{i-1}). \tag{6.1}$$

Accuracy

Let $\hat{P}$ be a recommender model which was trained over a set of user question sequences. Consider a new test sequence $x_1^t = x_1 x_2 \cdots x_t$.

We measure the accuracy of $\hat{P}$ with respect to the test sequence x_1^n as the proportion of correctly identified questions within the first N recommendations:

$$acc(\hat{P}, x_1^n) = \frac{1}{n} \sum_{i=1}^{n} |\{x_i\} \cap R(x_1^{i-1})| \tag{6.2}$$

where $x_1^0 = \emptyset$ and $R(s) = \arg\max_{q \in \mathcal{Q} \text{ and } q \notin s}^{N} \hat{P}(q|s)$ is the set of the first N "best" recommendations, given the context s.

Coverage

In general, catalog coverage represents the proportion of questions that the recommendation model can recommend. In our case, we define the catalog coverage as the proportion of questions that the recommender model $\hat{P}$ can recommend with a prediction value higher than a predefined threshold σ.

Overall, the recommender models introduced in chapter 5 can generate recommendations for *any user* (i.e. full user space coverage) and, eventually, *all* questions can be recommended, since the recommender repeatedly excludes already visited ones. But, towards the exhaustion of the database, the recommendations will have a very low prediction value. These recommendations are unreliable. Therefore, we introduce the prediction threshold σ.

In our evaluation, we generally set σ to be the lowest prediction value among the questions within the sequences used for training.

Since the user space coverage is equal for all recommender models, we will further refer to catalog coverage simply as "coverage".

Diversity

Generally, diversity is defined as the opposite of similarity. Within this context, we define the diversity as the average dissimilarity among each question pair within a recommendation.

6.4 Learning-oriented recommendation

Let $\hat{P}$ be a recommender model, s a user context and $R(s) = \arg\max_{q \in \mathcal{Q} \text{ and } q \notin s}^{N} \hat{P}(q|s)$ the set of the first N "best" recommendations given the context s.

Then, the diversity of $R(s)$ is defined as

$$div(R(s)) = \frac{2}{N(N-1)} \sum_{\substack{q_i, q_j \in R(s) \\ i<j}} [1 - sim_q(q_i, q_j)], \quad (6.3)$$

where $sim_q : \mathcal{Q} \times \mathcal{Q} \to [0,1]$ represents the semantic similarity measure between questions.

During the evaluation, we used the simple cosine similarity together with the semantic concept similarity defined by Lin [91]. In order to avoid further dependencies with our topic taxonomy, the Wordnet [119] lexical database was used instead, together with the Java library for interfacing with Wordnet – JWI [56] – and the Java library of the WordNet::Similarity [72].

Learning utility

As stated in the previous chapter, the learning utility refers to the *learning gain* of a user from a recommendation. One way of measuring learning utility is with user ratings. Since such an experiment can only be performed within a user study setting, a comparative metric is introduced instead that shows how good a model reflects the user learning process.

Consider two sets of equal size: S_{learn} a set of user question sequences based on the user's learning process and S_{rand} a set of randomly generated question sequences. Each of the sequence pairs from $S_{learn} \times S_{rand}$, corresponding to the same user, have the same length. Now let M be a recommendation model. We train this model with each of the two sequence sets using cross-validation and obtain the accuracy values:

- $a_{learn} = acc(M, S_{learn})$ and
- $a_{rand} = acc(M, S_{rand})$.

We define the learning utility of model M by comparing the normalized accuracy difference:

$$learnUtil(M, S_{learn}, S_{rand}) = \begin{cases} -a_{rand} & \text{, if } a_{learn} = 0 \\ \frac{a_{learn} - a_{rand}}{a_{learn}} & \text{, otherwise} \end{cases}. \quad (6.4)$$

This metric works only under the assumption that the set S_{learn} truly reflects the users' learning process. It shows how dependent model M is on receiving as input learning sequences.

6.4.4. Evaluation parameters

In order to evaluate the recommendation models against the measures defined above, we used the leave-one-out testing technique in combination with an n-fold cross-validation. In other words, one question sequence at a time was used for testing and the rest was used for training with an n-fold cross-validation to obtain the best model parameters (i.e. the best orders for the VLMCs).

Given the above defined metrics and the used evaluation technique, the following parameters were identified :

- N – the number of recommended items;
- σ – the prediction value threshold for computing the coverage;
- n – the number of folds used for cross-validation;
- $maxOrder$ – the maximum order of the VLMCs.

Abbreviations For a more compact representation, the following abbreviations of the recommender model names are introduced:

- S – Simple recommender,
- T – Topic-based recommender,
- KC – Knowledge- and cognitive process-based recommender,
- M – Mixed recommender,
- M-TL – Mixed learning oriented recommender,
- SH – Simple hierarchical recommender,
- H-K – Hierarchical knowledge-based recommender,
- H-C – Hierarchical cognitive process-based recommender,
- H-KC – Hierarchical knowledge- and cognitive process-based recommender,
- H-L – Hierarchical learning-oriented recommender,
- H – Hybrid recommender, and
- R – Random recommender.

6.4.5. Results

The results presented below were obtained with the following parameter settings:

- $N = 5$, which is a relatively common value among recommender systems;
- $\sigma =$ "the lowest prediction value among the questions within the sequences used for training";

6.4 Learning-oriented recommendation

- $n = 10$ – this is also a common choice in machine learning practice, but also given the size if the datasets, it seemed to be a reasonable value;

- $maxOrder = 10$ – according to our experiments, the order of the VLMCs never exceeded the value of 10.

The average log-loss, accuracy, coverage and diversity were computed for all 12 models, with each of the three datasets. Figure 6.1 shows the average log-loss of the models with the above defined parameters. One can notice, that over the three domains, the average log-loss maintains stability for each of the recommender models, i.e. there are no major differences between the results of the same model. The mixed models achieved too high average log-loss values and were, therefore, omitted from the plot. The lowest average log-loss was obtained by S, SH, H-L and H, but the difference with respect to the other models is relatively small. Their improved performance can be explained by the fact that these three models try to reflect more accurately the question order from the training sequences. Among the rest of the models, the H-L recommender achieved the best result.

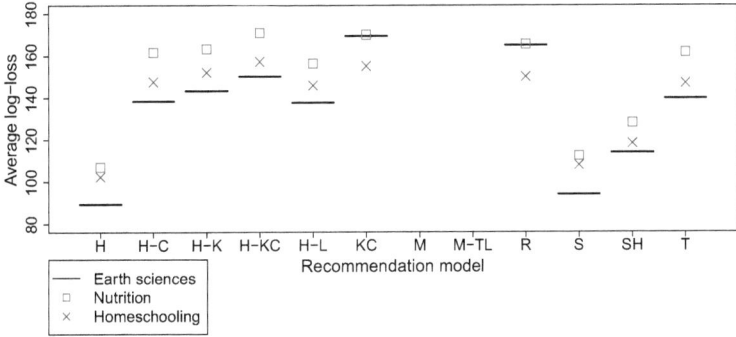

Figure 6.1.: Average log-loss of models for each dataset.

Figure 6.2 contains the accuracy values for each of the recommender models over the three datasets. Overall, a significantly higher accuracy was observed for the earth sciences domain. This might be related to the objectivity of the domain in comparison with the other two fields. Additionally, the nutrition domain curriculum is not as well established as the earth sciences one and there are many conceptual models formed around it.

Comparing the models with respect to the accuracy measure, the simple and the hierarchical models show an improved performance. Among all models, the same four – S, SH, H-L and H – obtained the best accuracy values. However, in the particular case of our learning-oriented QA system, high accuracy is not the only most desired feature.

Overall, the hierarchical models achieved better results than the mixed ones, which actually obtained an accuracy close to the random recommender. By comparing the results of the learning-oriented recommenders with the random one, we can conclude that these models genuinely reflect the learning behavior of users.

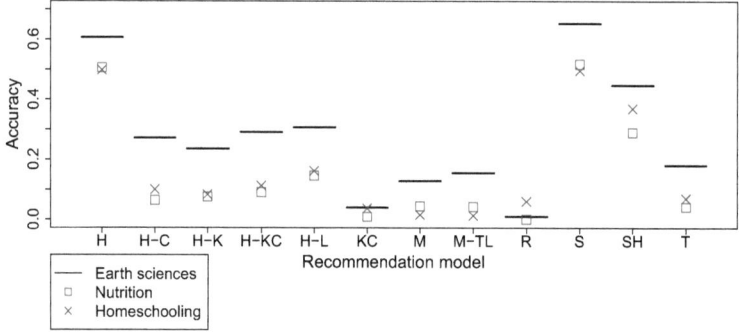

Figure 6.2.: Model accuracy for each dataset.

The highest catalog coverage was achieved by R, KC and T. Intuitively, if the training sequences cover all topics or all knowledge and cognitive-process dimensions, then also the corresponding recommenders will cover all existing questions. On the other extreme, the lowest coverage was obtained for S and SH. In this case, the hybrid one managed to reach a higher value due to the learning-oriented component. Overall, the recommenders which use on some level the three features (i.e. topic, knowledge and cognitive process) and the random recommender achieved the highest coverage rates (see Figure 6.3).

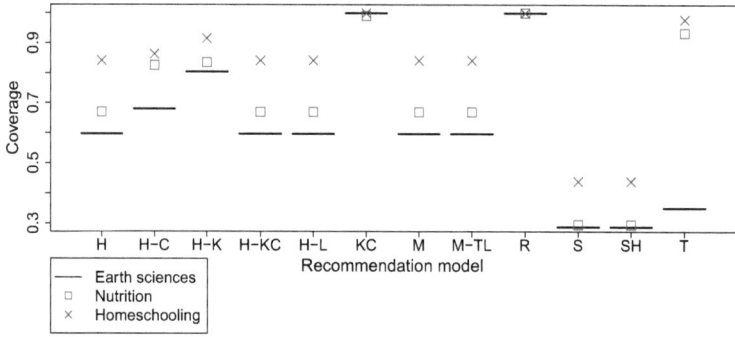

Figure 6.3.: Model coverage for each dataset.

6.4 Learning-oriented recommendation

Surprisingly, all models proved to deliver, on average, recommendations of similar diversity, with values between 0.35 and 0.61 (see Figure 6.4). This means that the questions within a recommendation were not too similar, but also not too different (from a semantic point of view) from one another. It might also be the case that the diversity oscillates around 0.5 over the entire dataset, not just for over the training sequences.

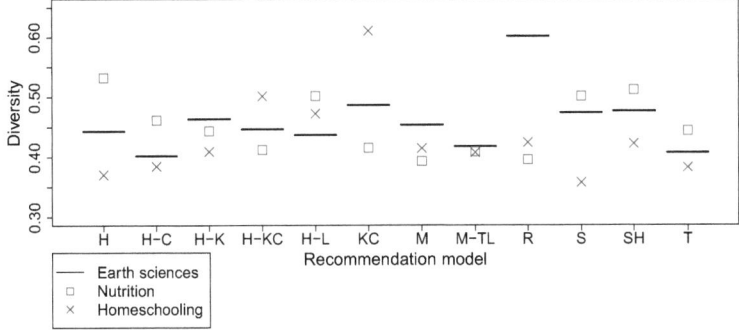

Figure 6.4.: Model diversity for each dataset.

Let us analyze now in more detail the performance of the recommendation models for each of the three datasets.

Earth sciences dataset

Figure 6.5 summarizes the performance of each recommender using three metrics: accuracy, coverage and diversity. As pointed out before, the highest accuracy is achieved by S, closely followed by H and then by SH and H-L. Although S and SH have a good accuracy performance, their catalog coverage scored the lowest value among all recommender models. The hierarchical ones have a fairly high coverage and, therefore, the hybrid model achieved the overall best performance, i.e with respect to all three evaluation metrics. By combining the simple recommender with the hierarchical learning-oriented recommender we managed to leverage the advantages of both models and achieve a good coverage and accuracy in the same time.

Figure C.7 (a), (b), (c) and (d) reflect the learning curves of the S, SH, H-L and H models, i.e. the increase in accuracy, coverage and diversity with the growing size of the training set. The learning curve starts with a dataset of 10 sequences, it learns a model using cross-validation, computes the three measurement values, adds a new sequence, recomputes the model and the values, and goes on until the entire user sequence database is covered.

Chapter 6   Results and Evaluation

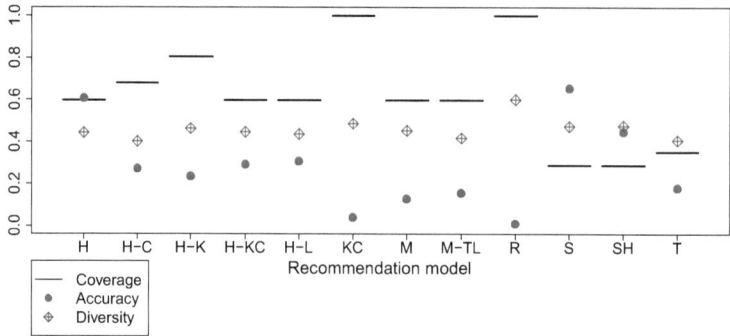

Figure 6.5.: Comparison of model performance over the earth sciences dataset.

A smooth and slow growth in accuracy is observed for all four models. This phenomenon is caused by the fact that the distinct questions among the sequences does not change much (see coverage), or even at all, as the number of training sequences increases, while the correlations between user sequences vary a lot. A higher accuracy might be obtained if the sequences don't have many questions in common and the coverage increases with the number of sequences.

Besides accuracy, the average log-loss also shows the predictive power of a recommender model. Figure 6.6 contains the learning curves with respect to the average log-loss. The decrease of the average log-loss means a decrease in the error rate with the growing number of training sequences.

Nutrition dataset

A similar performance pattern is observed also with the nutrition dataset (see Figure 6.7). The same four models: S, H, SH and H-L achieve, in this order, the best prediction performance (i.e. accuracy and average log-loss).

Although the coverage and diversity don't seem to have changed much, in comparison with the results obtained for the earth sciences dataset, a much lower accuracy was observed. This aspect might be related to the subjectivity of the nutrition domain, i.e. the questions are targeting more the user's opinion.

The learning curves of the best four recommender models can be found in Appendix C, Figure C.8.

Figure 6.8 represents the learning curve of each of the four recommender models with respect to the average log-loss.

6.4 Learning-oriented recommendation

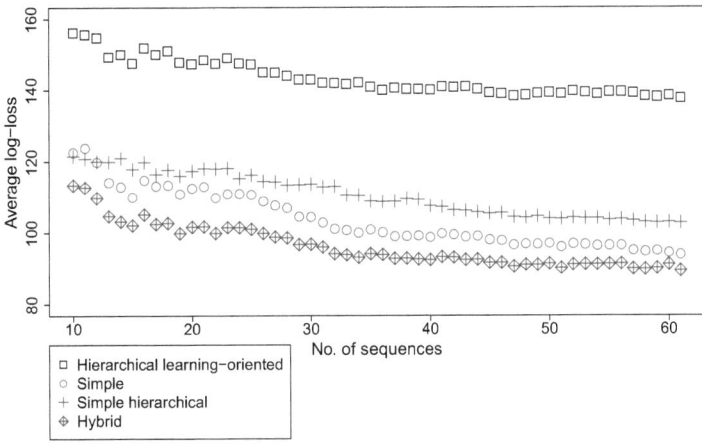

Figure 6.6.: Earth sciences – The learning curves of S, SH, H-L and H models with respect to the average log-loss.

Homeschooling dataset

The results obtained for this third dataset confirms the assertions stated for the previous two domains (see Figure 6.9). Although in this case a much higher catalog coverage is achieved, both the accuracy and the coverage follow the same pattern as before. The high coverage for this particular domain is directly influenced by the reduced size of the question database with respect to the number of training sequences. This aspect is also confirmed by the initial coverage (see Table 6.10).

The learning curves of the best four recommender models can be found in Appendix C, Figure C.9.

Figure 6.8 represents the learning curve of each of the four recommender models with respect to the average log-loss.

The influence of the topic mapping on the prediction performance

We mentioned before, that the performance of the models which are based on the question-topic mapping are highly dependent on it. The above results were obtained by mapping questions to their most specific matching topic, i.e. the deepest matching topic in the topic-tree. In some cases, only the leaf nodes were used. To show how the question-topic assignments influence some of the recommenders, we applied a "more general" mapping on the earth sciences dataset, i.e. questions were "pushed" up the topic-tree, and then compared the performance of the resulting models with

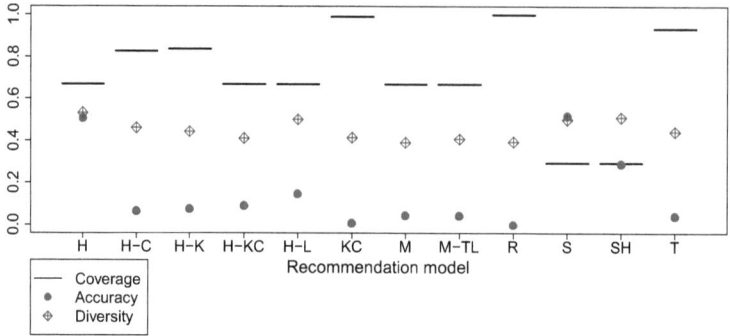

Figure 6.7.: Comparison of model performance for the nutrition domain.

the ones previously obtained (see Figure 6.11). One of the consequences of this operation, which is immediately observable, is the fact that now the number of questions per topic is much higher than before (see Table 6.12).

Mapping	No. of mapped topics	Avg. no. of questions in topic
Mapping$_1$	37	8.46
Mapping$_2$	9	34.78

Table 6.12.: Overview of the different topic mappings for the earth sciences dataset.

In general, the models which are based on the question-topic mappings perform worse when the average number of questions assigned to a topic is higher, which intuitively makes sense, since the probability of randomly selecting a question based on its topic becomes much smaller. Interestingly, the SH model performs for both the accuracy and average log-loss measures better because, by mapping more questions to a topic, the SH becomes more similar to the simple recommender. Therefore, the more "general" the question-topic assignments, the more similar the SH model gets to the simple recommender. Opposed to this, as the question-topic assignments become more "general", the rest of the topic-based models lose their prediction power.

Learning utility

In order to measure the learning utility for each recommendation model over all three datasets, as defined in subsection 6.4.3, the following experiment was performed. For each domain, the user learning sequences obtained from the surveys were randomly shuffled. In this case, S_{learn} is represented by the original set of sequences and S_{rand} will be the set of shuffled sequences.

6.4 Learning-oriented recommendation

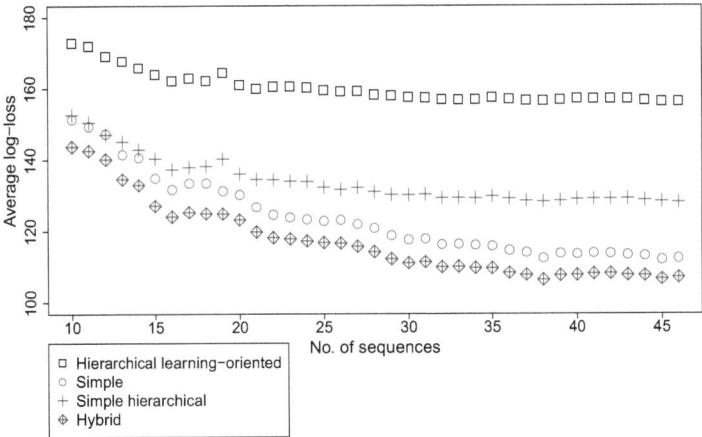

Figure 6.8.: Nutrition – The learning curves of S, SH, H-L and H models with respect to the average log-loss.

For each model and each domain, the learning utility was computed according to Equation 6.4. The result is shown in Table 6.13.

In general, a lower prediction performance was noticed when the models were trained with the randomly shuffled sequences, although some models, especially for the nutrition and homeschooling domains, achieved the same or almost the same accuracy (see Figure 6.12, Figure 6.13 and Figure 6.14). In fact, when the mixed models were trained on the shuffled sequences from the homeschooling dataset, the resulting accuracy was higher than before, therefore the negative learning utility. This might reflect the fact that these models don't perform better than the random model. The most significant accuracy decrease was observed for the same four models S, SH, H-L and H.

The resulting learning utility values don't show a common pattern over the three datasets, like the other evaluation measures. To have a better overview of the results, the average learning utility over the three domains was calculated for each recommendation model (see Table 6.13 and Figure 6.15). According to Table 6.13, the best performing models were the H-L and H-KC, followed by SH, H-C and S.

6.4.6. Comparison with the short-term recommendation

One open question still remains: what are the advantages of the learning-oriented recommender over the short-term recommender (i.e. the semantic similarity-based

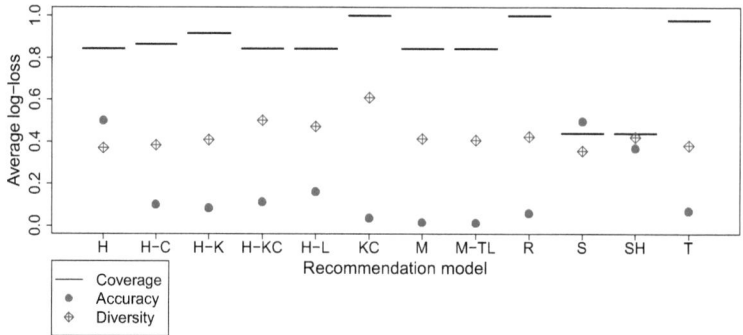

Figure 6.9.: Comparison of model performance for the homeschooling domain.

recommender)? For a fair evaluation, we would have to perform the same online rating experiment described in section 6.3, with the same input questions. Since a repeated experiment would be too expensive to perform, the most suitable is the one used for the learning-oriented recommender. While the coverage of the short-term recommender achieved higher values, the diversity is comparable to the one of the learning-oriented models.

To test the prediction power of the short-term recommender, we performed the same leave-one-out testing technique by generating N recommendations and computed the average accuracy. The parameter N was set to 5, like for the previous tests. As for the conversation recommender, there were 3 SiT and 2 SoT recommendations generated. The average log-loss is not applicable to this recommender because it is not based on a probabilistic model. A comparison of the short-term recommender's (S-T) accuracy with the accuracy of the rest of the models is shown in Figure 6.16. Table 6.14 gives an overview of the conversation recommender's prediction performance.

The results show that the short-term recommendation is not capable of modeling the user learning process.

6.4.7. Summary and conclusions

In this section, we analyzed and evaluated the performance of each of the eleven recommender models introduced in chapter 5 with respect to the measures defined in subsection 6.4.3 using three datasets from three different domains: earth sciences, nutrition and homeschooling education. Due to the lack of initial user browsing history, we randomly generated five subsets of 20 questions for each of the three domains and asked the users to order each of these 20 question-sets in the sequence that they, *personally*, would want to *ask* them or would want *learn about*. For each of

6.4 Learning-oriented recommendation

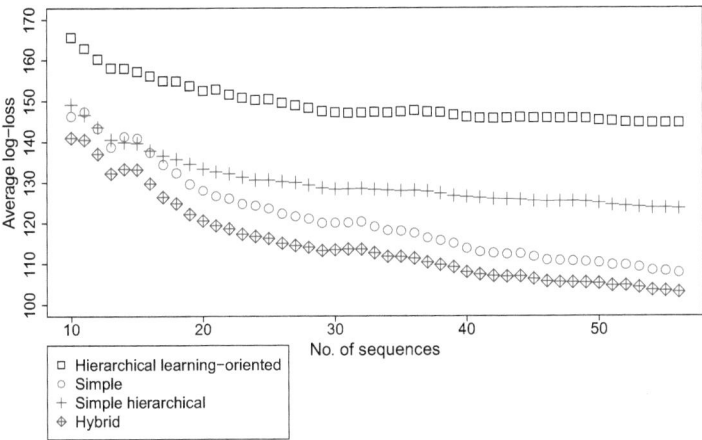

Figure 6.10.: Homeschooling – The learning curves of S, SH, H-L and H models with respect to the average log-loss.

the resulting 15 question-sets, an average of 11 participants, with a fairly balanced number of men and women, were registered. This resulted in about 55 question sequences for each domain, which were used to train and test the recommender models.

In the first part, an analysis of the survey results was made, in order to have an overview of the generated sequences and to identify early patterns and correlations between user answers. The results show that, in some cases, the users strongly agree on a particular question sequence, yet in other cases major discrepancies were identified. This can be explained by the unique and personal way humans understand certain concepts, i.e. the unique conceptual world map existing in each human mind. Additionally, some domain-specific questions are rather ambiguous and up for interpretation. The survey also captures user preferences and personal opinions and, therefore, there are no unanimous answers. For our evaluation purposes, this aspect was preferred over highly correlated question sequences, because it reflects real life situations. Hence, the learned models are not highly accurate, but despite the conflicting user opinions, some of them still proved to identify learning process patterns and use them to make useful recommendations.

Given the average log-loss, accuracy, coverage and diversity values of the recommender models for each of the three datasets, we identified four models that generally perform better than the other ones: the simple (S), simple hierarchical (SH), hierarchical learning-oriented (H-L) and hybrid (H) recommenders. When comparing these four models, on one hand, we notice that while S and SH achieve high

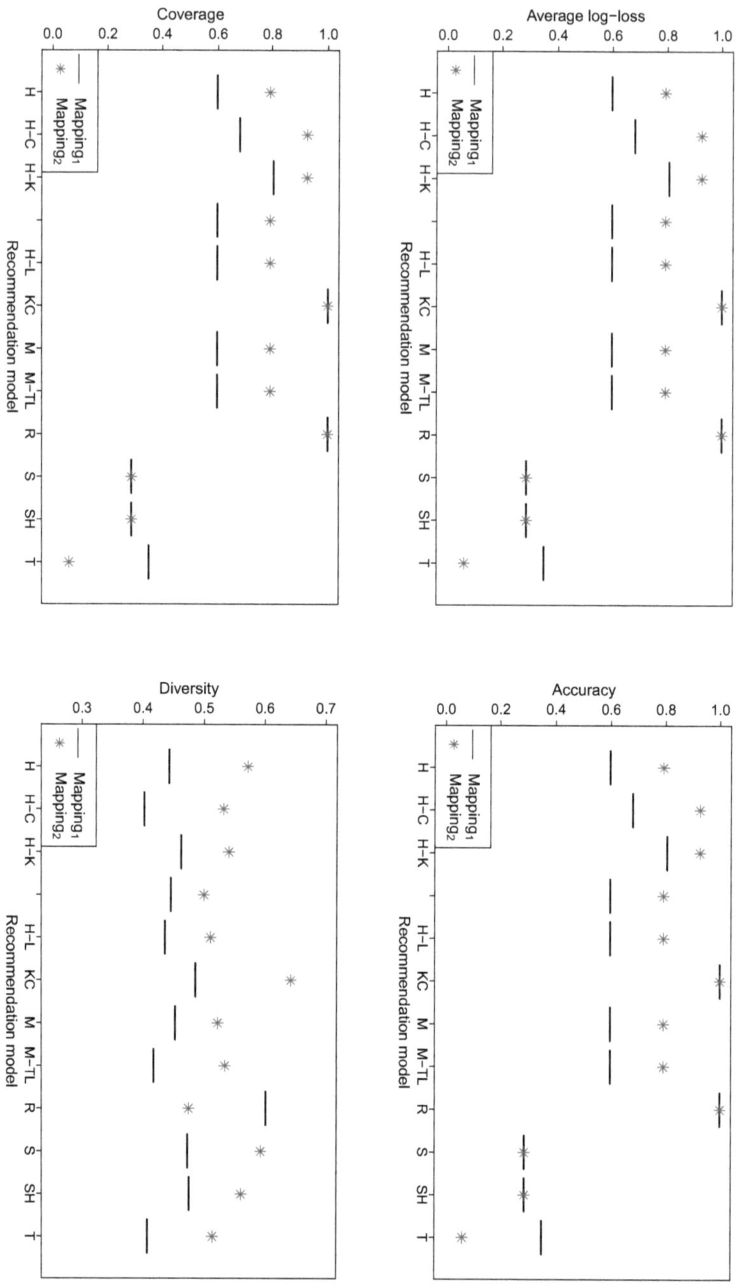

Figure 6.11.: Comparison of model performance for the earth sciences domain with respect to the topic mapping.

6.4 Learning-oriented recommendation

Model	Earth sciences	Nutrition	Homeschooling	Average
S	0.449	0.407	0.399	0.418
T	0.837	0.103	0.152	0.364
KC	0	0.125	0	0.042
M	0.752	0.238	-2.5	-0.503
M-TL	0.716	0.1	-3.067	-0.750
SH	0.631	0.228	0.437	0.432
H-K	0.718	0.057	0.043	0.272
H-C	0.719	0.339	0.239	0.432
H-KC	0.777	0.298	0.425	**0.500**
H-L	0.693	0.489	0.407	**0.529**
H	0.426	0.393	0.404	0.408
R	0	0	0	0

Table 6.13.: Summary of learning utility results over the three domains.

Dataset	Accuracy
Earth sciences	0.022
Nutrition	0.002
Homeschooling	0.025

Table 6.14.: Short-term recommendation accuracy for the three domains.

accuracy, their coverage is very low. On the other hand H-L has a lower accuracy, but a very good catalog coverage.

To evaluate the learning power of these models, we incrementally trained them and computed their prediction performance while increasing the size of the training set. Overall, both the accuracy and the average log-loss show a similar slow increase/decrease with the growing number of sequences in the training set. This means that all four models have the same learning power. The slow learning rate might be caused by the discrepancies between user answers, while the set of distinct questions in the training sequences does not grow almost at all with in the size of the training set. This aspect is proven by the almost constant coverage curve.

The average log-loss, accuracy, coverage and diversity measures are common measures used for the evaluation of any recommender system. In this section, a new metric called *learning utility* was introduced, which measures the capability of a recommendation model to mimic the users' learning process. The results show that the best learners are the H-L and the H-KC, followed by S, SH and H. This means that the most suitable intuition for modeling user learning goals is the third one introduced in section 5.4, i.e. learning patterns within question sequences can be determined by the *order* in which *topics* are tackled and then, *within each of these topics*, by the order in which questions are selected, either based on their unique identifier only or based on their *learning objectives*.

131

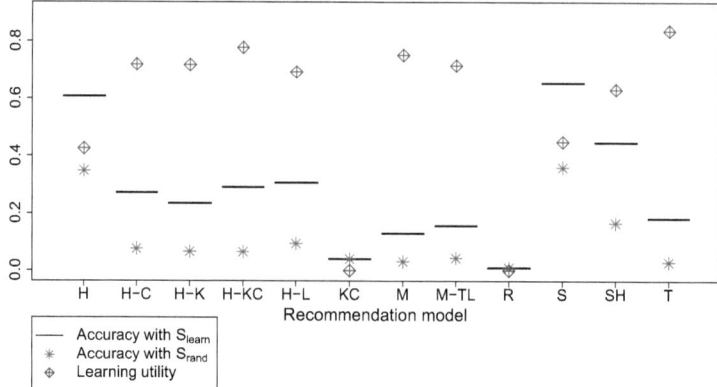

Figure 6.12.: Earth sciences – The accuracy and learning utility of models with respect to S_{learn} and S_{rand}.

At the beginning of chapter 5, it was also stated that the short-term recommendation is not capable of modeling the user learning process or even employ the users' browsing history to generate recommendations. This statement is supported by the low prediction performance of the short-term recommendation over the learning sequences, which were also used to train and test the learning-oriented recommenders.

6.4 Learning-oriented recommendation

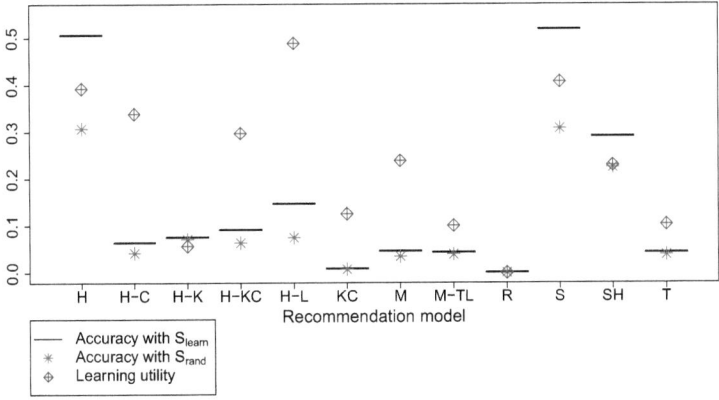

Figure 6.13.: Nutrition – The accuracy and learning utility of models with respect to S_{learn} and S_{rand}.

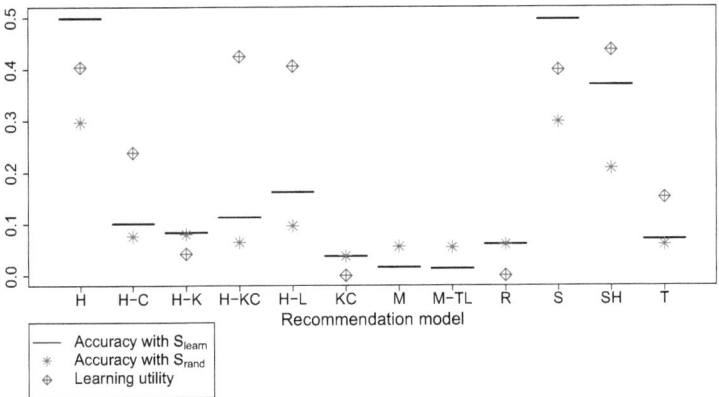

Figure 6.14.: Homeschooling – The accuracy and learning utility of models with respect to S_{learn} and S_{rand}.

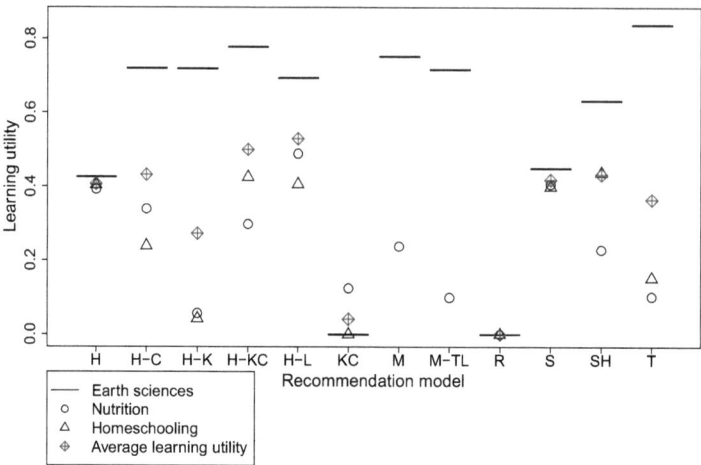

Figure 6.15.: Comparison of the learning utility for the three domains and their average.

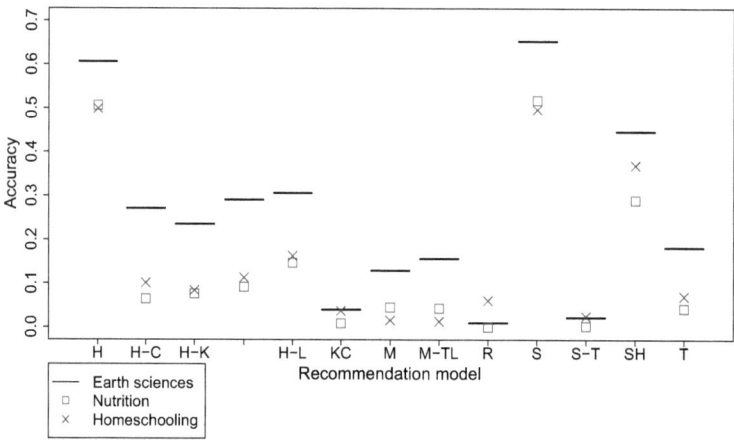

Figure 6.16.: Accuracy comparison of the short-term (S-T) recommender with the learning-oriented models, for the nutrition domain.

7. Conclusion and Future Work

7.1. Summary

The work documented in this thesis aims at covering a relevant research gap in the field of recommender techniques for QA systems.

Existing content-based and collaborative methods regard questions as abstract recommendation items without making use of any underlying knowledge and, therefore, lack the ability to guide the user through a meaningful learning experience. Traditional approaches generate recommendations based either on a utility value determined by the user's past choices or on the preferences of other users that share similar interests.

Although many variations and improvements of the two fundamental techniques were proposed in the past, they are not suitable for the purposes of a learning-oriented QA system.

In this thesis, two categories of recommendation techniques were introduced:

- the short-term recommender based on a semantic utility function and
- the long-term or learning-oriented recommender that uses a domain-specific topic taxonomy and Bloom's framework of learning objectives.

For the semantic utility function of the short-term recommender, a semantic four-layered similarity measure was defined that computes the semantic relatedness between two short fragments of texts (e.g. questions, in our case). Current research within this field has been mainly directed either towards concept similarity or document similarity, which deal with large textual objects. However, there are a few techniques that aim at measuring relatedness between sentences or short paragraphs. Nevertheless, there is still space for improvements.

In order to diversify the results retrieved by the short-term recommender, it was extended to explore the hierarchical structure of the domain-specific taxonomy. This approach is called conversation recommender, because it tries to give the user the impression of being in a conversation with another person. Despite the benefits that this recommender type provides, it was still not appropriate for the learning purposes of the QA system.

To engage and guide the user on a meaningful learning journey, the learning-oriented recommendation technique was introduced. This recommender type also uses Bloom's taxonomy to identify learning objectives and to model the users' learning process to generate useful recommendations. Existing evaluation measures for recommender systems are not capable of assessing the unique learning competence offered by the learning-oriented recommender. As a consequence, a new evaluation measure was defined – the learning utility – which measures how well a recommender models the learning process of the users.

Finally, the aforementioned three main contributions of this thesis were evaluated and their results were presented and discussed in detail.

7.2. Conclusions

For our evaluation purposes, three question datasets were considered, each covering a different field of study: nutrition, earth sciences and homeschooling education. The questions related to nutrition were provided by the nutrition expert Sasha Walleczek [150]. The other two datasets were extracted from the Wiki Answers [153] question database, whereas some of the earth sciences questions were also selected from MadSci [95].

The topic taxonomies were either manually constructed by an expert, like in the case of the nutrition domain, or a coarse structure was retrieved from the source (e.g., Wiki Answers) and then it was manually extended with more specific topics. As for the keywords assigned to topics, two sources were provided: first, the question and answers themselves and secondly, additional keywords were extracted from relevant Wikipedia [154] pages.

In order to reduce as much as possible the dependency of the evaluated methods on external factors, the question mappings to the topic taxonomy and to the two dimensions of the learning objectives were also manually created. However, this aspect does not eliminate completely the influence of the knowledge-base structure on the results, but simply increases its reliability. In fact, results show that the way questions are mapped to the topic space is highly relevant and influences every aspect of the recommender system: accuracy, coverage and diversity.

Semantic short-term similarity

To evaluate the relevance of the similarity measures introduced in chapter 3, we conducted a survey with 15 men and women. 50 pairs of question were randomly generated from the nutrition dataset of 318 questions. Survey participants were asked to compare and rate the relatedness of each pair by ranking them with a value between 0 and 4 (0="not related at all", 4="similar").

Then, the participants' ranking was compared against six different semantic similarity measures: existing similarity measures and the new four-layered semantic similarity measure.

The results show that the four-layered semantic similarity measure achieves higher correlation with the average survey ranking compared to the other methods. Although the recorded correlation values were relatively low, it does not contradict the

7.2 Conclusions

hypothesis that it reflects on some level the human perception, given the diversity of answers collected during the survey. Another reason behind these results is the complexity of the question dataset. Other evaluations of existing semantic similarity measures use a dataset of simple, short sentences that have a basic common understanding.

It has also been observed that the performance of the semantic short-text similarity measure is highly dependent on the knowledge-base: the structure of the topic-tree, the keyword-topic mappings and the corresponding keyword weights. This statement is also supported by [23], where it is argued that similarity assessment algorithms are ontology dependent.

Short-term recommendation

For the evaluation of the conversation recommender, the same knowledge-base with nutrition questions was considered. Recommendations were generated for all existing questions and for 50 of them, which were randomly selected, an experiment was conducted.

Users were asked to rate the recommended questions with a value between 1 and 5 (1= no match, 5=best match). The survey was answered by 38 people, all of which were not directly related to the chosen domain and, therefore, would represent the ideal customers. The outcome of the survey shows few outliers. Hence, a general agreement is observed on the relevance of recommendations.

Results show that the conversation recommender can be successfully adopted by QA systems. Based on the user ratings, we can conclude that it is capable of generating meaningful recommendations without having to know anything about the user's history nor his/her preferences. It also avoids the cold-start, new item and new user problems, which are very common with most recommender techniques. The system can generate suitable recommendations for new users as well, were no browsing history is available.

The catalog and user space coverage, as well as the diversity of recommendations, show that this recommender technique is well suited for QA systems. It allows users to have access to a wide spectrum of questions and to navigate through the entire database of questions.

In order to improve the quality of the retrieved recommendations, the content-based method needs be extended with collaboration filtering approaches. This is where the role of the learning-oriented recommender comes into play.

Learning-oriented recommendation

The evaluation of the learning-oriented recommender is not as easy task for at least two reasons. First, in order to train and learn the recommender model, a substantial history of user learning activity is needed, which is not influenced in any way by other recommenders or other external factors. Secondly, even if such question sequences that reflect the users' learning process were to be collected, there is no clear, well-established metric to evaluate the performance of the recommender from a learning perspective.

However, a first step was made towards a better understanding of the learning-oriented recommender's capabilities. From each of the above mentioned three datasets of questions (i.e. earth sciences, nutrition and homeschooling), five sets of 20 questions were randomly selected and users were asked to order each set according to their learning preferences – in the sequence that they, personally, would ask them or want to learn about.

As a result, about 50-60 question sequences were recorded for each of the three domains. Then, these sequences were used to train the defined recommender models using cross-validation, leaving each time one user sequence out for testing. Three well-known measures were used to evaluate the performance of the models: accuracy, coverage and diversity. The test was carried out for every question in the test sequence, generating each time N recommendations using the past subsequence. The predictions were compared to the actual values and the accuracy was calculated based on the number of "correctly" recommended questions. Additionally, for a further evaluation of the prediction performance, the average log-loss was also considered.

Based on the four measures, consistent results were obtained for all three datasets. The simple recommender – based on a variable length Markov chain of questions – obtained the best prediction performance, but the coverage was much higher for the learning-oriented models. The diversity was found almost constant for every tested recommender.

However, the four aspects were not enough to derive firm statements to support our initial hypothesis. In order to show that the learning-oriented recommender can model better the learning process of users, the learning utility was measured. The results show that among all recommender models the hierarchical learning-oriented model achieves the highest learning utility, and among all learning-based models the best accuracy and coverage.

The performance of the hierarchical learning-oriented recommender confirms the initial intuition: question sequences are first influenced by the underlying topic and the order in which these topics are tackled, then, within each topic, a particular order of learning objectives is observed (see Figure 1.1).

7.3. Impact and future work

The positive outcome of the evaluation process opens doors for new research opportunities. The hypothesis stated at the beginning of this work is now supported by solid arguments. Therefore, the transition from one question to the other is not influenced by their semantic relatedness alone, but it is also driven by a learning

7.3 Impact and future work

process – an interpretable sequence of learning goals. Nevertheless, there is still space for improvements.

Knowledge-base evaluation and improvement

As mentioned several times before, one of the important components that the learning-oriented recommender relies on, is the knowledge base: the topic taxonomy, Bloom's framework of learning objectives and the question mappings to these dimensions. During the evaluation presented here, only manual structures and assignments were considered.

Further research is needed to assess the importance of the knowledge-base, to identify its ideal structure for a better learning performance.

Additionally, it would be desirable to investigate the potential of an automatic topic-tree generation, and, more importantly the automatic assignment of questions to topics and to learning objectives, i.e. the extraction of the topic and the learning objective from questions.

Automated curriculum generation

At the beginning, we mentioned a novel research direction within the learning technology field: to use the learning patterns derived from the new recommender model in order to establish new fields of study and for the (semi-)automated construction of curricula for those domains.

With the information overload, new aspects of existing disciplines are identified or entirely unknown, unexplored fields of study are discovered. In the first case, a restructuring or extension of the current curriculum is required. The second case demands the settlement of the first building blocks.

Learning patterns represent relevant knowledge about these domains. Further research in this direction is expected to answer the question whether and how to exploit the learning-oriented recommender model for this purpose.

A. Appendix

Number of values m	Order l	Markov chain	MTD model
2	1	2	2
	2	4	3
	3	8	4
	4	16	5
3	1	6	6
	2	18	7
	3	54	8
	4	162	9
5	1	20	20
	2	100	21
	3	500	22
	4	2500	23
10	1	90	90
	2	900	91
	3	9000	92
	4	90000	93

Table A.1.: Maximal number of independent parameters for different Markov chains and MTD models [21].

Technique	Background	Input	Process
Collaborative	Ratings from C of items in S.	Ratings from c of items in S.	Identify users in C similar to c and extrapolate from their ratings the rating of s.
Content-based	Features of items in S.	Ratings from c of items in S.	Generate a classifier that fits c's rating behavior and use it on s.
Demographic	Demographic information about C and their ratings of items in S.	Demographic information about c.	Identify users that are demographically similar to c and extrapolate from their ratings the rating of s.
Utility-based	Features of items in S.	A utility function over items in S that describes c's preferences.	Apply the function to the items and determine s's rank.
Knowledge-based	Features of items in S. Knowledge of how these items meet a user's needs.	A description of c's needs or interests.	Infer a match between s and c's need.

Table A.2.: Recommendation techniques [41].

B. Appendix

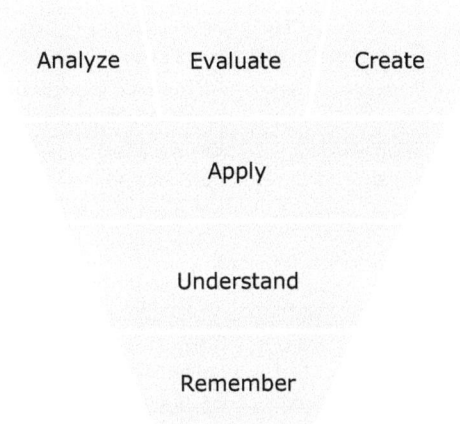

Figure B.1.: The cognitive process dimension of the revised version of Bloom's taxonomy [108].

Major types and subtypes	Examples
A. Factual knowledge – The basic elements students must know to be acquainted with a discipline or solve problems in it	
A1. Knowledge of terminology	Technical vocabulary, musical symbols
A2. Knowledge of specific details and elements	Major natural resources, reliable sources of information
B. Conceptual knowledge – The interrelationships among the basic elements within a larger structure that enable them to function together	
B1. Knowledge of classification and categories	Periods of geological time, forms of business ownership
B2. Knowledge of principles and generalizations	Pythagorean theorem, law of supply an demand
B3. Knowledge of theories, models and structures	Theory of evolution, structure of Congress
C. Procedural knowledge – How to do something, methods of inquiry, and criteria for using skills, algorithms, techniques and methods	
C1. Knowledge of subject-specific skills and algorithms	Skills used in painting with watercolor, whole-number division algorithm
C2. Knowledge of subject-specific techniques and methods	Interviewing techniques, scientific method
C3. Knowledge of criteria for determining when to use appropriate procedures	Criteria used to determine when to apply a procedure involving Newton's second law
D. Metacognitive knowledge – Knowledge of cognition in general as well as awareness and knowledge of one's own cognition	
D1. Strategic knowledge	Knowledge of outlining as a means of capturing the structure of a unit of subject matter in a textbook
D2. Knowledge about cognitive tasks, including appropriate contextual and conditional knowledge	Knowledge of types of tests particular teachers administer
D3. Self-knowledge	Knowledge that critiquing essays is a personal strength, whereas writing essays is a personal weakness

Table B.1.: The knowledge dimension according to Bloom's taxonomy (adapted after [10], page 46).

Appendix

Categories and cognitive processes	Alternative names	Definitions and examples
1. Remember – Retrieve relevant knowledge from long-term memory		
1.1. Recognizing	Identifying	Locating knowledge in long-term memory that is consistent with presented material
1.2. Recalling	Retrieving	Retrieving relevant knowledge from long-term memory
2. Understand – Construct meaning from instructional messages, including oral, written and graphic communication		
2.1. Interpreting	Clarifying, paraphrasing, representing	Changing from one form of representation to another
2.2. Exemplifying	Illustrating, instantiating	Finding a specific example or illustration of a concept or principle
2.3. Classifying	Categorizing, subsuming	Determining that something belongs to a category
2.4. Summarizing	Abstracting, generalizing	Abstracting a general theme or major point(s)
2.5. Inferring	Concluding, extrapolating, interpolating	Drawing a logical conclusion from presented information (e.g., in learning a foreign language, infer grammatical principles from examples)
2.6. Comparing	Contrasting, mapping, matching	Detecting correspondences between two ideas, objects, and the like
2.7. Explaining	Constructing models	Constructing a cause-and-effect model of a system
3. Apply – Carry out or use a procedure in a given situation		
3.1. Executing	Carrying out	Applying a procedure to a familiar task
3.2. Implementing	Using	Applying a procedure to an unfamiliar task

Table B.2.: The cognitive dimension according to Bloom's taxonomy (adapted after [10], page 67) – Part I.

Categories and cognitive processes	Alternative names	Definitions and examples
4. Analyze – Break material into constituent parts and determine how the parts relate to one another and to an overall structure or purpose		
4.1. Differentiating	Discriminating, distinguishing, focusing, selecting	Distinguishing relevant from irrelevant parts or important from unimportant parts of presented material
4.2. Organizing	Finding coherence, integrating, outlining, parsing, structuring	Determining how elements fit or function within a structure
4.3. Attributing	Deconstructing	Determine a point of view, bias, values, or intent underlying present material
5. Evaluate – Make judgment based on criteria and standards		
5.1. Checking	Coordinating, detecting, monitoring, testing	Detecting inconsistencies or fallacies within a process or product; determining whether a process or product has internal consistency.
5.2. Critiquing	Judging	Detecting inconsistencies between a product and external criteria, determining whether a product has external consistency;
6. Create – Put elements together to form a coherent or functional whole; reorganize elements into a new pattern or structure		
6.1. Generating	Hypothesizing	Coming up with alternative hypotheses based on criteria
6.2. Planning	Designing	Devising a procedure for accomplishing some task
6.3. Producing	Constructing	Inventing a product

Table B.3.: The cognitive dimension according to Bloom's taxonomy (adapted after [10], page 68) – Part II.

C. Appendix

Question	Order$_1$	Order$_2$
Does watching TV cause global warming?	19	20
What will probably happen over the next 100 years due to global climate change?	20	19
What is a greenhouse gas?	18	18
How old is the earth?	1	1
How hot is the center of the earth and how do you know?	4	2
Why is the inner core of the Earth solid even though it is hotter than the liquid outer core?	5	3
Can lightning cause earthquakes?	10	11
How normal is aftershock due to an earthquake?	8	4
What's the difference between cyclones and tornadoes?	12	12
When does a storm get named?	11	13
Does wild fire catastrophe have weather or geologic or humans cause?	14	9
What are some geographical processes associated with bush fires and wildfires?	15	10
How do wildfires start?	13	8
How many people died from volcanic eruption?	7	7
What cities are on tectonic plate boundaries?	6	5
Will Lyttleton volcano become active after an earthquake?	9	6
Why is the moon the primary cause of earth's tides?	2	16
How are animals affected by tides?	3	17
What is the function of the sun in the water cycle?	16	14
What does evaporation do in the water cycle?	17	15

Table C.1.: Examples of survey question ordering.

Question	Topic	Knowledge	Cognitive process
What was the biggest tsunami ever recorded?	tsunamis	factual	remember
What causes the phenomenon of the switching of the magnetic poles?	magnetic poles	conceptual	analyze
How did continental drift begin?	tectonics	factual	understand
How did the different land forms on earth get to exist?	surface	procedural	understand
How do earthquakes affect wildlife?	earthquakes	conceptual	analyze
What are the expected future continental movements?	tectonics	conceptual	evaluate
What is the difference between hurricanes and tornadoes?	hurricanes, typhoons and cyclones	conceptual	understand

Table C.2.: Examples of question mappings for the earth sciences domain.

Appendix

Question	Topic	Knowledge	Cognitive process
What is the difference between an allergy and a food intolerance?	allergy and intolerance	conceptual	understand
Should I eat often small meals or rather keep 5 hour breaks between meals?	lose weight	conceptual	evaluate
What role does the blood glucose level play in weight loss?	blood sugar	conceptual	remember
Is animal protein really unhealthy?	proteins	factual	evaluate
How can I reduce my cholesterol?	health	procedural	remember
Does the body absorb vitamins better from vegetables and fruits than from supplements?	beverages	factual	analyze
What food has no carbohydrates?	carbohydrates	factual	remember

Table C.3.: Examples of question mappings for the nutrition domain.

Question	Topic	Knowledge	Cognitive process
How much does it cost to enroll into homeschooling?	costs	factual	remember
What are the long-term effects of homeschooling?	effects	conceptual	analyze
Is homeschooling legal and accepted in most countries?	law	factual	evaluate
What are the benefits of homeschooling?	benefits	factual	understand
How can you convince your parents that you would be better off being home-schooled?	parents	procedural	remember
Can homeschooling help children with special needs?	special needs	conceptual	evaluate
Are home schooled students at a disadvantage socially?	socialization	conceptual	analyze

Table C.4.: Examples of question mappings for the homeschooling domain.

Appendix

Dataset	Part	Avg ♂	Avg ♀	Avg	Min	Max
Earth sciences	I	0.358	0.309	0.314	-0.439	0.910
	II	0.188	0.113	0.131	-0.925	0.910
	III	0.138	0.273	0.164	-0.695	0.874
	IV	0.344	0.126	0.151	-0.862	0.981
	V	0.171	0.359	0.199	-0.762	0.977
Nutrition	I	0.219	0.144	0.102	-0.662	0.734
	II	0.420	0.202	0.251	-0.759	0.789
	III	0.529	0.675	0.557	0.075	0.853
	IV	0.565	0.287	0.391	-0.531	0.892
	V	0.518	0.280	0.336	-0.370	0.905
Homeschooling	I	0.341	0.438	0.311	-0.346	0.829
	II	0.314	0.352	0.216	-0.394	0.798
	III	0.482	0.442	0.419	-0.248	0.847
	IV	0.239	0.289	0.219	-0.528	0.871
	V	0.614	0.543	0.553	-0.003	0.827

Table C.5.: Average, minimum and maximum correlations of question orderings.

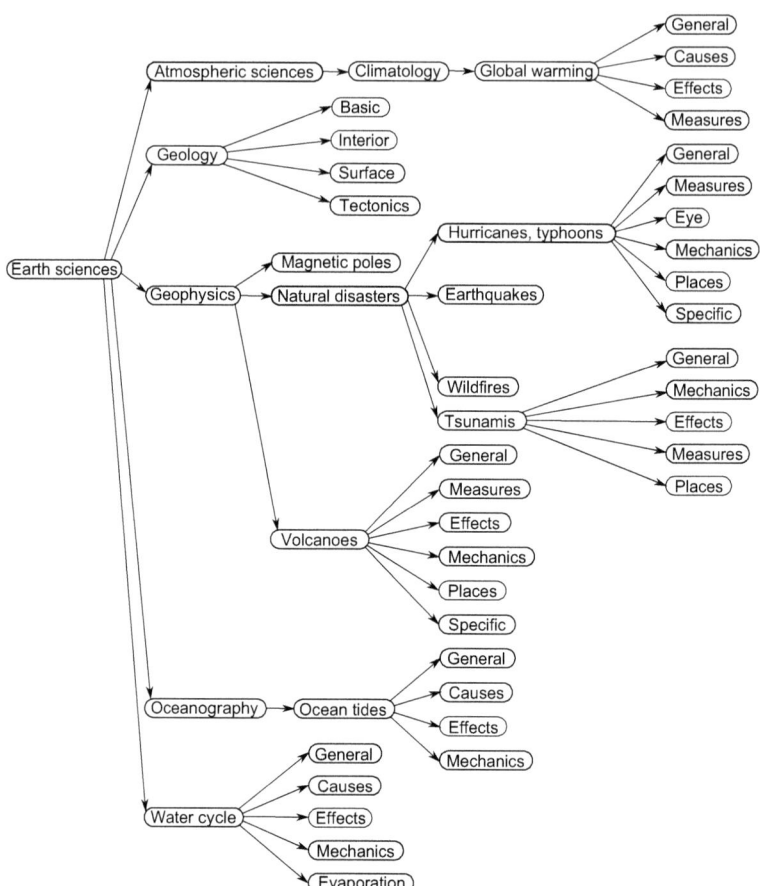

Figure C.1.: A taxonomy of the earth sciences domain.

Appendix

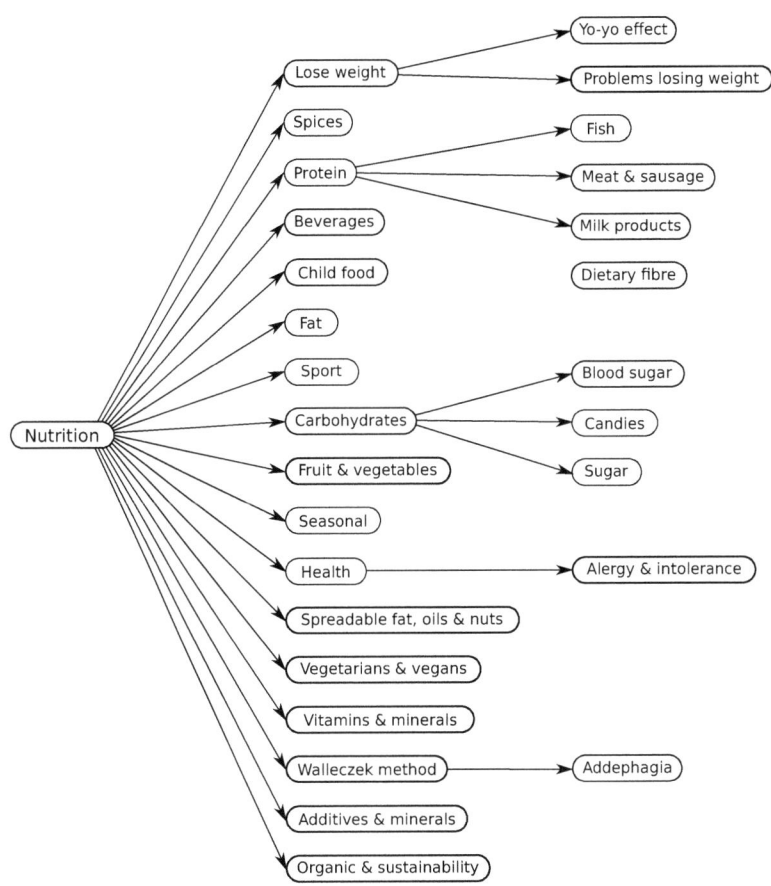

Figure C.2.: Example of nutrition taxonomy.

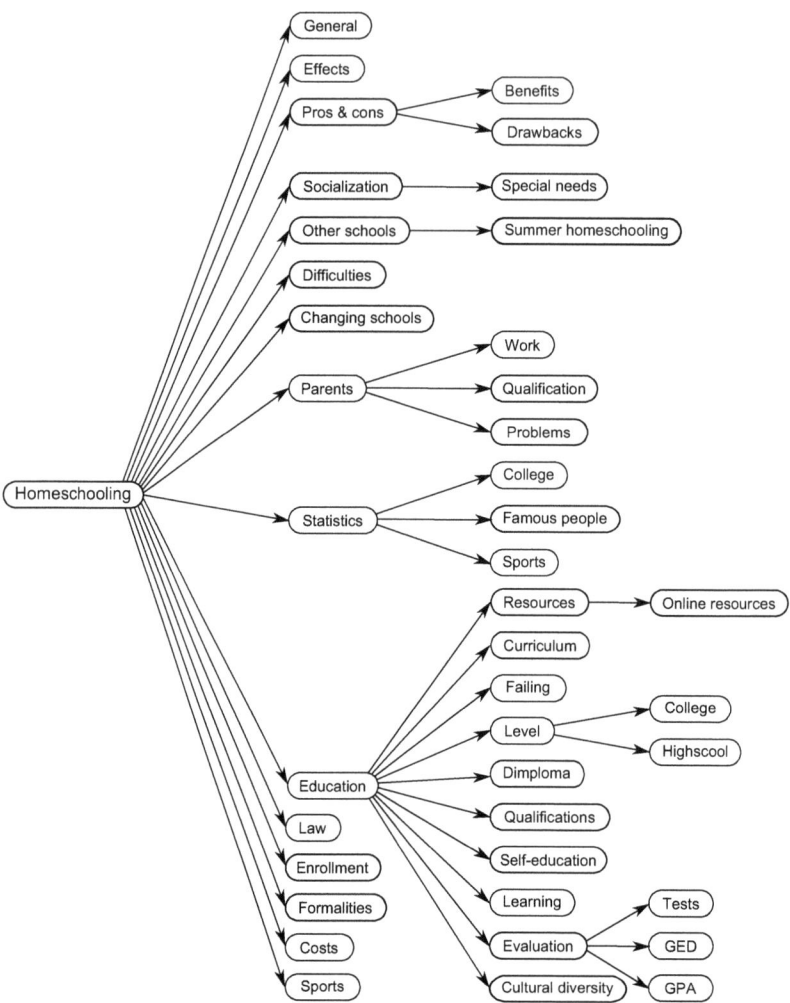

Figure C.3.: Example of homeschooling taxonomy.

Appendix

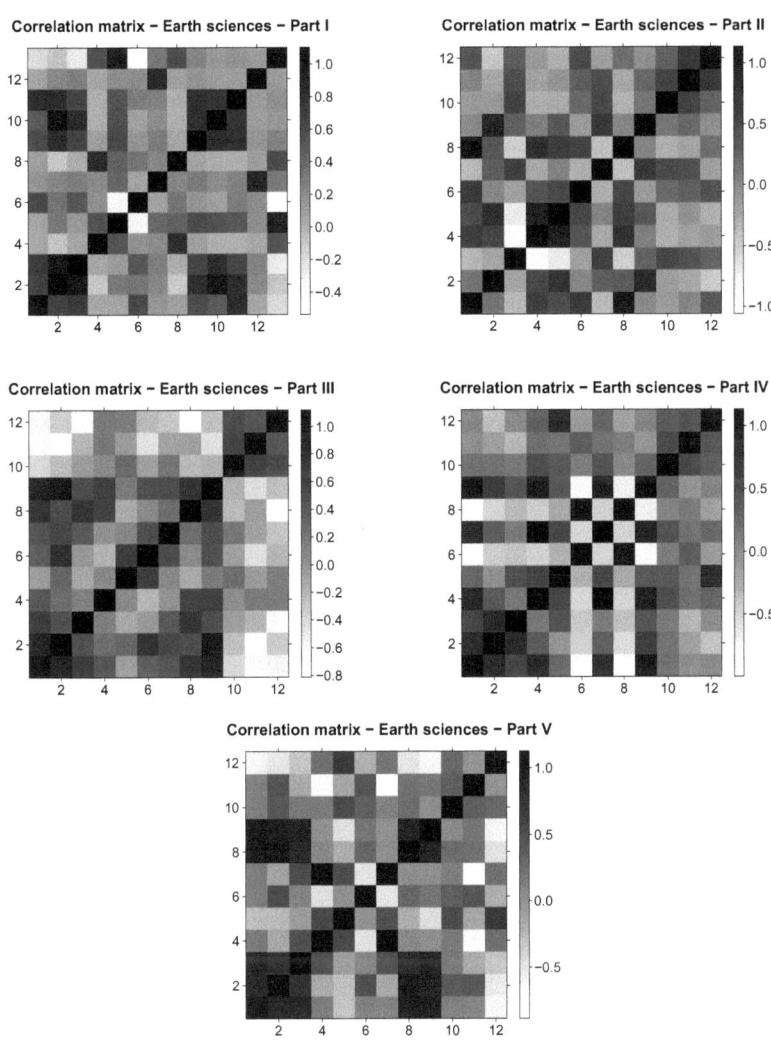

Figure C.4.: Correlation of user question orderings for the earth sciences domain.

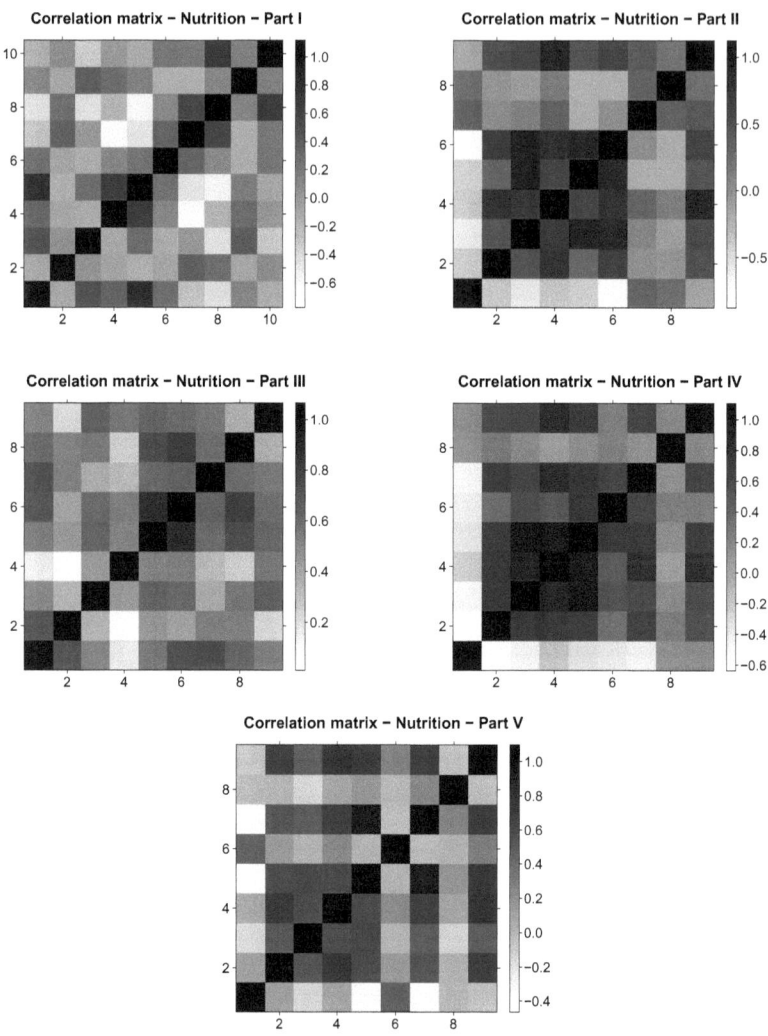

Figure C.5.: Correlation of user question orderings for the nutrition domain.

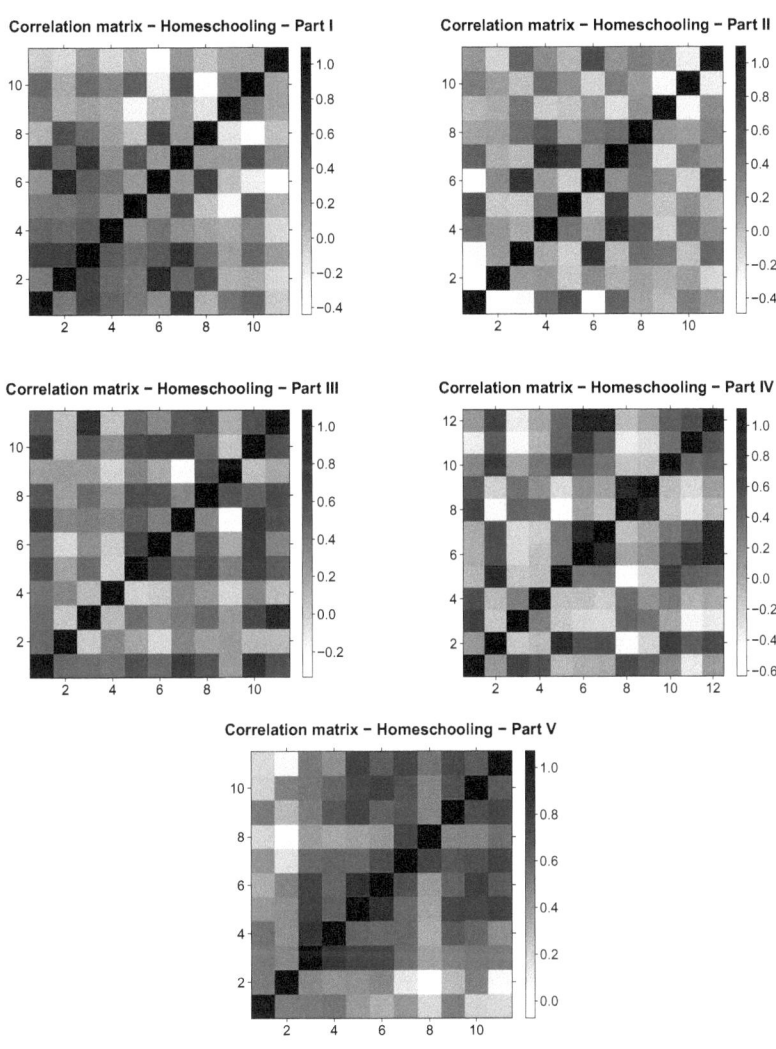

Figure C.6.: Correlation of user question orderings for the homeschooling domain.

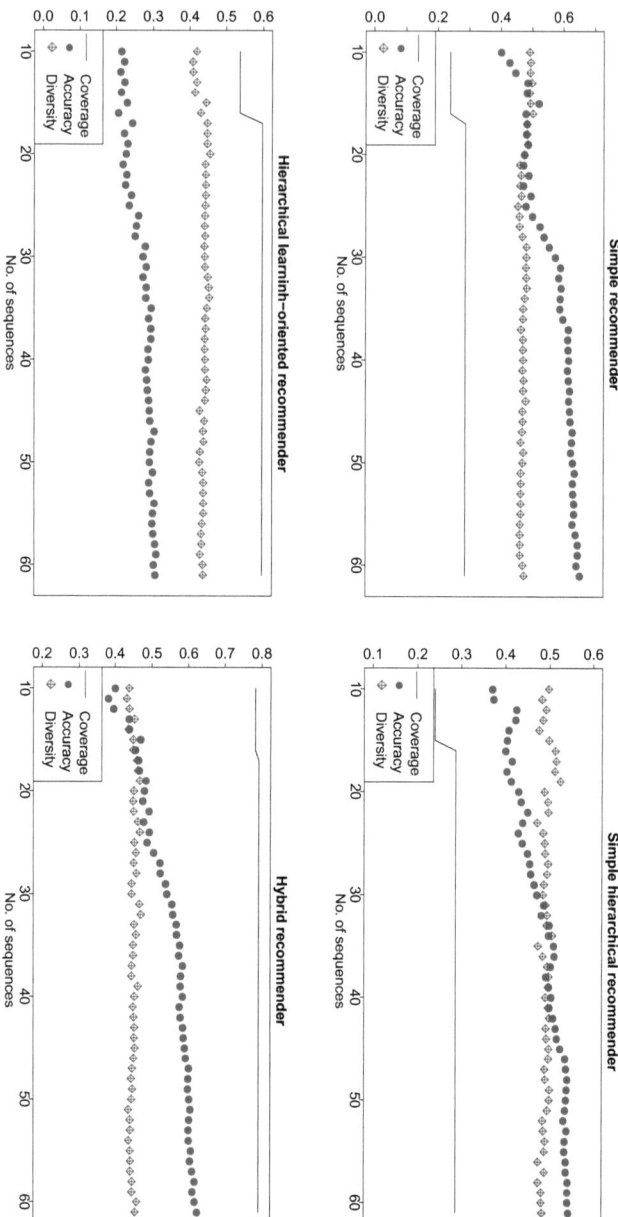

Figure C.7.: Learning curves for the earth sciences domain.

Appendix

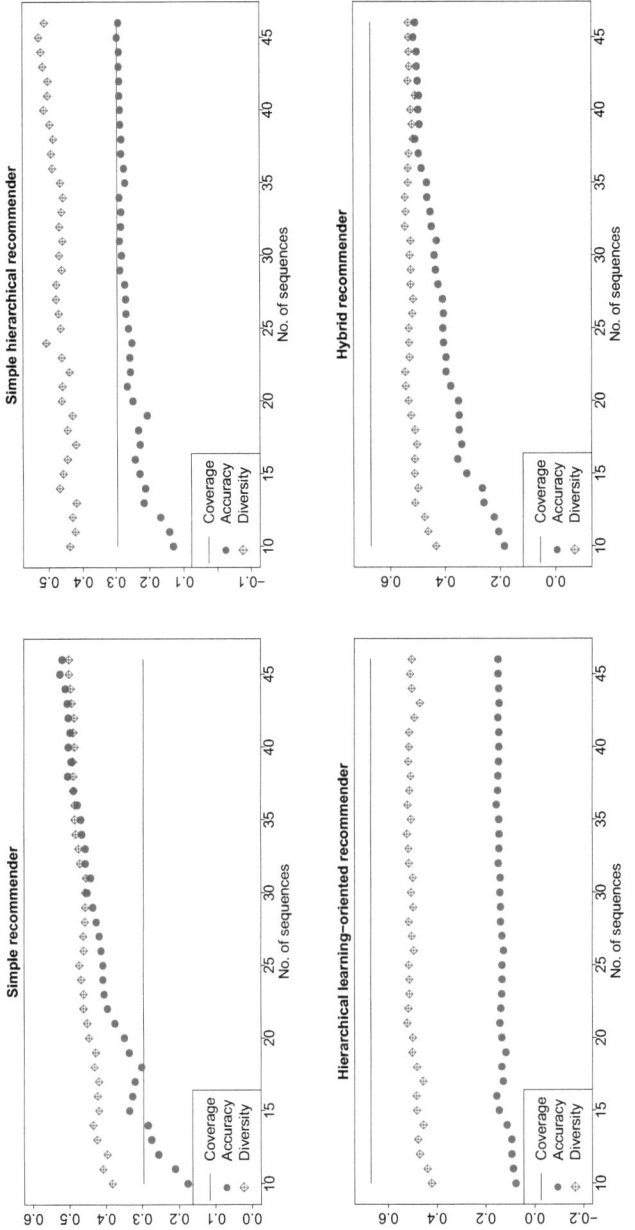

Figure C.8.: Learning curves for the nutrition domain.

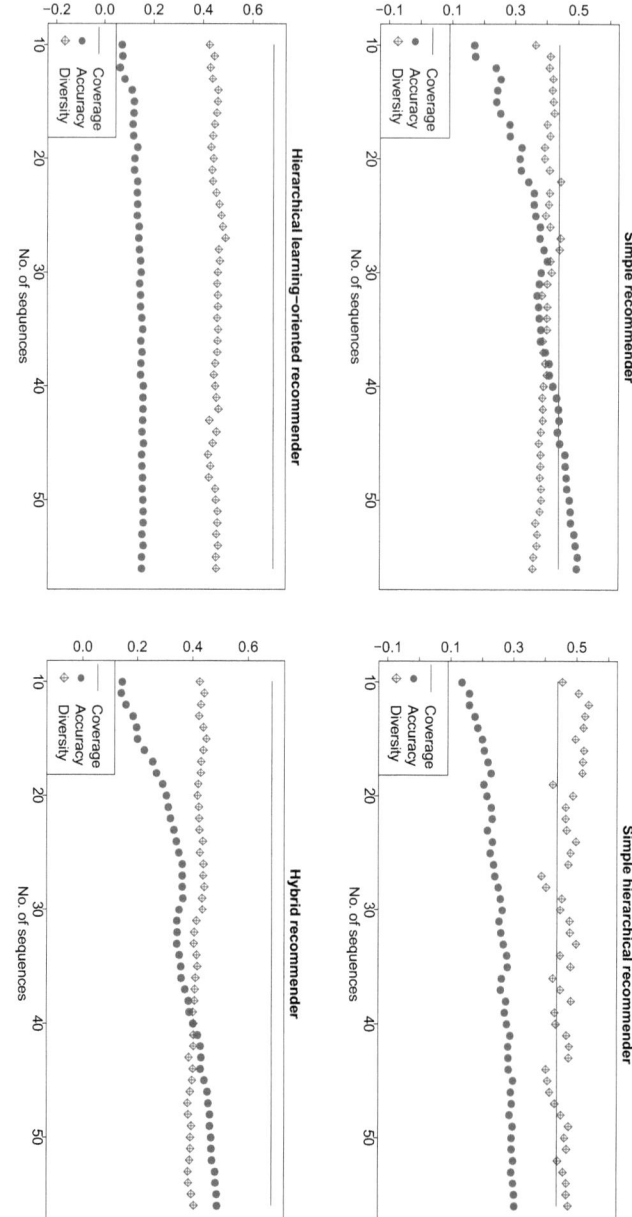

Figure C.9.: Learning curves for the homeschooling domain.

Bibliography

[1] AAINSQATSI, K. Bloom's rose — Wikipedia, the free encyclopedia. www.en.wikipedia.org/wiki/File:Blooms_rose.svg, 2008.

[2] ADOMAVICIUS, G., AND TUZHILIN, A. Multidimensional recommender systems: a data warehousing approach. In *Proceedings of the 2nd International Workshop on Electronic Commerce (WELCOM '01)* (2001).

[3] ADOMAVICIUS, G., AND TUZHILIN, A. Toward the next generation of recommender systems: A survey of the state-of-the-art and possible extensions. *IEEE Transactions on Knowledge and Data Engineering 17*, 6 (2005), 734–749.

[4] ADOMAVICIUS, G., AND TUZHILIN, A. Context-aware recommender systems. In *Recommender Systems Handbook*, F. R. et al., Ed. Springer Science+Business Media, LLC, 2011.

[5] AGICHTEIN, E., BRILL, E., AND DUMAIS, S. Improving web search ranking by incorporating user behavior information. In *Proceedings of the 29th annual international ACM SIGIR conference on Research and development in information retrieval* (New York, NY, USA, 2006), SIGIR '06, ACM, pp. 19–26.

[6] AGRAWAL, R., IMIELIŃSKI, T., AND SWAMI, A. Mining association rules between sets of items in large databases. In *Proceedings of the 1993 ACM SIGMOD International Conference on Management of Data* (New York, NY, USA, 1993), SIGMOD '93, ACM, pp. 207–216.

[7] AGRAWAL, R., AND SRIKANT, R. Fast algorithms for mining association rules in large databases. In *Proceedings of the 20th International Conference on Very Large Databases* (San Francisco, CA, USA, 1994), VLDB '94, Morgan Kaufmann Publishers Inc., pp. 487–499.

[8] AL-MUBAID, H., AND NGUYEN, H. A. A cluster-based approach for semantic similarity in the biomedical domain. In *Proceedings of the 28th IEEE EMBS Annual International Conference* (New York, USA, 2006), pp. 2713–2717.

[9] ALLISON, L., AND DIX, T. I. A bit-string longest-common-subsequence algorithm. *Information Processing Letters 23*, 6 (Dec. 1986), 305–310.

[10] ANDERSON, L., KRATHWOHL, D., AIRASIAN, P., CRUIKSHANK, K., MAYER, R., PINTRICH, P., RATHS, J., AND WITTROCK, M., Eds. *A taxonomy for learning, teaching, and assessing : a revision of Bloom's taxonomy of educational objectives*. Addison Wesley Longman, Inc., 2001.

[11] ANDERSON, L. W., SOSNIAK, L. A., AND BLOOM, B. S. *Bloom's Taxonomy: A Forty-year Retrospective*, vol. 93 of *Yearbook of the National Society*

for the Study of Education. 1994, ch. Reflections on the development and use of the taxonomy.

[12] ANSARI, A., ESSEGAIER, S., AND KOHLI, R. Internet recommendations systems. *Marketing Research* (2000), 363–375.

[13] BAEZA-YATES, R. Graphs from search engine queries. In *SOFSEM 2007: Theory and Practice of Computer Science*, J. Leeuwen, G. Italiano, W. Hoek, C. Meinel, H. Sack, and F. Plášil, Eds., vol. 4362 of *Lecture Notes in Computer Science*. Springer Berlin Heidelberg, 2007, pp. 1–8.

[14] BAEZA-YATES, R., HURTADO, C., AND MENDOZA, M. Query recommendation using query logs in search engines. In *Proceedings of the 2004 International Conference on Current Trends in Database Technology* (Berlin, Heidelberg, 2004), EDBT'04, Springer-Verlag, pp. 588–596.

[15] BAEZA-YATES, R., AND TIBERI, A. Extracting semantic relations from query logs. In *Proceedings of the 13th ACM SIGKDD International Conference on Knowledge Discovery and Data Mining* (New York, NY, USA, 2007), KDD '07, ACM, pp. 76–85.

[16] BAI, L., GUO, J., AND CHENG, X. Query recommendation by modelling the query-flow graph. In *Proceedings of the 7th Asian Conference on Information Retrieval Technology* (Berlin, Heidelberg, 2011), AIRS'11, Springer-Verlag, pp. 137–146.

[17] BÄR, D., ZESCH, T., AND GUREVYCH, I. A reflective view on text similarity. In *Proceedings of Recent Advances in Natural Language Processing* (Hissar, Bulgaria, september 2011), pp. 515–520.

[18] BAUM, L. E., PETRIE, T., SOULES, G., AND WEISS, N. A maximization technique occurring in the statistical analysis of probabilistic functions of Markov chains. *The Annals of Mathematical Statistics 41*, 1 (1970), 164–171.

[19] BEGLEITER, R., EL-YANIV, R., AND YONA, G. On prediction using variable order Markov models. *Journal of Artificial Intelligence Research 22* (2004), 385–421.

[20] BELL, T. C., CLEARY, J. G., AND WITTEN, I. H. *Text compression.* Prentice Hall, 1990.

[21] BERCHTOLD, A., AND RAFTERY, A. E. The mixture transition distribution model for high-order Markov chains and non-gaussian time series. *Statistical Science* (2002), 328–356.

[22] BERNHARD, D., AND GUREVYCH, I. Answering learners' questions by retrieving question paraphrases from social Q&A sites. In *Proceedings of the Third Workshop on Innovative Use of NLP for Building Educational Applications* (Stroudsburg, PA, USA, 2008), EANL '08, Association for Computational Linguistics, pp. 44–52.

Bibliography

[23] BERNSTEIN, A., KAUFMANN, E., BÜRKI, C., AND KLEIN, M. How similar is it? Towards personalized similarity measures in ontologies. In *7. Internationale Tagung Wirtschaftsinformatik* (2005), pp. 1347–1366.

[24] BILLSUS, D., AND PAZZANI, M. Learning collaborative information filters. In *Proceedings of the International Conference in Machine Learning* (1998).

[25] BIN, S., LIYING, F., JIANZHUO, Y., PU, W., AND ZHONGCHENG, Z. Ontology-based measure of semantic similarity between concepts. In *World Congress on Software Engineering* (2009), vol. 2, pp. 109–112.

[26] BLEI, D. M., GRIFFITHS, T. L., JORDAN, M. I., AND TENENBAUM, J. B. Hierarchical topic models and the nested Chinese restaurant process. *Advances in Neural Information Processing Systems* (2004).

[27] BLEI, D. M., NG, A. Y., AND JORDAN, M. I. Latent Dirichlet allocation. *Machine Learning Research 3*, January (2003), 993–1022.

[28] BLOOM, B., ENGLEHART, M. D., FURST, E. J., HILL, W. H., AND KRATHWOHL, D. *Taxonomy of educational objectives handbook I: The cognitive domain.* Longmans, New York, USA, 1956.

[29] BOLDI, P., BONCHI, F., CASTILLO, C., DONATO, D., GIONIS, A., AND VIGNA, S. The query-flow graph: model and applications. In *Proceedings of the 17th ACM Conference on Information and Knowledge Management* (New York, NY, USA, 2008), CIKM '08, ACM, pp. 609–618.

[30] BOLDI, P., BONCHI, F., CASTILLO, C., DONATO, D., AND VIGNA, S. Query suggestions using query-flow graphs. In *Proceedings of the 2009 Workshop on Web Search Click Data* (New York, NY, USA, 2009), WSCD '09, ACM, pp. 56–63.

[31] BOLDI, P., BONCHI, F., CASTILLO, C., AND VIGNA, S. From "dango" to "japanese cakes": Query reformulation models and patterns. In *Proceedings of the 2009 IEEE/WIC/ACM International Joint Conference on Web Intelligence and Intelligent Agent Technology - Volume 01* (Washington, DC, USA, 2009), WI-IAT '09, IEEE Computer Society, pp. 183–190.

[32] BOLDI, P., BONCHI, F., CASTILLO, C., AND VIGNA, S. Query reformulation mining: models, patterns, and applications. *Information Retrieval 14*, 3 (June 2011), 257–289.

[33] BONCHI, F., PEREGO, R., SILVESTRI, F., VAHABI, H., AND VENTURINI, R. Recommendations for the long tail by term-query graph. In *Proceedings of the 20th International Conference Companion on World Wide Web* (2011), WWW '11.

[34] BONCHI, F., PEREGO, R., SILVESTRI, F., VAHABI, H., AND VENTURINI, R. Efficient query recommendations in the long tail via center-piece subgraphs. In *Proceedings of the 35th International ACM SIGIR Conference on Research and Development in Information Retrieval* (New York, NY, USA, 2012), SIGIR '12, ACM, pp. 345–354.

[35] BORDINO, I., CASTILLO, C., DONATO, D., AND GIONIS, A. Query similarity by projecting the query-flow graph. In *Proceedings of the 33rd International ACM SIGIR Conference on Research and Development in Information Retrieval* (New York, NY, USA, 2010), SIGIR '10, ACM, pp. 515–522.

[36] BOUQUET, P., KUPER, G., SCOZ, M., AND ZANOBINI, S. Asking and answering semantic queries. In *Proceedings of Meaning Coordination and Negotiation Workshop (MCNW-04) in conjunction with International Semantic Web Conference* (2004).

[37] BREESE, J. S., HECKERMAN, D., AND KADIE, C. Empirical analysis of predictive algorithms for collaborative filtering. In *Proceedings of the 14th Conference on Uncertainty in Artificial Intelligence* (San Francisco, CA, USA, 1998), UAI'98, Morgan Kaufmann Publishers Inc., pp. 43–52.

[38] BÜHLMANN, P., AND WYNER, A. J. Variable length Markov chains. *Annals of Statistics 27* (1999), 480–513.

[39] BURGESS, C., LIVESAY, K., AND LUND, K. Explorations in context space: Words, sentences, discourse. *Discourse Processes 25*, 2-3 (1998), 211–257.

[40] BURKE, R. Knowledge-based recommender systems. *Encyclopedia of Library and Information Systems 69*, Suplement 32 (2000).

[41] BURKE, R. Hybrid recommender systems: Survey and experiments. *User Modeling and User-Adapted Interaction 12*, 4 (Nov. 2002), 331–370.

[42] CAO, H., HU, D. H., SHEN, D., JIANG, D., SUN, J.-T., CHEN, E., AND YANG, Q. Context-aware query classification. In *Proceedings of the 32nd International ACM SIGIR Conference on Research and Development in Information Retrieval* (New York, NY, USA, 2009), SIGIR '09, ACM, pp. 3–10.

[43] CAO, H., JIANG, D., PEI, J., CHEN, E., AND LI, H. Towards context-aware search by learning a very large variable length hidden markov model from search logs. In *Proceedings of the 18th International Conference on World Wide Web* (New York, NY, USA, 2009), WWW '09, ACM, pp. 191–200.

[44] CLEARY, J. G., IAN, AND WITTEN, I. H. Data compression using adaptive coding and partial string matching. *IEEE Transactions on Communications 32* (1984), 396–402.

[45] CONDLIFF, M., LEWIS, D., MADIGAN, D., AND POSSE, C. Bayesian mixed-effects models for recommender systems. In *Proceedings of the ACM SIGIR '99 Workshop on Recommender Systems: Algorithms and Evaluation* (August 1999).

[46] CORDÌ, V., LOMBARDI, P., MARTELLI, M., AND MASCARDI, V. An ontology-based similarity between sets of concepts. In *6th Joint Workshop "From Objects to Agents": Simulation and Formal Analysis of Complex Systems* (Camerino, Italy, 2005), pp. 16–21.

Bibliography

[47] CORTES, C., FISHER, K., PREGIBON, D., ROGERS, A., AND SMITH, F. Hancock: a language for extracting signatures from data streams. In *Proceedings of the 6th ACM SIGKDD International Conference on Knowledge Discovery and Data Mining* (2000).

[48] COVEY, S. R., MERRILL, A. R., AND MERRILL, R. R. *First things first*. Free Press, New York, USA, 2003.

[49] DELGADO, J., AND ISHII, N. Memory-based weighted-majority prediction for recommender systems. In *Proceedings of the ACM SIGIR '99 Workshop on Recommender Systems: Algorithms and Evaluation* (1999).

[50] DEMPSTER, A. P., LAIRD, N. M., AND RUBIN, D. B. Maximum likelihood from incomplete data via the EM algorithm. *Journal of the Royal Statistical Society, Series B 39*, 1 (1977), 1–38.

[51] DONATO, D. Graph structures and algorithms for query-log analysis. In *Proceedings of the Programs, Proofs, Process and 6th International Conference on Computability in Europe* (Berlin, Heidelberg, 2010), CiE'10, Springer-Verlag, pp. 126–131.

[52] DONG, H., HUSSAIN, F. H., AND CHANG, E. A hybrid concept similarity measure model for ontology environment. In *Proceedings of the Confederated International Workshops and Posters on the Move to Meaningful Internet Systems* (2009), pp. 848–857.

[53] EITER, T., AND MANNILA, H. Distance measures for point sets and their computation. *Journal Acta Informatica 34* (1997), 103–133.

[54] FAWCETT, T., AND PROVOST, F. Combining data mining and machine learning for efficient user profiling. In *Proceedings of the 2nd International Conference on Knowledge Discovery and Data Mining (KDD '96)* (1996).

[55] FELLBAUM, C., Ed. *WordNet - an electronic lexical database*. MIT Press, 1998.

[56] FINLAYSON, M. A. MIT Java Wordnet Interface (JWI) - a Java library for interfacing with Wordnet. projects.csail.mit.edu/jwi.

[57] FONSECA, B. M., GOLGHER, P. B., DE MOURA, E. S., AND ZIVIANI, N. Using association rules to discover search engines related queries. In *Proceedings of the First Conference on Latin American Web Congress* (Washington, DC, USA, 2003), LA-WEB '03, IEEE Computer Society, pp. 66–71.

[58] FRANK, E., PAYNTER, G. W., WITTEN, I. H., GUTWIN, C., AND ET AL. Domain-specific keyphrase extraction. In *Proceedings of 16th International Joint Conference on Artificial Intelligence* (1999), Morgan Kaufmann Publishers, pp. 668–673.

[59] GABRILOVICH, E., AND MARKOVITCH, S. Computing semantic relatedness using wikipedia-based explicit semantic analysis. In *Proceedings of the 20th International Joint Conference on Artifical Intelligence* (2007), pp. 1606–1611.

[60] GE, M., DELGADO-BATTENFELD, C., AND JANNACH, D. Beyond accuracy: evaluating recommender systems by coverage and serendipity. In *Proceedings of the fourth ACM conference on Recommender systems* (New York, NY, USA, 2010), RecSys '10, ACM, pp. 257–260.

[61] GETOOR, L., AND SAHAMI, M. Using probabilistic relational models for collaborative filtering. In *Proceedings Workshop Web Usage Analysis and User Profiling (WEBKDD '99)* (1999).

[62] GHAHRAMANI, Z. Learning dynamic Bayesian networks. In *Adaptive Processing of Sequences and Data Structures* (1998), Springer-Verlag, pp. 168–197.

[63] GIROLAMI, M., AND KABÁN, A. On an equivalence between PLSI and LDA. In *Proceedings of the 26th Annual International ACM SIGIR conference on Research and Development in Informaion Retrieval* (New York, NY, USA, 2003), SIGIR '03, ACM, pp. 433–434.

[64] GRAESSER, A., CHIPMAN, P., HAYNES, B., AND OLNEY, A. AutoTutor: an intelligent tutoring system with mixed-initiative dialogue. *Education, IEEE Transactions on 48*, 4 (2005), 612–618.

[65] GUNAWARDANA, A., AND SHANI, G. A survey of accuracy evaluation metrics of recommendation tasks. *Machine Learning Research 10* (December 2009), 2935–2962.

[66] HAASE, P., SIEBES, R., AND HARMELEN, F. V. Peer selection in peer-to-peer networks with semantic topologies. In *International Conference on Semantics of a Networked World: Semantics for Grid Databases* (2004).

[67] HACOHEN-KERNER, Y., , GROSS, Z., AND MASA, A. Automatic extraction and learning of keyphrases from scientific articles. In *Computational Linguistics and Intelligent Text Processing*, A. Gelbukh, Ed., vol. 3406 of *Lecture Notes in Computer Science*. Springer Berlin / Heidelberg, 2005, pp. 657–669.

[68] HE, Q., JIANG, D., LIAO, Z., HOI, S. C. H., CHANG, K., LIM, E., AND LI, H. Web query recommendation via sequential query prediction. In *Proceedings of the 2009 IEEE International Conference on Data Engineering* (Washington, DC, USA, 2009), ICDE '09, IEEE Computer Society, pp. 1443–1454.

[69] HOFMANN, T. Probabilistic latent semantic analysis. In *Proceedings of the 15th Conference on Uncertainty in Artificial Intelligence* (1999), pp. 289–296.

[70] HOFMANN, T. Probabilistic latent semantic indexing. In *Proceedings of the 22nd Annual International SIGIR Conference on Research and Development in Information Retrieval* (1999), pp. 50–57.

[71] HOFMANN, T. Collaborative filtering via Gaussian probabilistic latent semantic analysis. In *Proceedings of the 26th Annual International ACM SIGIR Conference* (2003).

[72] HOPE, D. Java Wordnet Similarity API - a Java implementation of WordNet::Similarity. www.sussex.ac.uk/Users/drh21.

Bibliography

[73] HUANG, Z., CHEN, H., AND ZENG, D. Applying associative retrieval techniques to alleviate the sparsity problem in collaborative filtering. *ACM Transactions on Information Systems 22*, 1.

[74] HULTH, A. Improved automatic keyword extraction given more linguistic knowledge. In *Proceedings of the 2003 conference on Empirical methods in natural language processing* (Stroudsburg, PA, USA, 2003), EMNLP '03, Association for Computational Linguistics, pp. 216–223.

[75] ISLAM, A., AND INKPEN, D. Second order co-occurrence PMI for determining the semantic similarity of words. In *Proceedings of the International Conference on Language Resources and Evaluation* (Genoa, Italy, 2006).

[76] ISLAM, A., AND INKPEN, D. Semantic text similarity using corpus-based word similarity and string similarity. In *ACM Transactions on Knowledge Discovery from Data* (2008), vol. 2(2), pp. 1–25.

[77] JIANG, J., AND CONRATH, W. Semantic similarity based on corpus statistics and lexical taxonomy. In *Proceedings of International Conference Research on Computational Linguistics* (Taiwan, 1997), pp. 19–33.

[78] KOLLER, D., AND FRIEDMAN, N. *Probabilistic Graphical Models: Principles and Techniques.* MIT Press, 2009, ch. Template-Based Representations.

[79] KOLLER, D., AND FRIEDMAN, N. *Probabilistic Graphical Models: Principles and Techniques.* MIT Press, 2009, ch. The Bayesian Network Representation.

[80] KOSORUS, H., BÖGL, A., AND KÜNG, J. Semantic similarity between queries in a QA system using a domain-specific taxonomy. In *Proceedings of the 14th International Conference on Enterprise Information Systems* (Wrocław, Poland, june 2012), pp. 241–246.

[81] KRATHWOHL, D. R. A revision of bloom's taxonomy: An overview. *Theory Into Practice 41*, 4 (2002), 212–218.

[82] LANDAUER, T. K., FOLTZ, P. W., AND LAHAM, D. Introduction to latent semantic analysis. *Discourse Processes 25*, 2-3 (1998), 259–284.

[83] LANDAUER, T. K., LAHAM, D., AND FOLTZ, P. Learning human-like knowledge by singular value decomposition: A progress report. In *Advances in Neural Information Processing Systems 10* (1998), MIT Press, pp. 45–51.

[84] LEACOCK, C., AND CHODOROW, M. *Combining Local Context and WordNet Similarity for Word Sense Identification.* In C. Fellbaum (Ed.), MIT Press, 1998, pp. 305–332.

[85] LEE, J. H., KIM, M. H., AND LEE, Y. J. Information retrieval based on conceptual distance in IS-A hierarchies. *Journal of Documentation 49*, 2 (1993), 188–207.

[86] LEE, M., PINCOMBE, B., AND WELSH, M. An empirical evaluation of models of text document similarity. In *Proceedings of the 27th Annual Conference of the Cognitive Science Society* (2005), pp. 1254–1259.

[87] LEE, W. N., SHAH, N., SUNDLASS, K., AND MUSEN, M. Comparison of ontology-based semantic-similarity measures. In *AMIA Annual Symposium Proceedings* (2008), pp. 384–388.

[88] LETHAM, B., RUDIN, C., AND MADIGAN, D. Sequential event prediction. Operations Research Center Working Paper Series OR 387-11, MIT, 2011.

[89] LI, Y., BANDAR, Z. A., AND MCLEAN, D. An approach for measuring semantic similarity between words using multiple information sources. *IEEE Transactions on Knowledge and Data Engineering 15*, 4 (2003).

[90] LI, Y., MCLEAN, D., BANDAR, Z. A., O'SHEA, J. D., AND CROCKETT, K. Sentence similarity based on semantic nets and corpus statistics. *IEEE Transactions on Knowledge and Data Engineering 18*, 8 (2006), 1138–1150.

[91] LIN, D. An information-theoretic definition of similarity. In *Proceedings of the 15th International Conference on Machine Learning* (1998), pp. 296–304.

[92] LOPS, P., DE GEMMIS, M., AND SEMERARO, G. Content-based recommender systems: state of the art and trends. In *Recommender Systems Handbook*, F. R. et al., Ed. Springer Science+Business Media, LLC, 2011.

[93] LUMENZ NETWORKS GMBH. www.lumenznetworks.org.

[94] MÄCHLER, M., AND BÜHLMANN, P. Variable Length Markov Chains: Methodology, Computing and Software. Research Report 104, Eidgenossische Technische Hochschule (ETH), CH-8091 Zürich, Switzerland, Mar. 2002.

[95] MADSCI. www.madsci.org.

[96] MANNILA, H., TOIVONEN, H., AND VERKAMO, A. I. Discovering frequent episodes in sequences. In *Proceedings of the 1st International Conference on Knowledge Discovery and Data Mining (KDD '95)* (1995).

[97] MANNING, C. D., AND SCHÜTZE, H. *Foundations of statistical natural language processing*. MIT Press, 1999.

[98] MARLIN, B. Modeling user rating profiles for collaborative filtering. In *Proceedings of the 17th Annual Conference on Neural Information Processing Systems (NIPS '03)* (2003).

[99] MCCANDLESS, M., HATCHER, E., AND GOSPODNETIC, O. *Lucene in Action, Second Edition: Covers Apache Lucene 3.0*. Manning Publications Co., Greenwich, CT, USA, 2010.

[100] MCCORMICK, T. H., RUDIN, C., AND MADIGAN, D. A hierarchical model for association rule mining of sequential events: An approach to automated medical symptom prediction. MIT Sloan Research Paper, MIT, 2011.

[101] MCCORMICK, T. H., RUDIN, C., AND MADIGAN, D. Bayesian hierarchical modeling for predicting medical conditions. *The Annals of Applied Statistics 6*, 2 (2012), 652–668.

Bibliography

[102] MELVILLE, P., MOONEY, R., AND NAGARAJAN, R. Content-boosted collaborative filtering for improved recommendations. In *Proceedings of the 18th National Conference on Artificial Intelligence* (2002).

[103] MILLER, G. A. Wordnet: A lexical database for English. *Communications of the ACM 38*, 11 (1995), 39–41.

[104] MURPHY, K. P. Dynamic Bayesian networks: Representation, inference and learning, 2002.

[105] NADSCHLÄGER, S., KOSORUS, H., BÖGL, A., AND KÜNG, J. Content-based recommendations within a QA system using the hierarchical structure of a domain-specific taxonomy. In *Proceedings of the 23rd International Workshop on Databases and Expert Systems Applications* (2012), pp. 88–92.

[106] NADSCHLÄGER, S., KOSORUS, H., REGNER, P., AND KÜNG, J. Semantic data integration and relationship identification using the hierarchical structure of a domain-specific taxonomy. In *Proceedings of the 23rd International Workshop on Databases and Expert Systems Applications* (2012), pp. 48–52.

[107] NAKAMURA, A., AND ABE, N. Collaborative filtering using weighted majority prediction algorithms. In *Proceedings of the 15th International Conference on Machine Learning* (1998).

[108] NESBIT. Bloom's cognitive domain — Wikimedia Commons. commons.wikimedia.org/wiki/File:BloomsCognitiveDomain.svg, 2006.

[109] NIINILUOTO, I. *Truthlikeness*. Reidel D. Pub. Comp., Dordrecht, Holland, 1987.

[110] NISENSON, M., YARIV, I., EL-YANIV, R., AND MEIR, R. Towards behaviometric security systems: Learning to identify a typist. In *Proceedings of the 7th European Conference on Principles and Practice of Knowledge Discovery in Databases*, N. Lavrač, D. Gamberger, L. Todorovski, and H. Blockeel, Eds., vol. 2838 of *Lecture Notes in Computer Science*. Springer Berlin Heidelberg, 2003, pp. 363–374.

[111] ODDIE, G. Verisimilitude and distance in logical space. In *The Logic and Epistemology of Scientific Change, Acta Philosophica Fennica 30*, I. Niiniluoto and R. Tuomela, Eds. Amsterdam, North-Holland, 1979, pp. 243–264.

[112] OLIVA, J., SERRANO, J. I., DEL CASTILLO, M. D., AND IGLESIAS, A. Sysmss: A syntax-based measure for short-text semantic similarity. *Data and Knowledge Engineering 70* (2011), 390–405.

[113] O'MAHONY, M., HURLEY, N., KUSHMERICK, N., AND SILVESTRE, G. Collaborative recommendation: A robustness analysis. *ACM Trans. Internet Technol. 4*, 4 (Nov. 2004), 344–377.

[114] O'SHEA, J., BANDAR, Z., CROCKETT, K., AND MCLEAN, D. A comparative study of two short text semantic similarity measures. In *Proceedings of the 2nd KES International Conference on Agent and Multi-agent Systems: Technologies and Applications* (2008), Springer Verlag, Berlin, pp. 172–181.

Bibliography

[115] O'SHEA, J., BANDAR, Z., CROCKETT, K., AND MCLEAN, D. Benchmarking short text semantic similarity. *International Journal of Intelligent Information and Database Systems 4*, 2 (2010), 103–120.

[116] PAZZANI, M. J. A framework for collaborative, content-based and demographic filtering. *Artificial Intelligence Review 13* (1999), 393–408.

[117] PENNOCK, D. M., AND HORVITZ, E. Collaborative filtering by personality diagnosis: a hybrid memory and model-based approach. In *Proceedings of the International Joint Conference on Artificial Intelligence Workshop: Machine Learning for Information Filtering* (August 1999).

[118] POPESCUL, A., UNGAR, L. H., PENNOCK, D. M., AND LAWRENCE, S. Probabilistic models for unified collaborative and content-based recommendation in sparse-data environments. In *Proceedings of the 17th Conference on Uncertainty in Artificial Intelligence* (2001).

[119] PRINCETON UNIVERSITY. Wordnet. www.wordnet.princeton.edu, 2010.

[120] QUERCIA, D., ASKHAM, H., AND CROWCROFT, J. TweetLDA: supervised topic classification and link prediction in Twitter. In *Web Science 2012, WebSci '12, Evanston, IL, USA* (2012), pp. 247–250.

[121] RABINER, L. R. A tutorial on hidden Markov models and selected applications in speech recognition. In *Proceedings of the IEEE* (1989), pp. 257–286.

[122] RABINER, L. R., AND JUANG, B. H. An introduction to hidden Markov models. *IEEE ASSp Magazine* (1986).

[123] RADA, R., MILI, H., BICKNELL, E., AND BLETTNER, M. Development and application of a metric on semantic nets. *IEEE Transactions on Systems, Man, and Cybernetics 19*, 1 (1989), 17–30.

[124] RADLINSKI, F., AND JOACHIMS, T. Query chains: learning to rank from implicit feedback. In *Proceedings of the eleventh ACM SIGKDD international conference on Knowledge discovery in data mining* (New York, NY, USA, 2005), KDD '05, ACM, pp. 239–248.

[125] RAFTERY, A. E. A model for high-order Markov chains. *Journal of the Royal Statistical Society B (47)*, 528–539.

[126] RESNICK, P., AND VARIAN, H. R. Recommender systems. *Commun. ACM 40*, 3 (Mar. 1997), 56–58.

[127] RESNIK, P. Using information content to evaluate semantic similarity in a taxonomy. In *Proceedings of IJCAI-95* (Montreal, Canada, 1995), pp. 448–453.

[128] RESNIK, P. Semantic similarity in a taxonomy: An information-based measure and its application to problems of ambiguity in natural language. *Journal or Artificial Intelligence Research 11* (1999), 95–130.

[129] RICCI, F., ROKACH, L., AND SHAPIRA, B. Introduction to recommender systems handbook. In *Recommender Systems Handbook*, F. R. et al., Ed. Springer Science+Business Media, LLC, 2011.

[130] RON, D., SINGER, Y., AND TISHBY, N. The power of amnesia: Learning probabilistic automata with variable memory length. In *Machine Learning* (1996), pp. 117–149.

[131] RUDIN, C., LETHAM, B., KOGAN, E., AND MADIGAN, D. A learning theory framework for sequential events and association rules. Operations Research Center Working Paper Series OR 394-12, MIT, 2012.

[132] RUDIN, C., LETHAM, B., SALLEB-AOUISSI, A., KOGAN, E., AND MADIGAN, D. Sequential event prediction with association rules. *Journal of Machine Learning Research - Proceedings Track 19* (2011), 615–634.

[133] SADIKOV, E., MADHAVAN, J., WANG, L., AND HALEVY, A. Clustering query refinements by user intent. In *Proceedings of the 19th International Conference on World Wide Web* (New York, NY, USA, 2010), WWW '10, ACM, pp. 841–850.

[134] SALTON, G., AND BUCKLEY, C. Term-weighting approaches in automatic text retrieval. In *Information Processing and Management* (1988), pp. 513–523.

[135] SANTOS, O. C., AND BOTICARIO, J. G., Eds. *Educational Recommender Systems and Technologies: Practices and Challenges*. IGI Global, 2011.

[136] SARULADHA, K., AGHILA, G., AND RAJ, S. A survey of semantic similarity methods for ontology based information retrieval. In *Second International Conference on Machine Learning and Computing* (2010), pp. 297–301.

[137] SCHEIN, A. I., POPESCUL, A., UNGAR, L. H., AND PENNOCK, D. M. Methods and metrics for cold-start recommendations. In *Proceedings of the 25th Annual International ACM SIGIR Conference* (2002).

[138] SENECAL, S., AND NANTEL, J. The influence of online product recommendations on consumers' online choices. *Journal of Retailing 80*, 2 (2004), 159 – 169.

[139] SHANI, G., BRAFMAN, R., AND HECKERMAN, D. An MDP-based recommender system. In *Proceedings of the 18th Conference on Uncertainty in Artificial Intelligence* (August 2002).

[140] SHANI, G., AND GUNAWARDANA, A. Evaluating recommendation systems. In *Recommender Systems Handbook*, F. R. et al., Ed. Springer Science+Business Media, LLC, 2011.

[141] SHU, L., LONG, B., AND MENG, W. A latent topic model for complete entity resolution. In *Proceedings of the 25th International Conference on Data Engineering, ICDE 2009, Shanghai, China* (Los Alamitos, CA, USA, 2009), IEEE Computer Society, pp. 880–891.

[142] SOBOROFF, I., AND NICHOLAS, C. Combining content and collaboration in text filtering. In *Proceedings of the International Joint Conference on Artificial Intelligence Workshop: Machine Learning for Information Filtering* (August 1999).

[143] SUN, Y., DENG, H., AND HAN, J. Probabilistic models for text mining. In *Mining Text Data*, C. C. Aggarwal and C. Zhai, Eds. Springer, 2012, pp. 259–295.

[144] SZPEKTOR, I., GIONIS, A., AND MAAREK, Y. Improving recommendation for long-tail queries via templates. In *Proceedings of the 20th International Conference on World Wide Web* (New York, NY, USA, 2011), WWW '11, ACM, pp. 47–56.

[145] TONG, H., AND FALOUTSOS, C. Center-piece subgraphs: problem definition and fast solutions. In *Proceedings of the 12th ACM SIGKDD International Conference on Knowledge Discovery and Data Mining* (New York, NY, USA, 2006), KDD '06, ACM, pp. 404–413.

[146] TSATSARONIS, G., VARLAMIS, I., AND VAZIRGIANNIS, M. Text relatedness based on word thesaurus. *Journal of Artificial Intelligence 37* (2010), 1–39.

[147] TURNEY, P. D. Learning algorithms for keyphrase extraction. *Information Retrieval 2*, 4 (May 2000), 303–336.

[148] VERBERT, K., MANOUSELIS, N., OCHOA, X., WOLPERS, M., DRACHSLER, H., BOSNIC, I., AND DUVAL, E. Context-aware recommender systems for learning: A survey and future challenges. *IEEE Transactions on Learning Technologies 99*, PrePrints (2012).

[149] VOLF, P. A. J. *Weighting Techniques in Data Compression: Theory and Algorithms*. PhD thesis, 2002.

[150] WALLECZEK, S. www.walleczek.at.

[151] WANG, G. H., WANG, Y. D., AND GUO, M. Z. An ontology-based method for similarity calculation of concepts in the semantic web. In *Proceedings of the 5th International Conference on Machine Learning and Cybernetics* (Dalian, China, 2006), pp. 1538–1542.

[152] WEN, J.-R., NIE, J.-Y., AND ZHANG, H.-J. Clustering user queries of a search engine. In *Proceedings of the 10th International Conference on World Wide Web* (New York, NY, USA, 2001), WWW '01, ACM, pp. 162–168.

[153] WIKI ANSWERS. wiki.answers.com.

[154] WIKIPEDIA. www.wikipedia.org.

[155] WILLEMS, F. M. J. The context-tree weighting method: extensions. *IEEE Transactions on Information Theory 44*, 2 (March 1998), 792–798.

[156] WILLEMS, F. M. J., SHTARKOV, Y., AND TJALKENS, T. The context-tree weighting method: basic properties. *IEEE Transactions on Information Theory 41*, 3 (May 1995), 653–664.

[157] WU, Z., AND PALMER, M. Verb semantics and lexical selection. In *Proceedings of the 32nd Annual Meeting of the Association for Computational Linguistics* (1994), pp. 133–138.

Bibliography

[158] YAMADA, I., HASHIMOTO, C., OH, J.-H., TORISAWA, K., KURODA, K., DE SAEGER, S., TSUCHIDA, M., AND KAZAMA, J. Generating information-rich taxonomy from Wikipedia. In *Proceedings of the 4th International Universal Communication Symposium (IUCS)* (2010), pp. 97–104.

[159] YU, K., XU, X., TAO, J., ESTER, M., AND KRIEGEL, H.-P. Instance selection techniques for memory-based collaborative filtering. In *Proceedings of the 2nd SIAM International Conference on Data Mining (SDM '02)* (2002).

[160] ZHANG, M., AND HURLEY, N. Avoiding monotony: improving the diversity of recommendation lists. In *Proceedings of the 2008 ACM conference on Recommender Systems* (New York, NY, USA, 2008), RecSys '08, ACM, pp. 123–130.

[161] ZHANG, Y., CALLAN, J., AND MINKA, T. Novelty and redundancy detection in adaptive filtering. In *Proceedings of the 25th Annual International ACM SIGIR Conference* (2002), pp. 81–88.

[162] ZHANG, Z., AND NASRAOUI, O. Mining search engine query logs for query recommendation. In *Proceedings of the 15th International Conference on World Wide Web* (New York, NY, USA, 2006), WWW '06, ACM, pp. 1039–1040.

[163] ZIV, J., AND LEMPEL, A. Compression of individual sequences via variable-rate coding. *IEEE Transactions on Information Theory 24*, 5 (1978), 530–536.

List of Notations

$\hat{P}$	learned probabilistic model
κ	knowledge
$\lambda(x_t, x_{t-1}, \ldots)$	function of the past that determines the VLMC
$\mathcal{CD}$	the cognitive process dimension
$\mathcal{H}$	history database
$\mathcal{KD}$	the knowledge dimension
$\mathcal{K}$	set of keywords
$\mathcal{LO}$	the set of learning objectives
$\mathcal{M}$	mapping relationship
$\mathcal{M}_\kappa$	mapping relationship between the question set and the knowledge dimension
$\mathcal{M}_\phi$	mapping relationship between the question set and the space of learning objectives
$\mathcal{M}_\rho$	mapping relationship between the question set and the cognitive process dimension
$\mathcal{M}_\tau$	mapping relationship between the question and topic space
$\mathcal{P}(\cdot)$	powerset
$\mathcal{Q}$	set of questions
$\mathcal{T}$	set of topics
ϕ	learning objective
ρ	cognitive process
σ	catalog coverage threshold
τ	topic

List of Notations

$acc(\hat{P}, x_1^n)$	accuracy of model $\hat{P}$ with respect to test sequence x_1^n
C	random variable over the cognitive process dimension
D	maximal memory length of a VLMC
$div(R(s))$	diversity of recommendation set $R(s)$
K	random variable over the knowledge dimension
k	keyword
L	random variable over the space of learning objectives
$l(\hat{P}, x_1^t)$	average log-loss of test sequence with respect to model $\hat{P}$
$learnUtil$	learning utility function
$maxOrder$	maximum allowed order of a VLMC during learning
N	number of recommendations
P	true probability distribution
p_κ	projection function on the knowledge dimension
p_ϕ	projection function on the space of learning objectives
p_ρ	projection function on the cognitive process dimension
p_τ	projection function on the topic space
$proj_\kappa$	projection function of question sequences on the knowledge dimension
$proj_\phi$	projection function of question sequences on the space of learnin objectives
$proj_\rho$	projection function of question sequences on the cognitive process dimension
$proj_\tau$	projection function of question sequences on the topic space
Q	random variable over the question space $\mathcal{Q}$
q	question
q_1^t	sequence of questions
$R(s)$	question recommendations with respect to context s

List of Notations

Sim	similarity function between a keyword and a keyword-set
sim_k	keyword similarity function
sim_q	question similarity function
sim_τ	topic similarity function
sim_{ks}	keyword-set similarity function
T	random variable over the topic space $\mathcal{T}$
u	recommendation utility function
$w(\tau, k)$	weight of keyword k within topic τ
X	random variable
$X^{(t)}$	instantiation of the random variable X at time t
x_1^t	test sequence of questions

Index

affective domain, 61
analyze, 64
apply, 64
association rule mining, 51
average log-loss, 58, 59, 87, 117

bag of words, 48
Baum-Welch algorithm, 60
Bayesian networks, 53
Bloom's taxonomy, 61

cognitive domain, 61
cognitive process dimension, 64
collaborative filtering, 19, 34
collaborative recommender system, 18
common-word order similarity, 46
concept similarity, 36
concept-set similarity, 39
conceptual knowledge, 63
content-based recommendation, 77
content-based recommender system, 17
context tree weighting, 58
context-aware search, 33
corpus statistics, 43
corpus-based text similarity, 35
cosine measure, 35
cosine similarity, 48, 49
create, 64
curricula, 61
curse of dimensionality, 57

decomposed context tree weighting, 58
demographic recommendation, 17
descriptive feature-based similarity, 35
Dice's coefficient, 49
directed graphical model, 50
document similarity, 40

dynamic Bayesian networks, 53
dynamic probabilistic models, 52

e-learning, 5
edge-based concept similarity, 36
educational process, 61
educational research, 61
evaluate, 64

factual knowledge, 63
forward-backward algorithm, 60

graph-based query recommendation, 25

hidden Markov model, 54, 59
high-order Markov chain, 56
hybrid recommender system, 20
hyperspace analogues to language, 42

information content, 37
information extraction, 60
information retrieval, 36
inverse document frequency, 48

Jaccard similarity coefficient, 48

Kalman filter, 54
knowledge dimension, 63, 144
knowledge-based recommendation, 17

latent Dirichlet allocation, 42
latent semantic analysis, 40
latent semantic indexing, 39
learning objective, 12, 61, 83
learning taxonomy, 61
learning-oriented recommender, 84, 89
least common super-concept, 37
Lempel-Ziv algorithm, 58
likelihood, 58, 87

longest common subsequence, 44
loss-less compression, 59

Markov assumption, 53
Markov chain, 54
Markov model, 32
maximum likelihood estimation, 60
memory-based recommendation, 19
metacognitive knowledge, 63
mixture transition distribution model, 54
mixture variable memory Markov model, 33
model-based recommendation, 19

natural language processing, 36, 60, 69

observation probability, 60
ontology, 38

prediction by partial match, 58
predictive models, 50
probabilistic latent semantic analysis, 41
probabilistic models, 52
probabilistic suffix tree, 58
procedural knowledge, 63
psycho-motor domain, 61

query instance, 26
query log, 29
query recommendation, 24, 31
query session, 26
query-flow graph, 28, 29
question answering, 5

recommendation, 15, 16, 24
recommendation technique, 17
recommender system, 15, 16
remember, 64

search engine, 24
search engine query graphs, 25
semantic compactness, 46
semantic relatedness, 46, 47
semantic short-text similarity, 67
semantic similarity, 35, 36

semantic text similarity, 44
sequence data, 50
sequential data, 50
sequential event prediction, 50
short-term recommendation, 77
short-text similarity, 43
similarity, 35
singular value decomposition, 41
structured lexical database, 43
syntactic similarity, 35, 48

taxonomy, 38, 69
temporal probabilistic models, 52
term frequency, 48, 70
term-query graph, 30
text similarity, 35
time series data, 50
time series modeling, 52
timeline discretization, 53
transition probability, 60

understand, 64
undirected graphical model, 50
URL cover, 26
user query session, 29
utility-based recommendation, 17

variable length hidden Markov model, 33
variable length Markov chain, 58, 84
variable length Markov chain learning methods, 58
variable length Markov model, 57
variable memory Markov model, 32
Viterbi algorithm, 60

wisdom of the crowds, 6
word co-occurance, 35

I want morebooks!

Buy your books fast and straightforward online - at one of world's fastest growing online book stores! Environmentally sound due to Print-on-Demand technologies.

Buy your books online at
www.morebooks.shop

Kaufen Sie Ihre Bücher schnell und unkompliziert online – auf einer der am schnellsten wachsenden Buchhandelsplattformen weltweit! Dank Print-On-Demand umwelt- und ressourcenschonend produziert.

Bücher schneller online kaufen
www.morebooks.shop

info@omniscriptum.com
www.omniscriptum.com

Printed by Books on Demand GmbH, Norderstedt / Germany